D0794119

DATE DUE

FE 12 04			

DEMCO 38-296

THE ARMENIA-AZERBAIJAN CONFLICT

R

THE ARMENIA-AZERBAIJAN CONFLICT

Causes and Implications

MICHAEL P. CROISSANT

PRAEGER

Westport, Connecticut
London

Library of Congress Cataloging-in-Publication Data

Croissant, Michael P., 1971–
   The Armenia-Azerbaijan conflict : causes and implications /
  Michael P. Croissant.
      p.   cm.
  Includes bibliographical references and index.
  ISBN 0–275–96241–5 (alk. paper)
   1. Nagorno-Karabakh Conflict, 1988–1994. 2. Armenia (Republic)—
Relations—Azerbaijan.   3. Azerbaijan—Relations—Armenia
(Republic) I. Title.
DK699.N34C76   1998
947.54—dc21   98–5238

British Library Cataloguing in Publication Data is available.

Library of Congress Catalog Card Number: 98–5238
ISBN: 0–275–96241–5

First published in 1998

Praeger Publishers, 88 Post Road West, Westport, CT 06881
An imprint of Greenwood Publishing Group, Inc.

Printed in the United States of America

The paper used in this book complies with the
Permanent Paper Standard issued by the National
Information Standards Organization (Z39.48–1984).

10 9 8 7 6 5 4 3 2

This book is dedicated with great love, appreciation, and deepest thanks to my parents, Faithann and Harold Croissant, to whom I owe so much.

Contents

Acknowledgments

I would like to thank several people for their support and guidance. I would like to express gratitude to Drs. William R. Van Cleave and J. D. Crouch II of the Center for Defense and Strategic Studies at Southwest Missouri State University, Dr. Marvin G. Weinbaum of the University of Illinois at Urbana-Champaign, and Dr. William Fierman of Indiana University for their immeasurable contributions to my education. Special thanks also goes to Bulent Aras, who provided me with many useful comments on the manuscript for this book. Much gratitude also goes to my family, whose tireless support has sustained me in good times and in bad. In particular, I am grateful for the love of my niece, Kelsey Egan Croissant, who suffers from a rare neurological disorder known as Rett Syndrome. Most of all, I want to thank my wife, Cynthia, not only for her creation of the maps for this book, but also for her unconditional love and patience. Without her this book would not have been possible.

Introduction

Ronald Reagan declared confidently in 1981 that "the West will not contain Communism, it will transcend Communism. We will not bother to denounce it, we'll dismiss it as a sad, bizarre chapter in human history whose last pages are even now being written." Reagan's prophesy was fulfilled a decade later, when the Soviet Union was dissolved formally after 74 years as the world's predominant Communist state. Owing to the momentous nature of the breakup of the Soviet empire, scholars will no doubt spend decades analyzing, interpreting, and debating the events of 1989–1991 and their effects on international politics. One important implication of the USSR's breakup, however, poses serious challenges to international peace and security today and will not await the judgment of history. Scattered throughout the area of the former Soviet Union (FSU) are several major sources of ethno-territorial conflict that are no longer kept under control by Communist rule. With the erosion and collapse of central authority in Moscow in the late 1980s and early 1990s, many of these potential zones of conflict exploded into violence and warfare that have killed thousands and driven millions of civilians from their homes.

Since the decline and fall of the USSR, numerous disputes have flared across the territory of the FSU. In Moldova, for example, ethnic Russians engaged in a violent campaign in 1991 and 1992 to create an independent "Transdniester Republic" with close links to Moscow. In Tajikistan, a bloody civil war involving rival clans, political groupings, and religious forces exploded in 1993 into what has been called a "second Afghanistan." Other areas torn by strife following the Soviet demise include Georgia and the Russian Federation itself.

While there is no shortage of actual or potential armed confrontations in the former USSR to analyze, the dispute between Armenia and Azerbaijan is worthy of particular note. Not only is the Armenia-Azerbaijan conflict one of the bloodiest and most intractable clashes to emerge from the breakup of the Soviet empire, but it is also perhaps the only post-Soviet conflict that poses a potentially explosive threat to peace and security on a regional—as opposed to a local—scale. With the implementation of *glasnost* and *perestroika* in the second half of the 1980s, Soviet leader Mikhail Gorbachev opened a Pandora's Box of grievances that had been suppressed by seventy years of Communist rule. Among the first regions to erupt into conflict was the Transcaucasus, where in early 1988 a dispute over the right of the ethnic Armenian population of the Nagorno-Karabakh Autonomous Oblast to secede from Azerbaijan resulted in bloodshed.

Encouraged by a perceived openness on the part of Gorbachev to redress "injustices" left over from the early Soviet period, the Armenians of Nagorno-Karabakh began an active campaign in 1988 both to reverse what they regarded as a grievous miscarriage of history—Stalin's 1923 attachment of the region to the Azerbaijan Soviet Socialist Republic (SSR)—and to remove themselves from arbitrary and denigrating rule from Baku. In a move unprecedented in Soviet history, the Karabakh Armenian authorities voted to undertake a peaceful unification with their brethren in the Armenian SSR, a move supported fully by the latter. Viewing the act as a potential threat to the territorial integrity of their republic, the Azerbaijanis resisted, and violence soon broke out between the two peoples in several cities and villages across both Armenia and Azerbaijan. Over the next three years and despite numerous attempts at settlement by the central authorities in Moscow, the conflict between the Armenians and Azerbaijanis grew beyond the realm of inter-communal violence. By the time of the Soviet Union's demise in late 1991, the dispute had spiraled into a full-scale clash between the two republics—a clash that has since defied resolution by the international community.

While the conflict between Armenia and Azerbaijan has manifested itself in a bloody struggle over the status of Nagorno-Karabakh, the post-Soviet geopolitics of the region have added complexity to the dispute and influenced its course. Situated in a region whose history is marked by incessant competition and conflict between rival imperial powers, Armenia and Azerbaijan are today surrounded by three major regional actors that have taken considerable interest in the course and implications of their dispute. Viewing the Armenia-Azerbaijan clash both as a potential threat to regional peace and security and as a potential opportunity through which to gain geopolitical influence, Russia, Turkey, and Iran have all become significant players in the conflict. On a handful of occasions between the middle of 1992 and late 1993, this phenomenon threatened to spark open involvement in the fighting by one or more of these players.

After two-and-a-half years of brutal combat that left more than twenty-five thousand people dead and nearly a million homeless, a cease-fire took hold in the region in May 1994. Although the cease-fire has been observed generally to the present day, a formal political settlement of the Nagorno-Karabakh conflict has remained elusive. While more than 20 percent of its territory—most of Nagorno-Karabakh included—is under the control of ethnic Armenian forces, Azerbaijan has used the cessation of hostilities to attract more than $35 billion in investment by Western oil companies seeking to tap its vast offshore energy reserves beneath the

Caspian Sea. The entry of Western oil majors has been followed by a heightened interest in the region by the governments of Europe and the United States, who seek to lessen their dependence on oil supplies from the volatile Persian Gulf.

With Western interest in the region on the rise, new impetus has been given to the quest for a political settlement of the Nagorno-Karabakh dispute. However, the entrance of Western powers has, in combination with the continuing competition of regional powers, served to complicate rather than ameliorate the situation. Large-scale international investment has not only emboldened Azerbaijan with the belief that Western governments will help it achieve diplomatically what it failed to achieve on the battlefield, but it has also begun to provide Baku with the capital to rebuild its military potential and thus to prepare for a potentially forceful solution to the Karabakh question. Armenia, on the other hand, has been excluded from regional oil development plans and thus stands to grow weaker by comparison.

Russia, too, is dissatisfied with the emerging geopolitical order in the Transcaucasus. Since late 1992, a consensus has emerged in Moscow on the necessity of maintaining a sphere of influence over the republics of the FSU. With its vast natural resource wealth and strategic location, the Transcaucasus has been of particular interest to Russian policy-makers; Moscow wishes to see neither the rise of a significant Turkish and Western political and economic presence in the region nor the emergence of truly independent states there. Thus, Russia's disenchantment with the developing situation has mirrored that of Armenia, albeit for different reasons.

The increasingly competitive nature of foreign engagement in the Transcaucasus is likely to have a negative influence on the Armenia-Azerbaijan conflict. The current maneuvering for allies and influence in the region has contributed to the rise of two blocs with competing interests and objectives. On one side are Russia, Iran, and a handful of smaller powers whose joint goal is to thwart the expansion of Turkish and Western influence in Transcaucasia and Central Asia. On the other side are Turkey and the Western powers, including the United States, who seek the unhindered development of Caspian oil and the subsequent emergence of truly independent states along Russia's southern flank. For obvious reasons, Azerbaijan has classed itself in the second group, while Armenia has out of geopolitical necessity been driven closer to Russia and Iran. As both the stakes and players in this struggle for influence increase, a potentially dangerous cold war in the region could emerge in the next century. As long as the Armenia-Azerbaijan conflict goes on without formal resolution, the potential will exist for the Nagorno-Karabakh dispute to explode into a regional war between rival blocs, resulting in a crisis of possibly global proportions.

This book will address the regional and international dynamics and implications of the Armenia-Azerbaijan conflict. Chapter one will serve as a primer by addressing the historical issues that underlie the current state of hostilities between Armenia and Azerbaijan. After assessing briefly the impact of geography upon the history and ethnicity of the Transcaucasus region, effort will be made to assess the roots of Armenian-Azerbaijani enmity. In particular, analysis will delve into how the two countries' animosity has come to focus primarily upon Nagorno-Karabakh. The decisive impact of Russian and Soviet nationality policies as well as divergent Armenian and Azeri interpretations of history on the development of the dispute will therefore be assessed to provide necessary background.

The second chapter will trace the Armenia-Azerbaijan conflict from its revival in 1988 to its serious escalation in the latter part of 1991. In particular, the impact of *glasnost, perestroika*, and, ultimately, the breakup of the USSR will be weighed with a view to comprehending the course of Armenian-Azerbaijani hostilities over the given period. Following discussion of the evolution of the Armenia-Azerbaijan dispute through late 1991, pause will be taken from chronological analysis in order to address a topic of major importance: The regional dynamics of the Nagorno-Karabakh conflict. Effort in the third chapter will focus on illuminating the factors at play in the geopolitical calculations of both the major regional powers—Russia, Turkey, and Iran—and the conflicting parties. Such analysis will lay the proper framework for an examination of the Armenia-Azerbaijan dispute from 1992 to 1994, for it is during this time period that Russian, Turkish, and Iranian interests emerged as significant factors in the course of the conflict.

Chapter four of this book will trace the direction of the Armenia-Azerbaijan conflict during the bloody warfare of 1992–1994, when the dispute nearly escalated beyond the two republics' borders. The fifth chapter will discuss the conflict since the cease-fire of May 1994, including the impact of oil and regional geopolitical competition on efforts by various international actors to achieve a peaceful settlement of the Nagorno-Karabakh dispute. Drawing upon insights gained from such examination, the sixth chapter will address both the prospects for, and likely repercussions of, renewed warfare between Armenia and Azerbaijan.

The Transcaucasus and the Surrounding Region

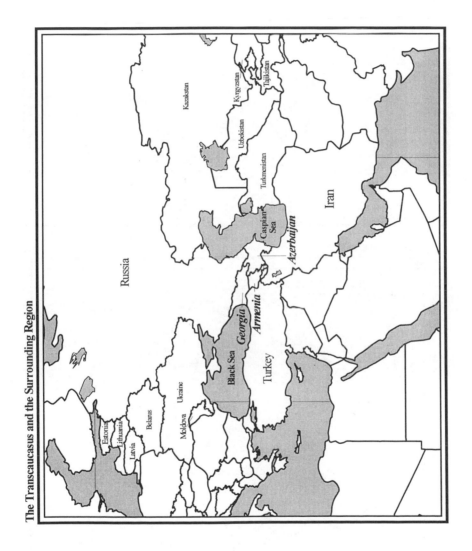

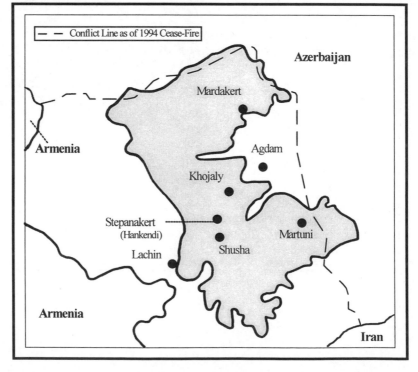

Abbreviations

ANM—Armenian National Movement
APCs—armored personnel carriers
APF—Azerbaijani Popular Front
ASSR—Autonomous Soviet Socialist Republic
AzCP—Azerbaijani Communist Party
CFE—Conventional Forces in Europe
CIS—Commonwealth of Independent States
CPSU—Communist Party of the Soviet Union
CSCE—Conference on Security and Cooperation in Europe
FSU—Former Soviet Union
NKAO—Nagorno-Karabakh Autonomous Oblast
NKR—"Nagorno-Karabakh Republic"
OSCE—Organization for Security and Cooperation in Europe
SOCAR—State Oil Company of the Azerbaijan Republic
SSR—Soviet Socialist Republic

Historical Origins of the Armenia-Azerbaijan Conflict

From the dawn of history, and doubtless long ages before, these mountain fastnesses were the refuge of vanquished races, the plains at their feet the camping-ground of conquering hordes.

—John F. Baddeley,
The Russian Conquest of the Caucasus

The conflict between Armenia and Azerbaijan has its origins in the late nineteenth century, when a multifaceted antagonism developed between the Armenians and Azeris under czarist Russian rule. However, the seeds of conflict were sown from earliest times as the Transcaucasus became a cauldron of ethno-cultural diversity and a locus of imperial rivalry. This chapter is dedicated to tracing the historical origins and development of the conflict through the late Soviet period.

REVIEW OF REGIONAL GEOGRAPHY AND HISTORY

Armenia and Azerbaijan are two of the three former Soviet republics that occupy the geographic area known as the Transcaucasus—the isthmus south of the Caucasus Mountains and between the Black and Caspian Seas. Although rugged and mountainous, the Transcaucasus is important geographically in that it represents a strategic land bridge between Europe and Asia. Over time, this geo-strategic location has made the Transcaucasus a crossroads of major human movement and a battleground of clashing empires.[1]

Owing to its location, Transcaucasia served from earliest times as a funnel through which traders, travelers, and entire peoples moved. The earliest wave of migration occurred sometime in the first millennium B.C., when Indo-Europeans, probably of the Hittite branch, entered the area and expanded south and eastward into Anatolia, Iran, and India.[2] The Hittites were followed later by a group of Indo-Europeans of Iranian stock, whose social and political influence left a deep imprint upon the culture of the Transcaucasus that survives up to the present.[3] Over the centuries that followed, scores of other peoples passed through or settled in Transcaucasia, including the Romans, Arabs, and Turks. While none of these groups eradicated completely the deeply rooted influences of pre-Islamic Iran, each left a lasting impact upon the area.

Although the entry of the Romans into the Transcaucasus dates back as early as 69 B.C., Roman influences did not become pervasive in the region until the fourth century A.D., when the Roman Empire adopted Christianity *en masse*. The Christianization of the region under Roman rule was uneven, however, centering mainly on what is now Georgia and Armenia. Islam took root in what is now Azerbaijan and the North Caucasus region following the invasion by Arab armies in 642 A.D.[4] Although the spread of Islam into Transcaucasia did not alter the indigenous peoples' cultural attraction to pre-Islamic Iran, it deepened significantly the existing split between the Christian and non-Christian peoples of the area.[5]

The next major wave of migration came in the eleventh century, when Turkic tribes began to flow through the area in great numbers as part of their large-scale migration into Asia Minor.[6] The Turks did not merely pass through the Transcaucasus, however; many tribes settled in the area, and it was incorporated wholly into the Seljuk Empire in 1071.[7] As was the case with each of the other major migrations through the area, the Turks left a lasting mark on the Transcaucasus: The linguistic Turkification of a number of the Muslim peoples of the region.[8] Over the centuries, in light of "the importance of language in determining the self-identity of peoples," this Turkification led many of the linguistically Turkified, but ethnically non-Turkic, peoples of the region to identify themselves as Turks.[9]

Since earliest times, Transcaucasia's geographic position as a bridge between continents has made it a crossroads for the movement of migrating peoples. Some of these peoples settled in the area, while others merely passed through or were forced out by warfare or other upheavals. Whatever the case, a gradual process occurred over history in which aspects of the migrants' identities, ranging from religion to language and culture, were adopted to varying degrees by the indigenous peoples of Transcaucasia. The main result of this process, which was accentuated by extensive inter-marriage and cross-breeding between the newcomers and local populations, was to make the Transcaucasus one of the most ethnically and culturally heterogenous areas of the world.

Regional geography has influenced the area's historical evolution in another significant way. In light of its strategic location, the Transcaucasus has been coveted by external powers almost continuously throughout history. Foreigners have eyed the region not only for the potential overland access it offers between Europe and Asia but also for its situation as a buffer zone between rival empires. To complicate matters, the historical process of migration and the intermingling of populations also made it inevitable that surrounding powers would share certain ethno-linguistic or cultural links with the peoples of Transcaucasia, often causing their interests in the region to transcend merely imperialistic motives. On countless occasions throughout history, these phenomena have made the Transcaucasus the locus of competition, and often battle, between surrounding powers.

Transcaucasia first became a sustained center of imperial rivalry in the first century B.C., when the region became a major battleground between the Roman Empire and the Arsacid dynasty of Iran.[10] For several centuries thereafter, the area, and Armenia in particular, continued to be an object of heated contention between Rome and successive Iranian dynasties.[11] With the passing of time, the Roman presence in the Transcaucasus was replaced by Byzantium and the Iranian presence by the Arabs; then, in 1071, the Byzantines were defeated by the Turks at the Battle of Manzikert, and Transcaucasia fell under the sway of the Seljuk Empire.[12]

Following the replacement of the Seljuks by the Mongols and then the Ottomans in the thirteenth century, the Transcaucasus became a locus of competition between an expansionist Ottoman Turkey and Safavid Iran by the early sixteenth century.[13] As a result of two successful wars with Iran in 1578 and 1603, Ottoman occupation of Transcaucasia was consolidated.[14] These Turkish gains lasted little more than a century, however, because a new power entered the competition for control of the region in the early 1700s: Russia.

Faced with further Ottoman expansion as the Safavid dynasty in Iran was weakened by internal strife and invasions by Afghan tribesmen, Peter the Great ordered the first major Russian expedition into Transcaucasia in 1722 in hopes of strengthening his military position against the Turks.[15] Russia's gains along the Caspian coast were recognized by the Russo-Turkish peace treaty of July 1724. However, Peter died a year later, and his successors pulled back from the Transcaucasus over the course of the next 45 years, favoring instead a newly strengthened Iranian dynasty as a counterbalance to the Ottoman Empire.[16]

Following the return of Russia to the Transcaucasus in the late 1700s, the region's history was marked for nearly the next two centuries by a three-way struggle for influence among Ottoman Turkey, imperial Russia, and Iran. Because both the Ottoman Empire and the Iranian dynasties were in relative decline at the time, much of this struggle was characterized by substantial Russian expansionism in the area: Christian Georgia was wrested from Ottoman hands in 1770–1773,[17] while two wars with Iran between 1804 and 1828 brought the Russian Empire's frontier with that state up to the Aras River (where it remained until the Soviet breakup).[18] Finally, as a result of significant gains in the Russo-Ottoman War of 1877–1878, Russian rule over most of Transcaucasia was consolidated.[19] After a brief interlude of independence brought about by Russia's departure from the Transcaucasus during the 1917 Bolshevik revolution, Georgia, Armenia, and Azerbaijan were incorporated into the Soviet Union in 1920, and the great centuries-long struggle for control of the region was put on hold.

Although this discussion gives only the briefest overview of the dynamics that have shaped the history and ethnicity of the Transcaucasus region, it is clear that the area has been somewhat of a "magnet" over the course of time. Situated strategically between Europe and Asia, it has attracted countless waves of human migrants and been the locus of almost continuous expansionism and competition between surrounding states. Inevitably, this reality has had a great impact upon the historical development of the region.

Subjected to centuries of foreign conquest and fragmented internally along ethnic and cultural lines, the peoples of the Transcaucasus have been virtual hostages to external dynamics throughout the region's long history of human habitation. Nation-states in the modern sense did not arise there until the early part of this century; for millennia before that, the region's inhabitants were mere vassals of their larger and more powerful neighbors. Unavoidably, such a state of affairs had a great impact upon the development of perceptions of self-identity and historical experience on the part of the Transcaucasian peoples. Indeed, this is especially the case for the two peoples concerned with in this study: The Armenians and Azeris.

Armenian Perceptions of Self-Identity

Modern Armenians trace their origins to a group of Indo-Europeans that migrated into what is now eastern Turkey and Transcaucasia in the sixth century B.C. Isolated in the mountains and valleys of the area, the early Armenians distinguished themselves on the basis of their common language (Armenian). More than a thousand years later, Ronald G. Suny notes, the Armenians emerged as a "unique, identifiable ethno-religious community" when they adopted their own exclusive form of Monophysite Christianity in the fourth century A.D.[20] In the centuries that ensued, the Armenians' commonality, as well as uniqueness, in religion and language formed the fundamental basis of their collective self-identity. This basic national consciousness was supplemented over time by historical experiences that arose largely out of geographically imposed conditions.

Like the other inhabitants of the Transcaucasus, the Armenians were subject to the effects of large-scale human migrations and frequent foreign conquests. As David Marshall Lang notes,

Armenia's strategic position has exposed her to repeated invasion. Situated immediately to the south of the Caucasian corridor, the Armenian highlands must be traversed or skirted by northern peoples driving south from the Eurasian steppes, or by any Near Eastern power moving north to control the Black Sea and Caspian littorals. Equally, Armenia must necessarily feature in rivalry between any dominant power in Asia Minor and the Bosphorus, and forces controlling Iran and Central Asia. From the time of Darius and Xerxes, this political tug-of-war has been an ever-present factor in Near Eastern affairs. In all such clashes of empires, the Armenians have found themselves between two warring camps.[21]

Unavoidably, this situation played a significant role in the development of the

Armenians' national character over the past 2,600 years.

Despite brief periods of unification and relative prosperity in medieval times, Armenia has for most of its history been under the dominion of foreign powers. While the list of rulers includes the Romans, Sassanids, Byzantines, Arabs, and Mongols, the most significant periods of foreign control from the standpoint of affecting the development of the Armenian national character were those under the Ottoman Turks and the Russians.

Falling under the rule of the Ottoman Empire in 1520, the majority of the Armenian people found their fate in the hands of the Turks for the next four centuries. While the empire was strong and expanding, the Armenians lived in relative peace despite being subject to special taxes and generally second-class standing under the law.[22] As Christians, they enjoyed a special protected status from the Sultan and were granted a fair degree of freedom to regulate their own affairs.[23] Moreover, the Armenians' religious identification with the Christian West, together with their standing as skilled artisans, merchants, and interpreters, allowed them to serve as intermediaries with Europe in economic matters—a role that gave them significant importance to the Sultan.[24]

While relations between the Armenians and their Turkish masters were mostly tranquil throughout the first hundred years of their association, the long decline of the Ottoman Empire from the seventeenth century sparked the growth of intolerance toward the Armenians. Faced with large-scale corruption in the bureaucracy and a growing threat to the European domains of the empire by the continental powers, the Turks began to see the Armenians as a potential pro-Western fifth column within their ranks. Although the Armenians did little to warrant such a characterization, the Ottomans eventually responded to the so-called "Armenian Question" with heightening levels of persecution and, from 1895 to 1896, with massacres of their Armenian subjects.[25] Finally, in what has been called the first holocaust of the modern era, the Turks sought a "final solution" to the "Armenian Question"—the destruction of Turkish Armenia—through a forced deportation of Armenians from eastern Anatolia in 1915–1916 that killed as many as 1.5 million people.[26]

The massacres at the hands of the Ottoman Turks left an indelible mark on the Armenian national character. Although it was not uncommon for them to be persecuted by their rulers, the Armenians had never previously faced an attempt at their destruction on a large scale. This reality, in addition to the fact that the European powers failed to come to the aid of their fellow Christians, heightened the Armenians' sense of both vulnerability and self-reliance that had evolved over centuries of foreign rule. Abandoned by Europe and pushed from their historic homeland in eastern Anatolia, the Armenians that survived the events of 1915–1916 were forced to cling to their existence in the mountains and valleys of Transcaucasian Armenia.

Another important episode in Armenian history occurred in the two centuries of Russian governance of Transcaucasian Armenia. Viewing imperial Russia as "an advanced civilization and society, a champion of Christendom against Islam, and the hope for emancipation," most Armenians welcomed the Russian annexation of the area between 1828 and 1878.[27] However, Russian policies toward the Armenians tended to fluctuate over time, giving them cause for feelings of insecurity.

Despite professions of protection for the Armenians as fellow Christians and potential allies against the neighboring Muslims, Russian leaders tended to let the extent of that protection be dictated by the necessities of the domestic and international situation. Thus, while still remaining loyal to the Russian Empire, the Armenians formed a nationalist movement in the late nineteenth century that focused on promoting their individuality based on a unique language and religion; cultural and spiritual ties with Russia were therefore de-emphasized.[28] Although this new movement posed no direct threat to Russia in light of the Armenians' rejection of separatism, the czarist authorities nonetheless began to regard the Armenians as revolutionaries. By the closing years of the nineteenth century, the heightening Russian suspicion of the Armenians brought about a policy of Russification toward them that included the seizure of Armenian Church properties and the closure of Armenian schools. The result was a growing cycle of mistrust and hostility between rulers and subjects that dissipated only with the coming of the First World War.[29]

Similar to the experience of their brethren across the frontier in the Ottoman Empire, the Armenians under Russian rule found that, despite professions of protection from their masters, they were nonetheless subject to persecution on the basis of their identity as Armenians. While their treatment by the Russians was not brutal and violent as it was under the Turks in the late nineteenth and early twentieth centuries, the Armenians viewed the inconsistency of czarist policies toward them as a sign that they could not always count on their larger Christian ally to the north. When the czar's policies turned toward attempted Russification, the Armenians' resolve to maintain their distinctiveness was only hardened.

Over the centuries, the net impact of the Armenians' experiences with Ottoman Turkish and imperial Russian rule, as well as those with all of their previous foreign masters, was to reinforce the Armenians' sense of solidarity. Lodged between rival empires and faced often with persecution or outright massacre, the Armenians sustained themselves for millennia on the feeling that they were a single, unique people with a common language, religion, and historical experience. Despite being subject to the disruptive effects of their geographical surroundings, the Armenians managed not only to survive, but to do so with their identity and character intact.[30]

Azeri Perceptions of Self-Identity

Tracing Azeri perceptions of self-identity is a much more difficult task than doing so for the Armenians. Unlike the Armenians, the Azeris had, until quite recently in historical terms, neither a common language and religion upon which to trace their national identity nor a sufficient stimulus to realize such an identity.

Indeed, the effects of historical migrations and imperial rivalries, which had such a large impact on the rise of a distinct Armenian identity, led the Azeris to develop a close sense of identification with, rather than distinction from, the two powers that ruled them historically—Turkey and Iran.[31] This affinity with the Turkic and Persian worlds retarded the development of a distinctly Azeri national identity.

Modern Azeri scholars trace their people's ancestry to the inhabitants of Caucasian Albania (not to be confused with the modern republic of Albania), an ancient state whose territories corresponded roughly to those of present-day Azerbaijan. At the time of the Arab conquest in 642 A.D., the people of these areas were under the strong cultural and political influence of Iran but were largely adherents of the Christian faith. With the arrival of the Arabs, a large portion of the Albanians converted to Islam while maintaining a firm cultural identification with their large neighbor to the south. Importantly, however, for the development of the conflict over Nagorno-Karabakh many centuries later, the Islamization of Caucasian Albania was not total; the people inhabiting the mountainous western half of the Albanian region known as Karabakh remained Christian and integrated with the Armenians, while those inhabiting the plains of eastern Karabakh converted to Islam.[32]

Although the ancient country of Caucasian Albania passed from the historical scene sometime in the ninth century, the inhabitants of the area (excluding those who were Armenianized) continued to identify closely with Iran. However, the coming of the Turks to the Transcaucasus in large numbers in the eleventh century brought about a gradual change in the ethnic and linguistic characteristics of the indigenous population. Many of the Turkic tribes that invaded the area settled there and inter-mingled substantially with the local people. Over many years, this interaction resulted in the replacement of the pre-existing language with a Turkic dialect and the growing self-identification of the indigenous people as Turks.[33] Thus, by the end of the eleventh century, the early Azeris looked culturally toward Iran, religiously toward the larger Muslim world, and linguistically and ethnically toward the Turkic world.[34]

In the opening years of the sixteenth century, imperial rivalry added a further degree of complexity to the self-identity of the early Azeris. After 1502, when the eastern Transcaucasus was made a part of the Shi'ite Safavid Empire in Iran, the majority of its Muslim inhabitants became adherents to the Shi'a faith. Thus, the Azeris' split with the mainstream Sunni Islamic sect clouded their sense of identification with the Sunni Turks and accentuated a dual sense of loyalty between the Persian and Turkic worlds; pulled toward Iran by religious and cultural affinity and toward Turkey by ethno-linguistic closeness, the development of a distinctly Azeri national consciousness was made difficult.

Nonetheless, the Azeris themselves did little in the way of promoting a sense of ethnic or cultural distinctiveness. Unlike the Armenians, they were content to view themselves in terms of their commonalities with—rather than differences from—the Turks and Iranians. Indeed, the terms "Azeri" and "Azerbaijani" were born only in the twentieth century upon the formation of the short-lived Republic of Azerbaijan in 1918, prior to which the Azeris were referred to as "Caucasian Tatars" or simply as "Tatars."[35] It was not until the late nineteenth century that a national consciousness began to develop among the "Azerbaijanis;" importantly, this development arose largely as a result of growing communal tensions with the Armenians during that time period.

THE DEVELOPMENT OF THE ARMENIA-AZERBAIJAN CONFLICT TO 1988

The roots of the hostility between the Armenians and Azerbaijanis exist in a complex, multifaceted antagonism that developed largely during czarist Russian rule. In the Russian Empire, economic and social developments in the late nineteenth century led to a growing division along class lines between the Armenians and Azerbaijanis: The latter were generally poor, unskilled, and rural, while the former inhabited the cities and occupied profitable positions as entrepreneurs and merchants. Benefitting disproportionately from economic advances—especially the establishment of a thriving oil industry in Baku at the close of the 1800s—[36] and from frequent favoritism on the part of their Russian rulers, the Armenians were able to rise to key economic and political positions in the major cities of Transcaucasia. Among the Azerbaijanis, these realities caused feelings of resentment that gradually coalesced into anti-Armenian feelings.[37] With the growth of pan-Turkism among the educated classes of Azerbaijanis in the late nineteenth century, these sentiments were given an intellectual basis.

Pan-Turkism took root among many educated Azerbaijanis in the late 1870s, largely in response to a policy of Russification toward the Azeris by the czarist administration.[38] A form of secular nationalism that had its roots in a declining Ottoman Empire in the late nineteenth century, pan-Turkism espoused the union of all Turkic peoples from the Balkans to western China and the promotion of a sense of national, linguistic, and historical commonality among them. The growth of this ideology among the Azerbaijanis of the Russian Empire fueled anti-Armenian sentiments not only because of its inherently racist nature, but also because Armenia itself was viewed as a geographic obstacle dividing the Turkic world.[39] Thus, according to Anahide Ter Minassian, "under the influence of a small Azeri intelligentsia connected to the landed nobility and the new industrial bourgeoisie, Azeri national consciousness developed not so much against the Russian colonizer as against the Armenian."[40]

The Armenians of the Russian Empire held feelings of animosity and contempt toward the Azerbaijanis as well. Following the experiences of their brethren under Ottoman Turkish rule, the Armenians of Transcaucasia began to equate the Azerbaijani Turks with the perpetrators of anti-Armenian policies in the Turkish empire—especially after the pogroms of 1895–1896 and the massacres of 1915–1916. Meanwhile, in promoting the Armenians' ethno-linguistic distinctiveness, the budding Armenian nationalist movement in Russia in the late nineteenth century tended to foment further anti-Turkish, and therefore anti-Azerbaijani, sentiment. The result was the proliferation of feelings of mistrust, suspicion, and enmity vis-à-vis the Azerbaijanis, feelings that were reciprocated in turn.

While the growth of animosity between the Armenians and Azerbaijanis of Transcaucasia in the late nineteenth and early twentieth centuries by no means made outright conflict between the two communities inevitable, czarist nationality policies tended to worsen their already tense relationship. True to its name, the czarist policy of divide-and-rule sought to promote jealousy and division among neighboring ethnic groups in order to ensure the monarchy's grip on power. When central authority waned during the Russian revolution of 1905, the tensions that had been building between the Armenians and Azerbaijanis exploded into violence throughout the Transcaucasus.

In early February 1905, riots broke out in Baku following the death of an Azeri at the hands of an Armenian policeman. For more than a month, mobs of Azeris rampaged through the Armenian quarter of the city while Russian authorities acquiesced. By the time the violence was brought to an end by the pleas of local religious leaders, 600 Azerbaijanis and 900 Armenians had been killed.[41] The lull in the bloodshed turned out to be only temporary, however; in May the violence reemerged in the town of Nakhichevan.[42]

As the rule of law crumbled throughout Transcaucasia through the fall of 1905, chaos returned to Baku and its environs. Hundreds of Armenian-owned oil wells were set ablaze by Azeris in late September, and the Armenians defended their properties forcefully.[43] Within a week, an estimated 1,500 people had been killed, and 1,026 of the region's 1,609 oil wells had been destroyed.[44] Tentative peace was restored to the Transcaucasus only with the collapse of the revolutionary movement in Russia at the end of 1905 and the gradual reestablishment of order throughout the empire by 1907. Yet, the first blood had been shed between the Armenians and Azerbaijanis, and the precedent for future conflict was set.

The explosion of 1905 was largely the product of class divisions reinforced along national lines and accentuated by czarist policies. Aside from being the first case of large-scale blood-letting between the Armenians and Azerbaijanis, one of the major, though perhaps indirect, results of 1905 was the addition of a territorial dimension to the two peoples' enmity.

For the Armenians, the 1905 violence at the hands of the Azerbaijani Turks and the corresponding inaction on the part of the Russians were further indications of their need for self-reliance as a people. This perception found expression in the growing Armenian nationalist movement in Transcaucasian Armenia, dominated by the Armenian Revolutionary Federation, or Dashnaktsutiun. Importantly, a major component of the Dashnaks' revolutionary program after 1905 was the need for Armenian autonomy in areas regarded as historically Armenian. At the time, much of the focus was on the heartland of Turkish Armenia, but two regions in Transcaucasian Armenia also stirred significant irredentist feelings: Nagorno-Karabakh and Nakhichevan—both of which were attached to Azerbaijan under the imperial Russian system of administration.[45] Significantly, Nagorno-Karabakh itself became a hotbed for the growth of Armenian nationalism following the violence of 1905.

While there had been little progress—or, for that matter, effort—on the part of the Azerbaijanis in developing a collective national consciousness prior to the late nineteenth century, the 1905 bloodshed and the subsequent growth of Armenian irredentism sparked the rise of Azerbaijani nationalism. The Azeris' contemptuous view of the Armenians as a privileged class enjoying the favoritism of the Russians was complimented thereafter by a perceived fear of Armenian claims to what were regarded as rightfully and historically Azerbaijani lands. Significantly, Nagorno-Karabakh was a major center for the growth of Azerbaijani nationalism. Thus, Armenian and Azerbaijani nationalist movements developed side by side in the mountainous area claimed by both peoples.[46]

Nagorno-Karabakh: The Seeds of Conflict

With a total area of 4,800 square kilometers, Nagorno-Karabakh is only 1.5 times larger than the smallest U.S. state, Rhode Island. It is a largely mountainous area situated at the easternmost edge of the highland known as the Armenian plateau. (In fact, the word "nagorno" is derived from the Russian word "nagorny," meaning "mountainous.") Although the ethnic makeup of Nagorno-Karabakh in the late Soviet period (140,000 Armenians and 48,000 Azeris) has led many observers to portray the situation as one of a "predominantly Armenian-inhabited enclave" attempting to break away from Azerbaijan, the Karabakh clash has far more to do with interpretations of history than with demographics.

Armenian scholars have amassed a wealth of historical evidence to support their claim that Nagorno-Karabakh has for centuries been a heartland of Armenian civilization. They claim that the area encompassing the western region of the modern Azerbaijani Republic, including Nagorno-Karabakh, belonged to the Armenians as far back as the formation of the Armenian people in the seventh century B.C.[47] Although conquered by the Medes in the sixth century B.C., the area was restored to Armenian control in the second century B.C. and thereafter became the province of Artsakh under the Artashes dynasty. In 387 A.D., the kingdom of Armenia was partitioned between Byzantium and the Sassanid Empire in Iran, with Artsakh becoming part of the Iranian province of Albania.[48] Although separated from the Armenian heartland, the inhabitants of the mountainous region were different from their brethren under Byzantine rule in that they were able to maintain a degree of autonomy over their affairs.

After nearly a century of tolerating Christianity in Albania, Sassanid Iran began a campaign of persecution and attempted assimilation of the Armenians after 461 A.D. However, Armenian princes populating the mountains of the former province of Artsakh organized a successful resistance, and for a brief period between the late fifth and early sixth centuries were able to reestablish Armenian autonomy there.[49] When the Sassanid presence in Transcaucasia was usurped by that of the Arabs in the seventh century, the Armenians of mountainous Karabakh continued to preserve their traditions and cling to a semi-autonomous existence while the rest of their countrymen were befallen by foreign rule. Over the next one thousand years, this precedent of Armenian autonomy was upheld, making Nagorno-Karabakh the only part of historic Armenia "where a tradition of national sovereignty was preserved unbroken until the late medieval period."[50] Thus, the Armenians' strong emotional and nationalistic attachment to the land is clear: As Richard G. Hovannisian notes, "while the rest of Armenia was submerged under foreign control, a flicker of freedom was maintained in Karabakh."[51]

In the thirteenth century, after having survived the Seljuk and Mongol invasions, an important Armenian family arose in Karabakh. Known as the Jalalians, they embarked on a campaign to restore major Armenian cultural works in the mountainous region, including monasteries and monuments. The descendants of the Jalalian family continued this action with fervor, particularly the five Armenian princes who achieved recognition by Shah Abbas of Persia as the local administrators of Karabakh in 1603.[52] Although subjects of the Shah, these princes "were largely autonomous in matters of defense and internal policy, justice and taxation,"[53] thereby maintaining a degree of freedom to preserve Armenian national traditions while the rest of their countrymen were subjugated under foreign rule.

Importantly, disunion amongst the five princes allowed the establishment of a foothold in mountainous Karabakh by a Turkic tribe around 1750. This event marked the first time that Turks were able to penetrate the eastern Armenian highlands; for the prior seven hundred years Turkic tribes had inhabited the plains of the southeastern Transcaucasus following their large-scale migration from Asia Minor.[54] Because members of these tribes came eventually to view themselves as Azerbaijanis, Armenian scholars cite this establishment of a Turkic presence in Nagorno-Karabakh as the initial arrival of the Azerbaijanis to the region. Importantly, however, modern Azerbaijani historians dispute this assertion and claim that Karabakh has long been an integral part of Azerbaijan.[55]

In the view of contemporary Azerbaijani scholars first articulated in Ziia Buniatov's 1965 monograph entitled *Azerbaijan in the Seventh-Ninth Centuries*, modern Azeris are descendants of the Caucasian Albanians.[56] It is alleged that in antiquity the Albanians were one of the three major peoples of Caucasia (along with the Armenians and Georgians) with a state extending from Lake Sevan eastward to the Caspian Sea, and from the Caucasus Mountains southwards to the Aras River.[57] Initially adherents of Christianity, the majority of the Albanian population converted to Islam in the seventh century A.D. and were linguistically Turkified four hundred years later.

Azerbaijani scholars of this view refuse to accept the Armenian claim that the inhabitants of mountainous Karabakh have been ethnically Armenian since earliest times, as compared to the people living on the plains to the east who are descendants of Islamized and Turkified Albanians. In contrast, it is argued that, beginning in the eighth century, immigrating Armenians forced the cultural, linguistic, and religious assimilation of the indigenous Albanian population of Karabakh.[58] Thus, Buniatov and others have argued that the modern Armenian inhabitants of

Nagorno-Karabakh are not Armenians *per se*, but are Armenianized Albanians, and thus, Azerbaijanis. According to Patrick Donabedian, the purpose of this approach is "to show that the Armenianness of Karabakh is only a myth and that the 'Albanians' who live there have no reason to challenge their membership [in] the Republic of Azerbaijan."[59]

It is beyond the scope of this book to weigh more fully the respective historical arguments of Armenian and Azerbaijani scholars. However, as Robert H. Hewsen points out, both sides are guilty of oversimplifying the ethnic history of the region: "The population of southeast Caucasia, whether under Armenian or Albanian rule, was highly mixed, and to label it as being essentially one or the other or even to divide it simply into two groups is well in advance of the evidence."[60] The Trans-caucasus is in fact a rich mosaic of ethnic groups produced over the millennia; the Russian Empire's 1897 census listed twenty-two separate nationalities residing in the region.[61]

The willingness of Armenian and Azerbaijani scholars to depict a clear ethnic history of the region where none exists is indicative of the passion attached to the Karabakh issue by both sides. For the Armenians, the nationalistic affinity for Nagorno-Karabakh developed over centuries of hardship brought about by foreign rule. Importantly, the Azerbaijanis' own attachment to the land is a much more recent historical phenomenon.

In a momentous event for the development of the Armenia-Azerbaijan conflict, Russia annexed the Nagorno-Karabakh region from Iran in 1805 as a result of the first Russo-Iranian War. Administered by the Iranians as a collective unit known as the Khanate of Karabakh, the region was populated largely by Armenians at the time of the Russian takeover. In an attempt to consolidate their rule, the Russians dissolved the numerous Iranian administrative units in the conquered territories and reorganized them into a handful of larger guberniia, or provinces. The former Khanate of Karabakh was expanded to include parts of the areas to the east, forming the Elisavetpol Guberniia.[62]

With the creation of the new province of Elisavetpol, the Russians linked the mountainous region of Karabakh with the plains to the east, which were inhabited predominantly by Azeris. This development was beneficial for the Azeris, the majority of whom were semi-nomadic herders; the highlands of Karabakh provided valuable pasturage for livestock during the summer months.[63] Over time, this arrangement had two significant consequences for the development of the Azerbaijanis' attachment to Nagorno-Karabakh.

By linking the highlands of Karabakh with the plains to the east, the Russians brought the economies and transportation networks of both areas closer together, with Nagorno-Karabakh becoming integrated gradually but completely into the economic system of eastern Transcaucasia.[64] The predominantly pastoral Azeris became dependent heavily upon this link, and it would later be used to justify the inclusion of Nagorno-Karabakh within the Azerbaijan Soviet Socialist Republic.[65]

Adding to the growth of Azerbaijani economic ties to the Karabakh highlands in the late nineteenth century was a growing emotional and nationalistic affinity for the area. Many of the great Azeri poets, composers, and writers hailed from the region,[66] and, more importantly, a semi-feudal landed aristocracy took root there that became a major focal point of the Azerbaijani nationalism that was developing during that time period.[67] In the aftermath of the communal violence between Armenians and Azerbaijanis in 1905, this aristocracy became a significant rallying force for Azerbaijani nationalism. Thus, for nationalistic—and to a lesser extent, economic—reasons, Nagorno-Karabakh came to occupy a dear place in the hearts of the Azerbaijanis while under Russian rule.

Although of major significance to the Azeris, Russia's conquest of Nagorno-Karabakh also had an important impact on Armenian claims to the area. While the mountainous region was annexed by St. Petersburg in 1805, the rest of Transcaucasian Armenia remained under Iranian rule until subdued by Russia in 1826. The Armenians of Nagorno-Karabakh were thus separated from their brethren to the west for 21 years, during which time they were incorporated into the Elisavetpol province where the Azerbaijanis held a majority.[68]

Of additional significance, the Russian reorganization of Iran's former Transcaucasian possessions brought with it the dissolution of the five Armenian principalities in the Karabakh highlands that had managed to maintain semi-autonomy under Iranian rule since 1603.[69] Thus, the tradition of Armenian semi-autonomy in Nagorno-Karabakh dating back to the second century B.C. was broken by St. Petersburg in 1805. Although a major blow, these events hardened the Armenians' connection to Nagorno-Karabakh, and the region became a focal point for the development of Armenian nationalism in the late nineteenth and early twentieth centuries.

The tiny region of Nagorno-Karabakh occupies a central place in the national consciousness of both the Armenian and Azerbaijani peoples. For the Armenians, Karabakh is "a refuge and bastion,"[70] the final stronghold where a tradition of national autonomy was preserved nearly uninterrupted; for the Azerbaijanis, Nagorno-Karabakh is both a key part of the ancient state to which they trace their ancestry and a focal point of their nationalism. Had relations remained good between the two peoples in the late nineteenth and early twentieth centuries, it is not certain whether overlapping claims to the territory of Nagorno-Karabakh would have resulted necessarily in conflict between them.

However, the growth of ill will during that time period, culminating in the violence of 1905, made it nearly inevitable that the region would become a bone of contention between the two neighboring peoples. With the proliferation of mutually reinforcing nationalisms in Nagorno-Karabakh among the Armenians and Azerbaijanis after 1905, all that was needed was a spark to set off an explosion of emotions on both sides. That spark came when the First World War brought chaos, destruction, and unexpected independence to Armenia and Azerbaijan.

Impact of the First World War

In the spring of 1918, Turkish troops capitalized on Russia's withdrawal from the Transcaucasus to begin an attack on eastern Armenia. Joined in the assault by Azerbaijani irregulars, the so-called "Army of Islam" set out to open a corridor between Turkey and Azerbaijan at Armenia's expense.[71] Although out-gunned and out-numbered, the Armenians put up stiff resistance and succeeded in stopping the Turkish advance at the battle of Sardarabad.[72] In the meantime, Georgia and Azerbaijan declared their independence on 26 and 27 May, respectively, and Armenia was left with little choice but to follow suit three days later.[73]

Despite the victory at Sardarabad, much of Armenia remained under Turkish occupation, and the authorities knew that they could not hold off another determined Turkish assault. By the Treaty of Batum, concluded on 4 June 1918, Armenia accepted crushing terms at the hands of the Ottomans: All Armenian claims to the historic heartland of eastern Turkey were repudiated, and the districts of Kars and Ardahan in Transcaucasian Armenia were ceded to Turkey. Together with the territorial losses imposed by the March 1918 Treaty of Brest-Litovsk, the Batum Treaty forced the Republic of Armenia to begin its existence on 4,500 square miles of bleak, rocky land inhabited by 600,000 people—most of them refugees who had fled the Turkish genocide in eastern Anatolia.[74]

Like Armenia, the Republic of Azerbaijan began its independence in the face of a chaotic situation. The oil-rich city of Baku had emerged as a stronghold of Bolshevism shortly after the October Russian Revolution, and friction between the Bolsheviks and the pan-Turkic Musavat party sparked a brief civil war in March 1918. During the so-called "March Days" that ensued, Armenian forces allied with the Bolsheviks to crush a Musavat bid to gain control of the city.[75] Equating the Musavats with the Turks, the Armenians set out to take revenge for the persecution and genocide suffered at the hands of the Ottomans. According to Firuz Kazemzadeh:

The brutalities continued for weeks. No quarter was given by either side: neither age nor sex was respected. Enormous crowds roamed the streets, burning houses, killing every passer-by who was identified as an enemy, many innocent persons suffering death at the hands of both the Armenians and the Azerbaijanis. The struggle which had begun as a political contest between the Musavat and the Soviet assumed the character of a gigantic race riot.[76]

While not an isolated incident in light of the Azerbaijanis' participation in the Ottoman Turkish offensive against Armenia in early 1918, the "March Days" played a major role in bringing pre-existing inter-communal tensions to the surface of Armenian-Azerbaijani relations. Moreover, with the checkered demographic pattern of the Trancaucasus leaving large numbers of Armenians and Azerbaijanis within the borders of each new state, the potential for ethnic conflict was great.

Although the pullout of Russian forces from the Transcaucasus following the October Revolution of 1917 marked the beginning of a major upheaval in the affairs of the Armenians and Azerbaijanis, the final defeat of Ottoman Turkey in October 1918 made an already frenzied situation worse. Under the terms of the

Mudros armistice of 30 October, Turkey agreed to pull its troops back from the Transcaucasus in order to make way for the forthcoming British military presence.[77] Before that presence was in place fully, however, the three states of Transcaucasia made a desperate scramble to incorporate disputed territories into their fledgling republics before the onset of the Paris Peace Conference, which was designated by the Allies as the forum through which all territorial disputes left over from the war were to be settled. While there was no shortage of such disputes among the Georgians, Armenians, and Azerbaijanis in 1918, Nagorno-Karabakh eclipsed all of the others in terms of the emotional and nationalistic fervor shown by the conflicting parties.

The spark that ignited the powder keg of Nagorno-Karabakh came in the spring of 1918, when the pan-Turkic "Army of Islam" invaded eastern Armenia. Prodded by their Azerbaijani allies, the advancing Turkish force pushed to the environs of Nagorno-Karabakh in August and demanded the Armenian citizenry's capitulation to Azerbaijani rule. By October, the Armenian resistance was overwhelmed by the Turks' superior numbers, and the Karabakh leadership was forced to submit to the "Army of Islam" in exchange for the promise of merciful treatment.[78] Azerbaijani-Turkish rule turned out to be anything but benevolent, however.

Within less than a week the Muslims unleashed a terror campaign against the townspeople marked by mass arrests, public hangings, and the forceful disarming of the populace. In response, the Karabakh Armenian leadership repudiated its acceptance of the Turks' terms and began an armed insurgency against them.[79] The Armenians' brutal guerilla campaign forestalled successfully the attempted Turkish conquest of Nagorno-Karabakh until Ottoman forces began their pullout from the Transcaucasus in the closing days of the First World War.[80]

With the departure of the Azerbaijanis' key ally from the area in November 1918, the Armenians saw a golden opportunity to make Nagorno-Karabakh a part of their fledgling country once and for all. However, before a popular Armenian partisan leader could march on the mountainous area and insure its incorporation into the republic, yet another new player emerged onto the regional scene: Great Britain.

The intercession of Britain into the emerging Armenia-Azerbaijan conflict was a fateful event for both sides. The British, motivated by strategic and economic concerns, embarked immediately upon a generally pro-Azerbaijani policy. On the one hand, it was believed that a strong and independent Azerbaijan allied with Britain would provide a valuable barrier against pan-Islamic—and, later, Soviet—encroachment upon the approaches to India and the newly acquired British mandates in the Middle East. On the other hand, it was perceived that unhindered British access to the vast oil reserves near Baku would require good relations between the two countries.[81] Thus, the British authorities determined that a policy friendly to the Azerbaijanis was necessary in the early days of its occupation of Transcaucasia.[82] In order to induce goodwill, the British set out to provide the Azerbaijanis with an important carrot: The attachment of Nagorno-Karabakh to the Republic of Azerbaijan.[83]

Initially, the Armenians' response was one of shock, for they had fought loyally on the side of the Allies during the war and felt that the British should have been sympathetic to their post-war claims in return.[84] As it became clear that Britain was playing into the hands of the Azerbaijanis on the matter of the disputed territories, the Armenians' disbelief was transformed into resistance.

On 12 February the Fourth Assembly of Karabakh Armenians was convened in the village of Shusha, its goal to reiterate the rejection of Azerbaijani sovereignty over Karabakh and secure the region's inclusion into the Armenian republic. Despite assurances from the local British commander that their rights and security would be upheld, the Karabakh Armenians promised to resist violently any attempt at "the forced establishment of Azerbaijani power on Armenian Karabakh."[85]

Frustrated in their efforts to secure Armenian acceptance of Baku rule, British commanders began gradually to acquiesce in the use of strong-arm measures on the part of the Azeris to achieve such acceptance.[86] On 20 May 1919, the British-appointed Azerbaijani Governor-General Sultanov had all transportation links leading from the highlands to the plain below cut, an act that amounted to a *de facto* blockade of Armenian Karabakh. At the same time, brigades of Kurdish irregulars were organized with the tacit support of Sultanov to begin a campaign of terror against Armenian villages.[87] By early summer, open conflict between the Azerbaijanis and the Armenians of Nagorno-Karabakh seemed imminent.

On 5 June 1919, clashes erupted finally between the two sides following the pullout of British forces from the Karabakh highlands.[88] Azerbaijani and Kurdish irregulars attacked a number of Armenian villages surrounding the stronghold of Shusha, killing as many as 600 Armenians and leaving several villages in ruin. Although Sultanov claimed that the troops were not under his control and therefore were not acting under his orders, it was made clear to the Armenians that Karabakh's fate would be decided by force barring their submission to Azerbaijani authority.[89]

By the middle of 1919, the situation in the region had begun to tilt gradually in favor of Azerbaijan. Outgunned and outnumbered, the Karabakh Armenians were unable increasingly to defend themselves, and the government of Armenia was facing problems of its own and could offer little assistance. Moreover, the British had announced their decision to pull out completely from the Transcaucasus despite the fact that the Paris Peace Conference had not yet begun to take up the question of the region and its territorial disputes; thus, the Armenians believed that whatever restraint the British may have had on the Azerbaijanis would evaporate entirely following their withdrawal.[90] Seeing the balance of power in the dispute shifting increasingly in favor of Azerbaijan, the Karabakh Armenians decided to open negotiations with their tormentors.

As a result of talks held through the summer of 1919, carried out under continued Azerbaijani threats to take the region by force, a 26-point document was signed providing for the provisional authority of Baku over a quasi-autonomous Nagorno-Karabakh pending the final determination of its status at the Paris Peace Conference.[91] For the Armenians the submission was a great emotional defeat, even though they believed that Baku rule would indeed be only temporary in nature. For the Azerbaijanis it was a national victory, because provisional rule was seen as a major step toward permanent control.

Impact of the Sovietization of Armenia and Azerbaijan

Following the conclusion of the agreement on provisional Azerbaijani administration of Nagorno-Karabakh in August 1919, tensions relaxed somewhat among the region's inhabitants. Governor-General Sultanov appointed an Armenian as his assistant in civil affairs, and three Armenians were selected to serve on the council established by the agreement. Also, the *de facto* blockade of Armenian areas was lifted with the re-opening of transportation links between the highlands and the eastern plains.[92] Despite the apparent normalization of life in Nagorno-Karabakh, however, underlying enmity remained. Among Armenian nationalists dominated by the Dashnak party, resentment toward the Karabakh leadership lingered for its ostensible submission to Baku rule. Among the Azerbaijanis, the desire to turn provisional administration of Nagorno-Karabakh into permanent rule continued to be strong. By early 1920, both sides had begun preparations for making a change in the *status quo*.

With his British overseers gone, Governor-General Sultanov sent an ultimatum to the Armenian National Council of Karabakh on 19 February 1920 demanding its unconditional agreement to the region's complete incorporation into Azerbaijan. However, Sultanov did not have enough military forces in place to force Armenian submission when the Council's expected rejection came.[93] Taking advantage of this shortfall, the Armenians began a major uprising in Nagorno-Karabakh on the night of 22 March.[94] What they could not have known at the time is that their rebellion would contribute indirectly to the conquest of Azerbaijan by Bolshevik forces.

Despite its pullout from Transcaucasia in late 1917, Russia never gave up its claim to the region, and Bolshevik leaders made it clear that they regarded its independence as only temporary.[95] Moscow's reconquest of the Transcaucasus was made possible, first, by a *modus vivendi* with Kemal Ataturk, the nationalist leader of post-Ottoman Turkey. Needing Russian arms and money in his battle against the occupying allied powers, Ataturk knew the necessity of having a land corridor with Soviet Russia. For its part, Moscow saw Turkey as a cohort in the struggle against the Western powers as well as a potential bridgehead for Communist expansion into the Near East. With a mutual pledge of non-interference in each other's internal affairs, the Turko-Soviet rapprochement was completed, spelling doom for the independence of the Transcaucasian republics.[96]

In an attempt to combat the Armenian uprising in Nagorno-Karabakh, Azerbaijan shifted the bulk of its military forces to the mountainous region in late March 1920, where it fought numerous engagements and laid waste eventually to the Armenian stronghold of Shusha.[97] Seeing a virtually undefended border before them, the Bolsheviks seized the opportunity to gain a foothold in Azerbaijan. The

Eleventh Red Army entered Baku unopposed on 27 April, and Azerbaijan became the first Soviet Socialist Republic (SSR) of Transcaucasia the next day.[98]

One of the first acts of the newly established Soviet government in Baku was to convey an ultimatum demanding the withdrawal of Armenian forces from Karabakh and the surrounding regions, "otherwise the Revolutionary Committee of the Soviet Socialist Republic of Azerbaijan will consider itself in a state of war with the republic of Armenia."[99] Given three days to decide, Armenia had little choice but to comply with the demand; the Eleventh Red Army entered Nagorno-Karabakh at the end of May 1920, in effect Sovietizing the mountainous region.

Notwithstanding the occupation of Nagorno-Karabakh by Soviet forces, the area's administrative incorporation into the Azerbaijan SSR did not take place at once. An Armenian delegation in Moscow at the time found Bolshevik leaders to be somewhat open-minded on the matter, and on 10 August 1920 an agreement was signed between Armenia and Moscow providing for the Soviet occupation of Karabakh and surrounding territories until an equitable and final solution could be reached on their status.[100] However, events made the accord obsolete the following month as Armenia found itself at war with Turkey.

At odds since the summer of 1919 over the contested provinces of eastern Anatolia, Armenia and Turkey became embroiled in open conflict in September 1920. In light of their numerical advantage and support from the Soviets, the tide of battle turned quickly in favor of the Turks, and the Armenians were forced to sue for peace on 18 November. Under the terms of the Treaty of Alexandropol, Armenia was forced to renounce its claims to eastern Anatolia and cede to Turkey the territories lost in the war. Further reduced in size at the hands of the Turks, Armenia was thrown into a political crisis marked by the fall of its government.[101] Seeing a ripe opportunity to gain control of yet another Transcaucasian republic, the Bolsheviks ordered the Eleventh Red Army to march on the Armenian capital of Yerevan, and Armenia became a Soviet Socialist Republic on 1 December 1920.[102] Thus, the question of Nagorno-Karabakh was transformed overnight from an inter-state dispute to an internal matter of the Soviet Union.

Throughout late 1920 and the first half of 1921, a curious series of events transpired that resulted in the incorporation of Nagorno-Karabakh into Azerbaijan. The first came on the day of Armenia's Sovietization, when the following telegram was sent to the government of Armenia from that of Soviet Azerbaijan: "As of today the border disputes between Armenia and Azerbaijan are declared resolved. Mountainous Karabakh, Zangezur and Nakhichevan are considered part of the Soviet Republic of Armenia."[103]

The telegram appeared to demonstrate great Soviet fraternalism by declaring that "boundaries had no meaning among the family of Soviet peoples."[104] However, it turned out to be a mere propaganda ploy aimed at encouraging the Armenians to view the Red Army as a savior as it entered Yerevan. Following the Sovietization of Armenia, Nariman Narimanov, the Bolshevik leader of Azerbaijan, repudiated the concession and reasserted his republic's claim to Nagorno-Karabakh.[105] In this he had the apparent support of Stalin, who wrote that "it is essential to take sides firmly with one of the two parties, in the present case, of course, Azerbaijan."[106]

In another peculiar event, the Caucasian Bureau of the Communist Party took up the question of Nagorno-Karabakh on 12 June 1921 and proclaimed: "Based on the declaration of the Revolutionary Committee of the Socialist Soviet Republic of Azerbaijan and the agreement between the Socialist Soviet Republics of Armenia and Azerbaijan, it is hereby declared that Mountainous Karabakh is henceforth an integral part of the Socialist Soviet Republic of Armenia."[107] Narimanov, who had been present at the meeting, was outraged and warned that the loss of Karabakh could foment anti-Soviet activity in Azerbaijan.

The Caucasian Bureau met again to consider the commission's recommendations and to settle once and for all the territorial conflicts in Transcaucasia. The fate of Nagorno-Karabakh was determined at two bizarre meetings. On 4 July, with Narimanov present, the Bureau decided by majority vote to transfer the region to the Armenian SSR. Also present was Stalin, then the Soviet Commissar for Nationalities, who did not participate in the debate. Although the exact details are not known, Stalin apparently made his opinion on the matter known to the Bureau members only after the meeting had adjourned. The next day, without deliberation or a formal vote, the Bureau released the following decision:

Proceeding from the necessity for national peace among Muslims and Armenians and of the economic ties between upper [mountainous] and lower Karabakh, of its permanent ties with Azerbaijan, mountainous Karabakh is to remain within the borders of the Azerbaijan SSR, receiving wide regional autonomy with the administrative center at Shusha, becoming an autonomous region.[108]

Thus, without stating its reasoning and apparently at Stalin's behest, the Bureau reversed itself abruptly and made Nagorno-Karabakh a part of the Azerbaijan SSR.

Much attention has been given to the question of why Stalin sought the inclusion of Nagorno-Karabakh within Azerbaijan. Armenian scholars claim that the stated reasons for the decision—the indispensability of economic links between mountainous Karabakh and eastern Transcaucasia and the necessity of maintaining peace between Armenians and Azerbaijanis—were "unconvincing and entirely insufficient for determining the fate of the whole region."[109] On the one hand, the economic argument has been viewed as bankrupt not only because of the fact that all of the Transcaucasus was linked in some way to Baku, which was the only major industrial center of the region, but also because economic ties between Armenia and Nakhichevan did not result in the latter's inclusion within Armenia. On the other hand, it has been pointed out that the decision presumed that peace between Armenians and Azerbaijanis could be possible only with the incorporation of Nagorno-Karabakh within Azerbaijan.[110]

The true motive behind Stalin's intervention in the decision on Nagorno-Karabakh's status was his principle of divide-and-rule. By placing the region within the borders of Azerbaijan, the Armenian inhabitants could be used as potential "hostages" to ensure the Armenian SSR's cooperation with the wishes of the Soviet leadership. By the same token, an "autonomous" Armenian enclave within Azerbaijan could serve as a potential pro-Soviet fifth column in the event of disloyalty by the Azerbaijanis.[111] In order to convert these potentialities into reality, Stalin created the Autonomous Oblast of Nagorno-Karabakh (AONK) on 7 July 1923 and drew its borders so as to leave a narrow strip of land separating it physically from Armenia.[112] As an autonomous area under Azerbaijani suzerainty, the AONK was granted the authority to administer its own affairs in the realm of culture and education, and parallel party and state organs were created and staffed by Armenians.[113] In 1937, the region's name was changed permanently to the Nagorno-Karabakh Autonomous Oblast (NKAO).[114]

The Sovietization of Armenia and Azerbaijan had a momentous impact on the development of the two republics' conflict over Nagorno-Karabakh. For the Armenians, Stalin's 1923 decision was a tremendous national loss; for the Azerbaijanis, it was a great victory, ratifying what was viewed as their historical right to rule the region. Although Armenian complaints about the situation were squelched during the Stalin years, the cause of unification between Armenia and Nagorno-Karabakh was again taken up during the "thaw" of the Krushchev period. A petition signed by 2,500 Karabakh Armenians was sent to Krushchev on 19 May 1964. Its lengthy text detailed Azerbaijan's "chauvinistic, pan-Turk policy" aimed at driving the Armenians out of their "ancestral homeland," and it concluded with a plea for prompt reincorporation into the Armenian SSR.[115] A second petition, signed by 13 prominent Karabakh Armenians, was sent to the Soviet leadership the following year, but both fell on deaf ears.[116]

Over the ensuing decades, the question of Nagorno-Karabakh was suppressed by strong central rule from Moscow. However, in a case where an underlying animosity between two peoples was fueled by a consuming attachment to the same piece of land, it was only a matter of time before the question would resurface violently. As the following chapter will point out, that time came in the late 1980s under the rule of Soviet leader Mikhail Gorbachev.

NOTES

1. Shireen T. Hunter, *The Transcaucasus in Transition: Nation-Building and Conflict* (Washington, DC: Center for Strategic and International Studies, 1994): 3.

2. Charles Burney and David Marshall Lang, *The Peoples of the Hills: Ancient Ararat and Caucasus* (New York: Praeger Publishers, 1971): 88.

3. See Nina G. Garosian, "Iran and Caucasia," in Ronald G. Suny, ed., *Transcaucasia: Nationalism and Social Change* (Ann Arbor: Slavic Publications, 1983): 7–23.

4. Touraj Atabaki, *Azerbaijan: Ethnicity and Autonomy in Twentieth-Century Iran* (London: British Academic Press, 1993): 7.

5. Hunter, *The Transcaucasus in Transition*, pp. 9–10.

6. Atabaki, *Azerbaijan*, p. 9.

7. Chantal Lemercier-Quelquejay, "Islam and Identity in Azerbaijan," *Central Asian Survey* 3, no. 2 (1984): 31.

8. Charles Warren Hostler, *The Turks of Central Asia* (Westport: Praeger Publishers,

1993): 18.

9. Hunter, *The Transcaucasus in Transition*, pp. 10–11.

10. Ibid., pp. 7–8.

11. Hugh Seton-Watson, *The Russian Empire, 1801–1917* (Oxford: Clarendon Press, 1967): 59.

12. Sydney Nettleton Fisher and William Ochsenwald, *The Middle East: A History*. 4th ed. (New York: McGraw-Hill, 1990): 148.

13. Ibid., pp. 184–185.

14. Lord Kinross, *The Ottoman Centuries: The Rise and Fall of the Turkish Empire* (New York: Morrow Quill, 1977): 276–277.

15. John F. Baddeley, *The Russian Conquest of the Caucasus* (1908; reprint, New York: Russell & Russell, 1969): 23–24.

16. Seton-Watson, *The Russian Empire*, pp. 60–61.

17. Kinross, *The Ottoman Centuries*, pp. 403–404.

18. See Muriel Atkin, *Russia and Iran, 1780–1828* (Minneapolis: University of Minnesota Press, 1980).

19. Richard G. Hovannisian, *Armenia on the Road to Independence, 1918* (Berkeley: University of California Press, 1967): 11–12.

20. Ronald G. Suny, *Looking Toward Ararat: Armenia in Modern History* (Bloomington: Indiana University Press, 1993): 7–9.

21. David Marshall Lang, *Armenia: Cradle of Civilization*. 3rd ed. (London: George Allen & Unwin, 1980): 38.

22. Richard G. Hovannisian, "The Historical Dimensions of the Armenian Question, 1878–1923," in Richard G. Hovannisian, ed., *The Armenian Genocide in Perspective* (New Brunswick: Transaction Books, 1986): 20.

23. James B. Gidney, *A Mandate for Armenia* (Oberlin: Kent State University Press, 1967): 8.

24. Hovannisian, *Armenia on the Road to Independence*, p. 24.

25. Hovannisian, "The Historical Dimensions of the Armenian Question," pp. 22–25.

26. Leo Kuper, "The Turkish Genocide of the Armenians, 1915–1917," in Hovannisian, ed., *The Armenian Genocide in Perspective*, pp. 52–53.

27. Hovannisian, *Armenia on the Road to Independence*, p. 7.

28. Ronald G. Suny, *Armenia in the Twentieth Century* (Chico: Scholar's Press, 1983): 10.

29. Suny, *Looking Toward Ararat*, pp. 44–51.

30. Gerard Chaliand and Yves Ternon, *The Armenians: From Genocide to Resistance* (London: Zed Press, 1981): 20–21.

31. Ronald G. Suny, "The Revenge of the Past: Socialism and Ethnic Conflict in Transcaucasia," *New Left Review*, no. 184 (November–December 1990): 16.

32. Lemercier-Quelquejay, "Islam and Identity in Azerbaijan," p. 29.

33. Sussan Siavoshi, "Ethnic Nationalism: The Case of Iran's Azerbaijan," *Current World Leaders* 34, no. 2 (April 1991): 256.

34. Peter B. Golden, "The Turkic Peoples and Caucasia," in Suny, ed., *Transcaucasia*, p. 45.

35. Patrick Donabedian, "The History of Karabagh from Antiquity to the Twentieth Century," in Levon Chorbajian, Patrick Donabedian, and Claude Mutafian, eds., *The Caucasian Knot: The History and Geopolitics of Nagorno-Karabagh* (London: Zed Books, 1994): 81–82.

36. By the early 1870s, the Armenians were the top buyers of oil lands in Baku. At the

same time, the Azerbaijanis occupied the lowest-paid and least-skilled positions in the industry. What resulted was an employer-employee relationship that subordinated poor Muslim workers to wealthy Armenian landholders. Suny, "The Revenge of the Past," p. 17; and Audrey L. Altstadt, "The Azerbaijani Turks' Response to Russian Conquest," *Studies in Comparative Communism* 19, no. 3–4 (Autumn–Winter 1986): 270.

37. Suny, *Looking Toward Ararat*, p. 199.

38. Mir Yacoub, *Le Problème du Caucase* (Paris: Librairie Orientale et Américaine, 1933): 29–44.

39. Christopher J. Walker, *Armenia and Karabagh: The Struggle for Unity* (London: Minority Rights Publications, 1991): 84.

40. Anahide Ter Minassian, "The Revolution of 1905 in Transcaucasia," *Armenian Review* 42, no. 2 (Summer 1989): 14.

41. Caroline Cox and John Eibner, *Ethnic Cleansing in Progress: War in Nagorno-Karabakh* (London: Institute for Religious Minorities in the Islamic World, 1993): 25.

42. Audrey L. Altstadt, *The Azerbaijani Turks: Power and Identity Under Russian Rule* (Stanford: Hoover Institution Press, 1992): 40.

43. See Luigi Villari, *Fire and Sword in the Caucasus* (London: T. Fisher Unwin, 1906): 191–208.

44. Christopher J. Walker, *Armenia: The Survival of a Nation* (New York: St. Martin's Press): 76–77.

45. Hovannisian, *Armenia on the Road to Independence*, pp. 21–23.

46. Suny, *Armenia in the Twentieth Century*, p. 16.

47. H. S. Anassian, "Une Mise Au Point Relative À L'Albanie Caucasienne," *Revue Des Études Arméniennes* 6 (1969): 305.

48. Walker, *Armenia and Karabagh*, pp. 73–74.

49. Ibid., pp. 75–76.

50. Ibid., p. 79.

51. Richard G. Hovannisian, "Nationalist Ferment in Armenia," *Freedom at Issue*, no. 105 (November–December 1988): 29.

52. Manuel Sarkisyanz, *A Modern History of Transcaucasian Armenia* (Nagpur, India: Udyama Commercial Press, 1975): 30–31.

53. Walker, *Armenia and Karabagh*, pp. 78–79.

54. Donabedian, "The History of Karabagh from Antiquity to the Twentieth Century," p. 74.

55. Timoutchine Hadjibeyli, "La Question du Haut Karabagh: Un point de vue azer-baidjanais," *Le Monde Musulman à l'épreuve de la frontière*, no. 48–49 (1988): 282.

56. Ziia M. Buniatov, *Azarbaijan VII–IX asrlarda* (1965; reprint, Baku: Azarbaijan dovlat nashriiiaty, 1989). See also Farida Mamedova, *Politicheskaia istoriia i istoricheskaia geografiia Kavkazskoi Albanii* (Baku: Elm, 1986); and Kemal Aliev, *Kavkazskaia Albaniia: I v. do n. e.- I v. n. e.* (Baku: Elm, 1974): 83–123.

57. G. Vorochil, "De l'histoire de l'Albanie caucasienne et de l'écriture albanaise," *Bedi Kartlisa: revue de kartvélologie* 32 (1974): 279.

58. Nora Dudwick, "The Case of the Caucasian Albanians: Ethnohistory and Ethnic Politics," *Cahiers du Monde russe et soviétique* 31, no. 2–3 (April–September 1990): 379.

59. Donabedian, "The History of Karabagh from Antiquity to the Twentieth Century," p. 64.

60. Robert H. Hewsen, "Ethno-History and the Armenian Influence Upon the Caucasian Albanians," in Thomas J. Samuelian, ed., *Classical Armenian Culture: Influences and Creativity* (Pennsylvania: Scholars Press, 1982): 33.

61. Minassian, "The Revolution of 1905 in Transcaucasia," p. 2.

62. Victor Porkhomovsky, "Historical Origins of Interethnic Conflicts in Central Asia and Transcaucasia," in Vitaly V. Naumkin, ed., *Central Asia and Transcaucasia: Ethnicity and Conflict* (Westport: Greenwood Press, 1994): 25.

63. Donabedian, "The History of Karabagh from Antiquity to the Twentieth Century," p. 79.

64. Hunter, *The Transcaucasus in Transition*, pp. 97–98.

65. Igrar Aliev, *Daghlyg Garabagh: tarikh, faktlar, hadislar* (Baku: Elm, 1989): 103.

66. Audrey L. Altstadt, "Nagorno-Karabagh: 'Apple of Discord' in the Azerbaijan SSR," *Central Asian Survey* 7, no. 4 (1988): 71.

67. Nora Dudwick, "Armenian-Azerbaijani Relations and Karabagh: History, Memory, and Politics," *Armenian Review* 46, no. 1–4 (1993): 87.

68. Porkhomovsky, "Historical Origins of Interethnic Conflicts," p. 25.

69. Mark Malkasian, *Gha-ra-bagh! The Emergence of the National Democratic Movement in Armenia* (Detroit: Wayne State University Press, 1996): 19.

70. Donabedian, "The History of Karabagh from Antiquity to the Twentieth Century," p. 62.

71. Cox and Eibner, *Ethnic Cleansing in Progress*, p. 27.

72. Walker, *Armenia*, pp. 254–255.

73. Hovannisian, *Armenia on the Road to Independence*, pp. 188–191.

74. Richard G. Hovannisian, "Caucasian Armenia Between Imperial and Soviet Rule: The Interlude of National Independence," in Suny, ed., *Transcaucasia*, pp. 261–262.

75. Ronald G. Suny, *The Baku Commune, 1917–1918: Class and Nationality in the Russian Revolution* (Princeton: Princeton University Press, 1972): 218.

76. Firuz Kazemzadeh, *The Struggle for Transcaucasia, 1917–1921* (New York: Philosophical Library, 1951): 73.

77. A secret Anglo-French agreement signed on 23 December 1917 awarded "the Cossack territories, the territory of the Caucasus, Armenia, Georgia, (and) Kurdistan" to Britain as "zones of influence." Quoted in Walker, *Armenia*, p. 259.

78. Richard G. Hovannisian, *The Republic of Armenia, Volume I: The First Year, 1918–1919* (Berkeley: University of California Press, 1971): 85.

79. James G. Mandalian, "The Transcaucasian Armenian Irredenta," *Armenian Review* 14, no. 2–59 (Summer 1961): 8–9.

80. Cox and Eibner, *Ethnic Cleansing in Progress*, p. 29.

81. Hovannisian, *The Republic of Armenia, Volume I*, p. 157; and Manuel S. Hassassian, *The Historical Evolution of the Armenian Question and the Conflict Over "Nagorno-Karabagh" "Artsakh"* (Jerusalem: Palestinian Academic Society for the Study of International Affairs, 1988): 42–43.

82. Akaby Nassibian, *Britain and the Armenian Question, 1915–1923* (New York: St. Martin's Press, 1984): 154–155.

83. At the time (late 1918), it was believed that the Republic of Armenia would be awarded the historically Armenian provinces of eastern Turkey at the forthcoming peace conference. In the eyes of the British, therefore, it only seemed fair to award the Azerbaijanis Nagorno-Karabakh. Hovannisian, "Nationalist Ferment in Armenia," p. 31.

84. Artin H. Arslanian, "Britain and the Question of Mountainous Karabagh," *Middle Eastern Studies* 16, no. 1 (January 1980): 93.

85. "The Fifth Assembly of the Armenians of Karabagh to General Shuttleworth, Commander of the British forces in the Caucasus," 25 April 1919, in Gerard J. Libaridian, ed., *The Karabakh File: Documents and Facts on the Question of Mountainous Karabakh,*

1918–1988 (Cambridge: The Zoryan Institute, March 1988): 17–19.

86. Hovannisian, *The Republic of Armenia, Volume I*, pp. 172–173.

87. Walker, *Armenia and Karabagh*, pp. 95–96.

88. Mandalian, "The Transcaucasian Armenian Irredenta," p. 10.

89. Hovannisian, *The Republic of Armenia, Volume I*, pp. 176–177.

90. Arslanian, "Britain and the Question of Mountainous Karabagh," p. 94.

91. Walker, *Armenia and Karabagh*, p. 96.

92. Hovannisian, *The Republic of Armenia, Volume I*, p. 188.

93. Walker, *Armenia and Karabagh*, p. 98.

94. Tadeusz Swietochowski, "The Problem of Nagorno-Karabagh: Geography Versus Demography Under Colonialism and in Decolonization," in Hafeez Malik, ed., *Central Asia: Its Strategic Importance and Future Prospects* (New York: St. Martin's Press, 1993): 146.

95. Richard Pipes, *Russia Under the Bolshevik Regime* (New York: Alfred A. Knopf, 1993): 160.

96. Richard Pipes, *The Formation of the Soviet Union: Communism and Nationalism, 1917–1923* (Cambridge: Harvard University Press, 1964): 222–223; and Christopher J. Walker, "Between Turkey and Russia: Armenia's Predicament," *The World Today* 44 (August–September 1988): 143.

97. Walker, *Armenia and Karabagh*, pp. 98–99.

98. Pipes, *The Formation of the Soviet Union*, pp. 226–227.

99. Quoted in Walker, *Armenia*, p. 284.

100. Walker, *Armenia and Karabagh*, p. 103.

101. Mandalian, "The Transcaucasian Armenian Irredenta," pp. 24–25.

102. Pipes, *The Formation of the Soviet Union*, pp. 232–233.

103. "Telegram sent by the Soviet Azerbaijani government to the Armenian republic regarding the decision to cede Armenian territories," in Libaridian, ed., *The Karabakh File*, p. 34.

104. Richard G. Hovannisian, "Mountainous Karabagh in 1920: An Unresolved Contest," *Armenian Review* 46, no. 1–4 (1993): 27.

105. Cox and Eibner, *Ethnic Cleansing in Progress*, p. 31.

106. Quoted in Walker, *Armenia and Karabagh*, p. 107.

107. "Announcement of Armenian-Azerbaijani agreement on disputed territories," in Libaridian, ed., *The Karabakh File*, p. 35.

108. Quoted in Altstadt, *The Azerbaijani Turks*, p. 118.

109. Vardges Mikaelian and Lendrush Khurshudian, "Several Issues Concerning the History of Mountainous Karabagh," *Armenian Review* 43, no. 2–3 (Summer–Autumn 1990): 62.

110. Ibid., pp. 62–63.

111. Cox and Eibner, *Ethnic Cleansing in Progress*, p. 31.

112. Walker, *Armenia and Karabagh*, p. 109.

113. Altstadt, *The Azerbaijani Turks*, p. 126.

114. Altstadt, "Nagorno-Karabagh," p. 67.

115. "Petition from the Armenians of Mountainous Karabagh to Prime Minister Nikita Krushchev," 19 May 1964, in Libaridian, ed., *The Karabakh File*, pp. 42–46.

116. Claude Mutafian, "Karabagh in the Twentieth Century," in Chorbajian et al., *The Caucasian Knot*, p. 147.

2

The Armenia-Azerbaijan Conflict, 1988–1991

Soviet patriotism is the greatest of our values. Any manifestations of nationalism and chauvinism are incompatible with it.

—General-Secretary Mikhail S. Gorbachev,
February 1988

Following Stalin's incorporation of Nagorno-Karabakh into the Azerbaijan SSR in 1923 and the refusal of his successors to revisit the issue, the question of the region's status was seemingly put to rest by years of strong central rule from Moscow. However, in the hearts and minds of the Armenians and Azerbaijanis, the question of Nagorno-Karabakh never receded in importance: The Armenians retained a strong desire for unification with their brethren in the mountainous area and vice versa, while the Azerbaijanis retained an equally strong desire to retain sovereignty over the land. Therefore, when the "thaw" of the Gorbachev period arrived, tensions and irredenta that had been just below the surface of Armenian-Azerbaijani relations were released, resulting in a spiraling cycle of violence and bloodshed between the two republics that outlasted the Soviet Union itself.

GLASNOST, *PERESTROIKA*, AND THE REAWAKENING OF THE ARMENIA-AZERBAIJAN CONFLICT

After becoming the General-Secretary of the Communist Party of the Soviet Union (CPSU) in 1985, Mikhail S. Gorbachev set out to lead his country out of the "stagnation" of the Brezhnev era. Seeing the USSR's lagging economy as a potential long-term threat to its superpower status, Gorbachev embarked on a program of economic restructuring known as *perestroika*. In tandem with this policy was *glasnost,* or "openness," which was intended both to stimulate the Party and to mobilize popular support for reforms by allowing public debate of formerly taboo issues.[1] In his preoccupation with the revitalization of the Soviet economic and political systems, however, Gorbachev unleashed forces that had unintended consequences for the future of the Soviet empire.

One of the major undesigned results of Gorbachev's reform policies was the reawakening of the nationalities question in the USSR in the late 1980s. On the one hand, the allowance of a degree of public debate and openness in the media led inevitably to the expression of long simmering grievances among the Soviet Union's numerous ethnic groups. Indeed, Gorbachev's own explicit criticism of Stalinist nationality policies seemed to sanction greater debate on the issue.[2] On the other hand, Gorbachev's program of political "democratization" gave impetus to the rise of grass-roots political movements in the republics. Numerous informal and unofficial movements devoted to various political and social causes arose, particularly those committed to environmental issues, and common nationality served as a natural basis for their organization.[3] Thus, Gorbachev's reforms set in motion processes that promoted, directly or indirectly, the rise of nationally based movements in the republics, movements whose goals often clashed with the interests of other national groups. Such was the case particularly between Armenia and Azerbaijan, as reawakening nationalism and irredenta on the part of the former brought the question of Nagorno-Karabakh to the surface of relations between the two republics once again.

Initially, the Armenian nationalist movement that emerged in 1987 coalesced around issues related to the republic's terrible environmental condition.[4] However, two events occurred in the latter part of the year that led the Armenians to believe that a "window of opportunity" had opened on the possibility of realizing unification with the Nagorno-Karabakh Autonomous Oblast (NKAO). First, Heydar Aliyev, the former Communist party chief of Azerbaijan, was removed from his post in the Politburo in October,[5] possibly signaling to the Armenians that the last high-level opponent of their claims to Nagorno-Karabakh was out of the way. Several weeks later, Abel Aganbegyan, a senior economic advisor to Gorbachev, suggested while on a trip to London that Moscow was willing to treat the Armenian demand for unification with Karabakh sympathetically.[6] Although later denied, this comment, together with Aliyev's dismissal and the growing climate of openness in general, gave the Armenians cause to believe that a redressing of the territorial "injustices" imposed by Stalin was on the horizon.

In the latter part of 1987 the Armenians' growing optimism for union with Nagorno-Karabakh was given a powerful voice in the budding Armenian nationalist movement. Demonstrations in Yerevan and Stepanakert (the NKAO capital) in support of peaceful unification became more and more frequent, drawing first hundreds and then thousands of people. In August a petition signed by more than 75,000 Armenians was sent to General-Secretary Gorbachev, pleading for the Soviet leader "to reattach Mountainous Karabakh to Socialist Armenia."[7]

Events took a new turn in October, when Armenian villagers residing just outside the borders of the NKAO were beaten by Azeris after opposing the nomination of an Azerbaijani for the position of president of the local kolkhoz. When news of the incident reached Yerevan, thousands of people took to the streets in protest.[8] As 1987 came to an end, the populace of Soviet Armenia and the NKAO were mobilizing around the cause of unification.

The early months of 1988 were crucial in forging the subsequent course of Armenian-Azerbaijani relations. Mass rallies that had become frequent in late 1987 now became a common occurrence in the Armenian and NKAO capitals, drawing tens of thousands of participants often toting pictures of the Soviet leader.[9] Azerbaijan viewed the Armenian moves with hostility, and Azerbaijani party officials complained to Moscow that the rallies threatened the republic's territorial integrity. Mass Armenian demonstrations were responded to sporadically by the Azerbaijanis, and emotions ran high on both sides. Amid a climate of growing nationalism and heightening tension in the Transcaucasus, a milestone event for the development of the Armenia-Azerbaijan conflict occurred on 20 February 1988, when the Soviet of People's Deputies of Nagorno-Karabakh passed a resolution by a vote of 110–17 requesting the oblast's transfer to the Armenian SSR. (See Appendix A.) Nominally just a "rubber stamp" for official party policy, the soviet's action was unprecedented, causing a chain reaction of nationalistic fervor on both sides.

In Armenia, the news of the Nagorno-Karabakh soviet's request was greeted with elation, but not celebration. With no immediate reaction—either positive or negative—coming out of the Kremlin, demonstrations were called every day for a week, with crowds numbering in the hundreds of thousands taking to the streets of Yerevan and calling for union with the NKAO.[10] When it did come on 23 February, Moscow's response was met with disbelief in Armenia: "Having examined the information about developments in the Nagorno-Karabakh Autonomous Region, the CPSU Central Committee holds that the actions and demands directed at revising the existing national and territorial structure contradict the interests of the working people in Soviet Azerbaijan and Armenia and damage inter-ethnic relations."[11] After having put high hopes in Gorbachev and his reforms, the Armenians found those hopes dashed once the issue of Nagorno-Karabakh was forced.

The Central Committee's rejection of union between Armenia and the NKAO spawned mass demonstrations in Yerevan and Stepanakert through the end of the month. Seeing a potential crisis in the making, Gorbachev intervened personally on 26 February and allegedly promised to find a "just solution" to the question of Nagorno-Karabakh.[12] As if to give Gorbachev one last chance to justify their hopes in him, the Armenians agreed to discontinue the mass gatherings for a month.[13]

Just as it appeared that calm might prevail in Yerevan and Stepanakert, the Azerbaijanis were reacting in their own way to the Nagorno-Karabakh soviet's request for union with Armenia. Despite the Central Committee's apparent resolution of the matter in their favor, crowds of Azeris—responding apparently to the killing of two Azeri youths on the outskirts of the NKAO—took to the streets of Sumgait and from 27 to 29 February embarked on a binge of havoc in the city's Armenian quarter.[14] After three nights of violence, which the Azeri authorities did little to suppress, the official death toll stood at 32—26 of whom were Armenians—[15] although other sources numbered the dead in the hundreds.[16] Thus, after almost 70 years of uneasy but generally peaceful co-existence under Soviet rule, the Armenians and Azerbaijanis turned upon each other once again with lethal violence, marking the opening blows in a bloody and intractable clash that outlasted the very forces that helped lead to its resurgence.

Impact of the Sumgait Violence

Among the first visible effects of Sumgait was a growing exodus of refugees from Armenia and Azerbaijan. Fearing further anti-Armenian violence in other cities across Azerbaijan, tens of thousands of Armenians began leaving the republic for Armenia.[17] Similarly, large numbers of Azeris living in Armenia began returning to their home republic out of fear of reprisals for the Sumgait incidents.[18] In both cases, the refugees often found themselves in an inhospitable environment upon their arrival. Unemployment was rampant, and resentment toward the other side ran high. Over time, the refugees became a radicalizing force that fueled bloody inter-communal clashes through 1990.[19]

Contributing further to the hardening of each side's disposition and to the escalation of violence in the wake of Sumgait was a growing disillusionment with Moscow's handling of the crisis. The primary source of this discontentment was the Kremlin's general tendency to respond in half-measures to the Karabakh Armenians' bid for self-determination, seeking to calm the situation while shying from the search for a permanent solution to the problem suitable to both sides. However, such a course of action was satisfactory for neither side, and it fed— rather than stifled—the spread of violence and the growth of nationalism and separatism in Armenia and Azerbaijan.

From the outset, the Kremlin based its position on the question of Nagorno-Karabakh on Article 78 of the Soviet constitution: "The territory of a union republic may not be altered without its consent. The boundaries between union republics may be altered by mutual agreement of the union republics concerned, subject to confirmation by the USSR."[20] In the case of Nagorno-Karabakh, in which Baku refused to recognize the right of the Karabakh Armenians to self-determination and thus rejected their attempt to secede from the Azerbaijan SSR, it was clear that such a constitutional mechanism would be incapable of yielding a solution suitable to all involved parties. The Gorbachev regime was thus in a nearly impossible position from the onset.

Complicating further the apparent intractability of the NKAO dispute in constitutional terms were Gorbachev's own short-comings regarding the nation-alities question in general. As Richard Pipes notes, the General-Secretary had little appreciation for either the intensity or complexity of the animosity between many of the USSR's more than one hundred ethnic groups, and while the Soviet leader was willing to a certain extent to acknowledge grievances on the part of the republics, he had "no sympathy whatsoever for separatist tendencies."[21] Thus, Gorbachev's own failings—which often bounded on outright impatience— tended to make the Nagorno-Karabakh problem worse, for he proved unwilling to give serious consideration to anything but the most token moves aimed at calming the populace.

Indeed, rather than recognizing the frequent mass demonstrations in Armenia and the NKAO as manifestations of the popular will, he branded the activities as "extremism" aimed at undermining his reforms. On occasions of violence between Armenians and Azerbaijanis, Gorbachev fingered the blame at assorted "hooligan elements" and "anti-*perestroika* forces."[22] Seemingly ignorant of the complexity of the Nagorno-Karabakh problem and the grievances between Armenia and Azerbaijan, the General-Secretary committed his regime to a policy of reacting to developments rather than heading them off through the search for a suitable solution. Thus, the next two years were marked by continued conflict between the Armenians and Azerbaijanis that the Soviet leadership proved ill equipped to deal with adequately.

The Soviet government first took up the matter of Nagorno-Karabakh in March 1988, when, in keeping with his earlier promise to Armenian activists to seek a "just solution" to the dispute, Gorbachev brought the issue before both the USSR Supreme Soviet and the CPSU Central Committee. The result was a pair of resolutions aimed apparently at buying time for the Soviet leadership by offering meager concessions to the Armenians of the NKAO.[23] Among the measures promised were boosted investment in housing, industry, and social services and an increase in the availability of Armenian-language television and books.[24]

Although the prospect of increased economic, social, and cultural development for Nagorno-Karabakh was welcomed in principle by the Armenians, any measure short of full union was inadequate for the growing nationalist movement in the republic. Consequently, the Gorbachev regime's program for the NKAO was rejected wholly, and for most Armenians it marked the end of their support for the Soviet leader and his reforms.[25] Thereafter, the Armenian movement was driven by the so-called Karabakh Committee, an informal grouping of eleven nationalist intellectuals formed in early 1988.

With the overwhelming support of the populace, the Karabakh Committee became a *de facto* opposition to the Armenian Communist Party by espousing a program including union between the republic and the NKAO, democratization, economic reform, and national sovereignty within the framework of a new Soviet confederation.[26] Faced with the greatest challenge to its authority since 1921, the Armenian Communist Party was forced to give ground to the increasingly mobilized population and its unofficial leadership.

On 15 June 1988, following five hours of stormy debate, the Supreme Soviet of the Armenian SSR passed a resolution calling for the USSR Supreme Soviet to approve the annexation of Nagorno-Karabakh by Armenia in accordance with the NKAO's request of 20 February. Expectedly, the Supreme Soviet of Azerbaijan responded two days later with a resounding rejection of the oblast's transfer on the grounds that such a move would violate the Soviet constitution.[27] With the issue at an impasse, all eyes turned to Moscow.

Echoing his earlier statements on the Karabakh question, Gorbachev's keynote speech at the Nineteenth Party Congress condemned what he branded "attempts to abuse *glasnost* with the aim of recarving state borders."[28] When news of the Congress' rejection of any change in inter-republican boundaries reached Armenia, the population was galvanized into action.

Vowing not to let the issue fade from Moscow's attention, the Karabakh Committee called a large-scale general strike in Yerevan on 3 July, and a number of demonstrators proceeded to the nearby Zvartnots Airport intent on disrupting its operations.[29] Two days later, Soviet Ministry of Internal Affairs troops blitzed the airport, leaving two dead and more than forty injured.[30] Already dissatisfied with the Kremlin's handling of the Nagorno-Karabakh question, the violent intervention of Soviet troops served to fuel Armenian anger with—and alienation from—Moscow.

As tensions in the Transcaucasus were turned up another notch with the events of late June and early July 1988, the Armenians of Nagorno-Karabakh made one last bid for peaceful unification with the Armenian SSR through constitutional means. In a move unprecedented in Soviet history, the NKAO Soviet of People's Deputies voted on 12 July in favor of unilateral secession from Azerbaijan.[31] Although the Azerbaijan SSR Supreme Soviet Presidium rejected the move as illegal almost immediately,[32] the Karabakh Committee called a temporary halt to the general strike pending an ultimate decision from Moscow.[33] With a major crisis building between Armenia and Azerbaijan, Gorbachev convened a special session of the USSR Supreme Soviet Presidium on 18 July to consider the matter of Nagorno-Karabakh.

After eight hours of heated debate characterized by the same lack of understanding of the Nagorno-Karabakh problem shown previously by Gorbachev,[34] the Presidium passed a resolution reaffirming the attachment of the NKAO to Azerbaijan while promising the acceleration of the development plans for the oblast outlined in Moscow's previous directives.[35] (See Appendix B.) Almost immediately, the Karabakh Committee, with the full support of most of Armenia and the NKAO, declared the resolution unacceptable, making it clear that a suitable constitutional solution to the Nagorno-Karabakh question was not likely to be found. For the next few months an uneasy calm prevailed in Yerevan and Stepanakert as the Karabakh Committee pondered its next move.

A new wave of ethnic unrest struck Nagorno-Karabakh in mid September 1988 following a week-long general strike that brought the NKAO capital to a virtual standstill. Contending that the arrival of large numbers of Azeri refugees from Armenia was part of an Azerbaijani scheme to increase the oblast's Azeri population,[36] the Karabakh Armenians vowed to strike until the refugees were evacuated to the Azerbaijan SSR.[37] Amid a climate of growing tensions, clashes broke out in the town of Khojaly on 18 September, claiming 33 Armenian and 16 Azerbaijani casualties. Fearing the spread of violence to Armenia itself, the Soviet authorities declared a state of emergency in the region and deployed Ministry of Internal Affairs troops to Yerevan.[38]

As ethnic tensions and sporadic violence between Armenians and Azeris grew in the closing months of 1988, a number of important events took place that had a decisive impact on inter-communal relations in Armenia and Azerbaijan and on the two republics' ties with Moscow. First among these events were the so-called "November days" in the capital of Baku, where Azerbaijani nationalism awoke in highly visible form.

After facing nearly a year of Armenian attempts to annex Nagorno-Karabakh peacefully, the Azerbaijani people had become mobilized by the fall of 1988 in defense of the territorial integrity of their republic. Among their grievances was the de facto loss of Azerbaijani sovereignty over the NKAO in the wake of the USSR Supreme Soviet Presidium's July decision to speed development plans for the oblast. In accordance with those plans, Russian official Arkadiy Volskiy was dispatched to the region by Moscow late in the summer and given extraordinary powers to administer the NKAO development program. Thereafter, "a gradual but steady separation of the region from Azerbaijani control was implemented" despite the fact that Nagorno-Karabakh remained within the borders of the Azerbaijan SSR.[39] For Baku, this deprivation of authority was a step toward the NKAO's ultimate separation from the republic.

Contributing to Azerbaijan's perceived loss of sovereignty over Nagorno-Karabakh was a widespread feeling of anger and frustration with the handling of the crisis by both the Kremlin and Azerbaijani party officials. In the eyes of the Azeris, the Communists had allowed the Nagorno-Karabakh issue to drag on into November when the problem had become clear in February, failed to fulfill the tenets of the Soviet constitution requiring the protection of inter-republican borders, and allowed the publishing of one-sided reports in the media "ignoring the position of Azerbaijanis living in the Armenian SSR."[40] By the fall of 1988, these grievances caused Azeri discontent with Soviet rule to be translated into growing nationalist fervor.

Another major force rallying the Azerbaijani people around the cause of Nagorno-Karabakh was the Armenian nationalist movement itself. In the prior nine months, the Azeris had watched as mass rallies in Yerevan and Stepanakert were effective at bringing Armenian calls for unity with the NKAO to the notice of the central authorities in Moscow. By November, the Azerbaijanis had come to realize that comparable means could be used to voice their own grievances and to guard their republic's territorial integrity. In a sense, therefore, reaction to, and emulation of, the Armenian nationalist movement were significant factors in the development of a similar movement in Azerbaijan.[41]

The week of 17–23 November 1988 witnessed the awakening of Azerbaijani nationalism as Azeris numbering in the hundreds of thousands took to the streets of Baku. Although broader issues facing the Azerbaijan SSR, such as environmental concerns and corruption among local party officials, were of significance, the dominant rallying cry of the demonstrators was the retention of Azerbaijani sovereignty over Nagorno-Karabakh.[42] When news of the USSR Supreme Court's death sentence for an Azeri involved in the Sumgait violence of February reached the crowds on 21 November, demonstrations gained in intensity and spread to surrounding cities. With ethnic tensions already high, a new exodus of refugees between the two republics was sparked by the disorder, making a bad situation worse.[43]

The second crucial event of the latter months of 1988 was the devastating earthquake that struck northwestern Armenia on the morning of 7 December. Measuring 6.9 on the Richter Scale, the tremor flattened large portions of several Armenian cities, leaving as many as 25,000 dead and hundreds of thousands homeless.[44] Far from overshadowing the issue of Nagorno-Karabakh, however, the disaster had the effect of polarizing Armenian attitudes further.

The Armenians' dissatisfaction with Communist rule that had surfaced around the Karabakh question in the previous months was accentuated greatly in the wake of the December earthquake. Countless apartment blocks of substandard quality had become mass graves for Armenians in the affected areas, and rescue services proved inadequate to respond to the disaster. Therefore, when General-Secretary Gorbachev arrived at the scene on 10 December after cutting short a visit to the United States, he was greeted with hostility and anger at the central government's response to the crisis.[45] However, seeing the Armenian disaster as a potential opportunity to behead the growing nationalist movement there, the Soviet leader had all eleven members of the Karabakh Committee and a handful of other Armenian activists arrested on charges of fomenting public disorder. With their unofficial leadership incarcerated without trial amid a large-scale national catastrophe, Armenian opposition to Soviet rule was only galvanized.

The year 1988 set many processes into motion in Armenia and Azerbaijan. Long-simmering grievances—especially those related to the Nagorno-Karabakh question—were unleashed in violent form by the onset of *glasnost* and *perestroika*, and sporadic inter-ethnic clashes caused tensions to rise greatly. As a consequence, Armenian and Azerbaijani nationalism emerged as powerful forces aimed at one another as well as at Moscow. By year's end, attitudes had jelled to an extent that peaceful coexistence between the two peoples seemed a virtual impossibility.

1989 in Review

The second year of the newly awakened Armenia-Azerbaijan dispute was marked by a number of significant events that both deepened the two peoples' hostility toward one another and widened their respective splits with Moscow. While inter-ethnic clashes increased in frequency and intensity during 1989, the most important developments of the year centered around the legalization of the

Armenian and Azerbaijani nationalist movements and the Kremlin's ongoing efforts to resolve the Nagorno-Karabakh question without modifying inter-republican borders. As a result of these events, by year's end the Armenians and Azerbaijanis began to act increasingly without regard for the wishes or policies of the Soviet government.

With the leadership of the Karabakh Committee in Soviet custody by the end of 1988, General-Secretary Gorbachev moved swiftly to find an interim solution to the crisis over Nagorno-Karabakh. Consequently, a 12 January 1989 decree of the USSR Supreme Soviet Presidium endowed the NKAO with a "special admin-istrative status" that put the region under the direct control of a six-person com-mittee answerable to Moscow.[46]   Headed by Gorbachev's personal envoy, Arkadiy Volskiy, the body was "entrusted with the leadership of local organs of state power and administration of the NKAO."[47]

The apparent logic behind the Kremlin's move was clear: Gorbachev hoped that removing the Karabakh Armenians from Baku's rule would satisfy their demands, while leaving the NKAO within Azerbaijan's borders would do the same for the demands of the Azeris. At the official level, the Soviet leader turned out to be right as the Communist leadership of both Armenia and Azer-baijan endorsed the measure.[48] However, at the popular level, the January ruling was greeted with spite on both sides.

Following the disastrous December earthquake and the subsequent imprison-ment of the leading Armenian nationalists, the Armenian movement for unifica-tion with Nagorno-Karabakh quieted somewhat as the populace was forced to confront difficult new domestic realities. The initial popular reaction to the January 1989 establishment of a "special administrative status" for the NKAO was therefore rather muted. However, when agonizingly slow progress towards recovery from the earthquake damage was made by the spring of 1989, the Armenians returned to the streets in large numbers to take up once again the cause of self-determination for the Armenians of the NKAO.

On 24 April 1989, the Armenian holiday marking the anniversary of the Turkish genocide turned into a mass protest calling for the release of the jailed leaders of the Karabakh Committee. When the Soviet leadership decreed in mid May to continue and strengthen the NKAO's special status, mass demonstrations and sporadic violence broke out across Armenia and Nagorno-Karabakh.[49] Seeking perhaps to appease the protestors, Moscow set free the leadership of the Karabakh Committee on 31 May and allowed the group's legalization the follow-ing month as the Armenian National Movement (ANM).[50]

Empowered by their new-found freedom and official status, the leadership of the ANM set out to overturn the Volskiy committee that had been administering the NKAO since January. With the ANM's active support, the Armenians of Nagorno-Karabakh organized and held unauthorized elections on 16 August for a 78-member National Council intended to replace the Moscow-appointed board.[51] The following month, the Armenian Supreme Soviet, which by that time had been forced to adopt the nationalists' program,[52] passed a resolution recognizing the National Council as the sole and legitimate representative of the Armenian population of the NKAO.[53] When Moscow and Baku balked at their efforts, the National Council members set out to establish a parallel government for Nagorno-Karabakh, and one of its activities that would later prove to be of major importance was the creation of Armenian paramilitary self-defense units in the NKAO.[54]

While the Armenians' negative response to the January decision of Moscow regarding Nagorno-Karabakh was formidable, so too was that of the Azerbaijanis. With *de facto* Azerbaijani authority over the NKAO broken in the latter half of 1988, the granting of a special status for the oblast marked the *de jure* loss of Azerbaijani sovereignty over a part of the republic's territory. In the eyes of the increasingly mobilized populace, such a course of events was completely unacceptable, and by the spring of 1989, a new political force arrived on the scene to give direction to this popular discontent.

The rise of the Azerbaijani Popular Front (APF) in March 1989 was similar in many respects to that of the Karabakh Committee the previous year. Like its Armenian predecessor, the APF drew its leadership from a handful of nationalist intellectuals and espoused a program of increased Azerbaijani sovereignty. Calling also for the reassertion of direct Azerbaijani control over the NKAO, the APF viewed the activities of the Moscow-appointed Volskiy committee as overt interference in the domestic affairs of the republic.[55] With the Azerbaijani Communist Party continuing to support tacitly the Kremlin's policies on the issue, the Front became a popular—though unsanctioned—political force in the summer of 1989.

Beginning in August, the Popular Front organized a series of industrial strikes throughout the republic aimed at forcing the local government's capitulation to a number of demands. In particular, the APF sought official recognition by the Azerbaijani Communist Party and the reassertion of direct Azerbaijani control over Nagorno-Karabakh.[56] Experiencing little progress at achieving its goals, the APF demonstrated its growing power by coordinating a rail blockade of Armenia and the NKAO starting in September.[57] Dependent on rail traffic through Azerbaijan for some 85 percent of its food and fuel needs,[58] Armenia felt the blockade's effects immediately and deeply, especially in the earthquake-ravaged areas.[59] Within weeks, the stoppage of rail service brought about what one report called a "catastrophic situation" in the republic,[60] raising the likelihood of retaliatory measures by the Armenians.

Faced with unabating strikes and rallies in the republic and outcry from Moscow over its failure to stop the rail blockade,[61] the Azerbaijani Communist Party entered reluctantly into negotiations with the APF in October. In return for a guarantee to end the rail stoppage, the APF secured the party's recognition as a legal organization and the withdrawal of its support for Moscow's special rule of Nagorno-Karabakh.[62] Emboldened by its new status, the Popular Front induced the convening of an extraordinary session of the Azerbaijan Supreme Soviet on 5 October at which a "law on the sovereignty of the republic" was passed.[63]

Significantly, the law provided for the extension of Azerbaijani sovereignty over all parts of the republic, including the NKAO, and made any territorial changes contingent upon a referendum. Furthermore, the law bestowed upon Azerbaijan the right "to withdraw freely from the USSR," also pending the results of a popular referendum.[64] Thus, Azerbaijan's national sovereignty law posed an immediate challenge to Moscow's handling of the Nagorno-Karabakh crisis as well as to the Soviet system of government in general.

By the closing months of 1989, the Kremlin was faced with institutionally recognized nationalist movements in both Armenia and Azerbaijan that had taken steps in direct contradiction to Soviet policy. Furthermore, like their Armenian counterparts, the Azerbaijanis had begun to organize independent militias, and the prospects for a deadly escalation of violence between the two republics was heightened greatly. Moscow was thus forced to intervene again with political measures. As had been the case over the previous two years, however, the Soviet leadership responded with moves that had the effect of promoting, rather than mitigating, further conflict.

On 28 November 1989, the USSR Supreme Soviet voted essentially to restore the *status quo ante* by abolishing the Volskiy committee and reinstating direct Azerbaijani rule over the NKAO.[65] To facilitate this restoration, a republic-level oversight committee staffed primarily by ethnic Azeris was created to take over the day-to-day administration of Nagorno-Karabakh until local party organs could be revived.[66] Moreover, authority for security functions in the NKAO was delegated to Azerbaijani agencies in an apparent effort to restore order in the oblast.[67] Thus, Moscow's move represented essentially a capitulation to the demands of the Azerbaijanis.

Although welcomed in Baku,[68] the November decision of the central authorities to reinstate Azerbaijani control over the NKAO was met with outrage in Armenia and Nagorno-Karabakh. With the ANM now a major political force in Armenia, an extraordinary joint session of the Armenian Supreme Soviet and the National Council of Nagorno-Karabakh was convened to formulate a response.[69] What emerged from the session on 1 December was a move of further defiance to the authority of Moscow and Baku: The proclamation of a "United Armenian Republic" consisting of the Armenian SSR and the NKAO.[70] Decried quickly by Baku as an illegal and "impermissible interference in the Sovereign Azerbaijan SSR's affairs,"[71] the declaration accentuated further the Armenian-Azerbaijani political duel for control over Nagorno-Karabakh. (See Appendix C.)

A number of questions arise as to the reasons behind the central authorities' decision to restore Azerbaijani sovereignty over Nagorno-Karabakh at the end of 1989. One possible motive is that Gorbachev sought to restore the *status quo ante* out of frustration with the Nagorno-Karabakh question, hoping to wash his hands of the matter.[72] However, since reinstating Azerbaijani sovereignty over the NKAO held little promise of abating, let alone ending, the Karabakh dispute, it is doubtful that Gorbachev was willing or able to simply turn his back on the issue. Thus, a more compelling explanation for Moscow's move must be found.

By allowing the establishment of what was essentially military rule of the NKAO by Azerbaijan, it is possible that Gorbachev was laying the groundwork for a forcibly imposed settlement to the dispute. With authority for administration and security of Nagorno-Karabakh placed wholly within the hands of the Azerbaijanis, the Soviet leader must have expected a resurgence of violence to result, whether it be in the form of an armed revolt by the Karabakh Armenians, the forceful suppression of NKAO separatism by Azerbaijan, or outright conflict between Armenia and Azerbaijan. Whatever the eventuality, Moscow could have portrayed any renewal of violence as a direct result of its November withdrawal from the administration of Nagorno-Karabakh, thereby justifying forceful Soviet intervention and a centrally imposed settlement. Whether or not such a train of thought occupied the minds of Gorbachev and other Soviet leaders will likely never be known, but the events of late 1989 and early 1990 saw both an escalation in Armenian-Azerbaijani violence and a subsequent large-scale Soviet military intervention in Azerbaijan.

"Black January" in Azerbaijan and Its Aftermath

What came to be known as "Black January" in Azerbaijan—the bloody take-over and occupation of Baku by Soviet troops on 20 January 1990—was the culmination of heightening nationalist fervor in Armenia and Azerbaijan and growing inter-communal violence in border settlements and in the Azerbaijani capital itself. By the time it was over, "Black January" had brought inter-ethnic tensions and anti-Moscow feelings to a new level in both republics, propelling Armenia and Azerbaijan further down the road toward open warfare.

The third year of the resurgent Armenia-Azerbaijan conflict began with what the Azerbaijanis perceived as yet another provocative parliamentary act by the Armenians. On 9 January a joint session of the Armenian Supreme Soviet and the NKAO National Council discussed a 1990 budget for the Armenian SSR that included for the first time economic and social development funds for Nagorno-Karabakh.[73] The announcement of the Armenian intention to adopt a unified budget for Armenia and the NKAO was met with a predictable response from the Azerbaijani Supreme Soviet, which "categorically condemn[ed]" the act as "open interference in the internal affairs of [the] Azerbaijan SSR, which is a sovereign republic."[74]

The Soviet leadership sided with Baku, and on 10 January the USSR Supreme Soviet Presidium passed a resolution annulling the Armenian budgetary act as well as the 1 December 1989 proclamation of a "United Armenia."[75] However, the Gorbachev regime did nothing to enforce the resolution, thereby displaying to the Azerbaijanis what Audrey Altstadt called "another toothless roar from the Kremlin."[76]

In apparent response to Soviet actions perceived as inadequate for dealing with Karabakh separatism, Azeri mobs attacked three Armenian villages on the border of the oblast on 11 January.[77] Gunfire and hostage-taking took place on both sides, and Moscow radio reported the destruction of two bridges in the NKAO.[78] Two days later, the violence spread to Baku, and "Black January" began in earnest.

On 13 January a mass demonstration was held in Baku to protest Armenian moves on Nagorno-Karabakh and the perceived inadequate response to those moves by Moscow and the Azerbaijani Communist Party. The apparent catalyst for violence came when reports reached the crowd that an Armenian man had murdered an Azeri with an axe while attempting to defend his family from forced eviction from their Baku apartment.[79] Thereafter, large groups of Azeris—most of them refugees seeking revenge upon the Armenians for their squalid living conditions—broke away from the rally and went on a rampage in the Armenian quarter of the city.[80] In two nights of carnage, which neither the local authorities nor the 12,000 Soviet Interior Ministry troops stationed in Baku did anything to stop, more than 74 people died, the majority of them Armenians,[81] and the rest of Baku's estimated Armenian population of 50,000 was evacuated hastily by air and sea.[82]

The first stirrings of a Soviet response to the bloodshed in Azerbaijan came on 15 January, when the USSR Supreme Soviet Presidium declared a state of emergency in the NKAO and surrounding areas.[83] Inexplicably, the state of emergency was not expanded to include Baku until five days later, by which time the anti-Armenian pogroms had all but ended.[84] During the delay, however, Moscow had mobilized an additional force of 11,000 Soviet Army and Interior Ministry troops for dispatch to the Azerbaijani capital,[85] where the fateful events of "Black January" ran their course.

After the destruction of the central television station and the cutting of phone and radio lines by Soviet special forces, heavily armed troops smashed through barricades erected by Popular Front supporters and entered Baku during the night of 19–20 January 1990.[86] In a bloody assault that Robert Kushen equates with one on "an enemy position intended for military destruction,"[87] Soviet forces took control of the Azerbaijani capital after a five-hour battle that left more than a hundred Azeris dead and over a thousand wounded.[88]

Stunned by the level of bloodshed in Baku, the APF proclaimed a day of national mourning, issued a call for a general strike, and organized a haphazard blockade of Baku harbor.[89] Moreover, an extraordinary all-night session of the Azerbaijani Supreme Soviet on 21–22 January resulted in the adoption of a resolution demanding the immediate withdrawal of Soviet troops and threatening secession from the USSR if the demand was not met.[90] Moscow's response was not only to ignore the Azerbaijani ultimatum, but also to arrest a number of the Popular Front's leaders and disperse the blockade of Baku harbor by force.[91] Thereafter, the capital of the Azerbaijan SSR fell under martial law enforced by Soviet occupation troops.[92]

"Black January" had a momentous impact on the parties involved in the Armenia-Azerbaijan conflict. The brutal use of Soviet troops in Baku and the repression of the APF did not root out the Azerbaijani nationalist movement or reestablish strong links with the center. On the contrary, according to Altstadt, "those actions broke whatever bonds of limited trust [that] remained between the rulers in Moscow and their subjects in Azerbaijan."[93] However, the state of emergency in Baku backed by the presence of Soviet troops allowed the Azerbaijani Communist Party to reassert its authority in the republic despite having lost virtually all popular support.[94]

Soon after the intervention of Soviet forces in Baku, the Kremlin sacked the top leadership of the Azerbaijani Communist Party (AzCP) and installed Ayaz Mutalibov as the new First Secretary.[95] Mutalibov realized quickly that in order to reestablish the party's legitimacy among the populace, he would have to adopt popular goals. Therefore, in the months following "Black January" the Azerbaijani leader embraced a program that included calls for the reassertion of direct Azerbaijani rule over Nagorno-Karabakh, the withdrawal of Soviet troops and the lifting of the state of emergency in Baku, and the purge of "unprincipled party members." However, in light of the combined fact that Moscow had never tolerated independent Communist parties in the republics and that the AzCP's hold on power was contingent almost entirely upon the continued presence of Soviet forces in Baku, Mutalibov's post-January policies were likely an attempt to put on the appearance of catering to popular opinion in order to bolster the party's credibility and authority in Azerbaijan. At the practical—as opposed to the rhetorical—level, the AzCP's policies became more and more synchronized with those of Moscow as 1990 progressed, culminating ultimately in Operation "Ring" in mid 1991.[96]

In Armenia, pre-existing feelings of disenchantment with the policies of Moscow were fueled greatly by the events of "Black January." Most infuriating to the Armenians was the fact that Soviet Interior Ministry troops stationed in Baku had stood by and watched as the anti-Armenian pogroms ran their course and that the army's intervention was ordered only after the violence had ended. Over the following months, this anger was translated into acts that had a fateful impact both on the Armenia-Azerbaijan conflict and on Armenia's relations with Moscow.

After the events of Sumgait and the Zvartnots airport in 1988, the Armenians' confidence in—and trust of—the Soviet military had declined considerably. However, the refusal of Soviet Interior Ministry forces to intervene to stop the Baku pogroms in January 1990 marked the end of the Armenians' acceptance of the military's authority and protection. Determined to take charge of defending Armenian interests, large groups of Armenians began forming independent militias.

The first half of 1990 saw the emergence of a handful of unofficial militias in Armenia, the largest and most active of which was the 5,000-strong so-called Armenian National Army (ANA).[97] Guided, in the words of the ANA's leader, by the need to "ensure national self-defense,"[98] the militias laid the foundation for the formation of an independent Armenian army. Beginning in late March, armed groups on patrol in Nagorno-Karabakh and along the border with the

Nakhichevan Autonomous Soviet Socialist Republic (ASSR) came into conflict with Azeri villagers, resulting in numerous deaths.[99]

In a significant turn of events, by early spring the militias' operations began to focus more and more on acquiring arms from local Soviet forces. Attacks on Soviet military convoys, weapons depots, and border checkpoints came to be a regular occurrence, resulting in the confiscation of large numbers of automatic rifles, rocket launchers, grenades, and other weaponry by the militias.[100] Despite a Gorbachev decree calling for the dissolution of "armed units not envisaged under Soviet legislation,"[101] attacks aimed at taking possession of Soviet weapons continued unabated.[102]

Amid a climate of growing defiance and militancy on the part of the independent militias,[103] the first non-Communist Armenian government in 70 years came to power on 5 August 1990. Levon Ter-Petrosyan, a founding member of the Karabakh Committee and leader of the ANM, was elected to the chairmanship of the Armenian Supreme Soviet and set out immediately to reestablish order in the republic.[104] However, Ter-Petrosyan soon found that the Armenian militias were not eager to give up their arms.

Faced with the continued refusal of the militias to comply with Gorbachev's disbandment order, the Armenian Supreme Soviet declared a state of emergency throughout the republic on 29 August and instructed all unauthorized armed formations to hand over their weapons and dissolve themselves immediately.[105] Backed by a substantial force of Armenian Interior Ministry troops, officials were finally able to disband the ANA following the arrest of its leader and the occupation of its headquarters.[106] Although the situation stabilized somewhat thereafter, sporadic raids both on Soviet forces and on Azerbaijani settlements continued through late 1990.[107]

While attempting to forestall a Soviet intervention similar to that in Baku by disbanding the militias, Armenian officials began to prepare for the republic's separation from the USSR. Just weeks after Ter-Petrosyan took power as the new chairman of the Armenian Supreme Soviet, Armenia declared on 23 August 1990 its intention to become a sovereign and independent state.[108] Among other things, the declaration renamed the Armenian SSR the Armenian Republic, nullified all but Armenian laws on its territory, and called for the establishment of independent armed forces, internal troops, and police units.[109] In a further snipe at Moscow and Baku, the decree also cited the earlier proclamation of a "United Armenia" as the basis for Nagorno-Karabakh's inclusion as an integral part of the new Armenian Republic.[110]

Armenia's moves toward independence were only one part of a larger problem for Soviet President Mikhail Gorbachev in the latter half of 1990. Faced with separatism elsewhere in the Soviet Union, particularly in the Baltics, and with a growing challenge from right-wing elements within the Communist Party, the Soviet leader was forced to steer a precarious course on the future of his country. In an effort to hold the USSR together, Gorbachev unveiled the draft of a new Union treaty in the closing months of 1990 that offered greater autonomy to the republics. For Armenia and Azerbaijan, this attempt by Moscow to redraw the relationship between the center and the peripheries became a key element propelling the two republics toward open warfare in 1991.

1991: ESCALATION TO OPEN WARFARE

The year 1991 saw a marked escalation in violence between the Armenians and Azerbaijanis. Beginning with Operation "Ring" in April, clashes expanded from the inter-communal disorders that characterized the previous three years into direct confrontations between armed units of both southern Soviet republics. By the time of the USSR's breakup in late 1991, Armenia and Azerbaijan were poised on the brink of full-scale war.

Operation "Ring"

In late 1990 and early 1991, the efforts of Armenian and Azerbaijani policymakers were focused not on the issue of Nagorno-Karabakh, but on the all-important question of the future of their republics and of the Soviet Union itself. Gorbachev had set 17 March 1991 as the date of an all-Union referendum meant to pass judgment on a new draft Union treaty that promised greater autonomy to the republics, and debate in the Supreme Soviets of Azerbaijan and Armenia took up the question first of whether or not to participate in the vote.

In Azerbaijan, the previous September had seen an overwhelming victory for the Communists in what numerous opposition figures charged were rigged parliamentary elections.[111] Still dependent largely upon Moscow for its continued grip on power, the Azerbaijani government headed by Ayaz Mutalibov became an early supporter of Gorbachev's efforts to revive the Soviet Union.[112] Thus, on 7 March the Azerbaijani Supreme Soviet voted to take part in the all-Union referendum to be held ten days later.[113]

In contrast with its eastern neighbor, Armenia was unsatisfied with the Soviet leader's attempts to redefine the relationship between Moscow and the republics. Armenia's Supreme Soviet voted on 31 January to boycott the all-Union action,[114] and on 1 March it went one step further, stating not only that the referendum's results would not have legal force on the territory of the republic,[115] but also that Armenia was beginning the formal process of secession from the USSR.[116] Thus, by March 1991 it was clear that the Armenians and Azerbaijanis were taking fundamentally divergent approaches to the future of their republics and of the Soviet Union.

The 17 March referendum resulted in a victory for President Gorbachev with a vote of more than 75 percent in favor of the new Union treaty.[117] According to official statistics, which were disputed hotly by the nationalist opposition, more than three-fourths of the Azerbaijani populace took part in the vote, of whom 92 percent voted "yes."[118] However, true to its claim of 31 January, Armenia boycotted the referendum, as did Georgia, Moldova, and the Baltic republics. In an apparent effort to frustrate further moves by Armenia toward independence, Moscow colluded with Baku to exploit one of the Armenian government's most vulnerable Achilles' heels: The Armenian population within the borders of Azerbaijan.

In the closing months of 1990, Azerbaijani special-purpose militia brigades began a systematic campaign of harassment against Armenian villages in and around the NKAO. Raids on collective farms and the theft of livestock were among the detachments' common practices, presumably in an attempt to demoralize the Armenian population of Azerbaijan and prompt it to leave for Armenia. On many occasions, Azerbaijani forces found themselves in heated combat with the Armenian militias that continued to operate despite Gorbachev's July decree. The situation deteriorated sharply in early 1991, with Soviet Interior Ministry forces often being caught in the middle of skirmishes between the two sides.[119] In an apparent attempt to stem the spread of violence, the Soviets introduced elements of the 23rd Motorized Rifle Division of the Fourth Army into a five-kilometer strip along the Armenia-Azerbaijan border in early April. Within a matter of weeks, however, these Soviet forces shifted their activities from those of a buffer force to those of an active participant in the hostilities.[120]

Although the details are unknown, it is alleged that Mutalibov approached Soviet military and security officials in the third week of April 1991 and offered the prospect of combined Soviet-Azerbaijani operations in and around Nagorno-Karabakh. Justifiable under the legal pretext of implementing the July 1990 presidential decree on the disbandment of unauthorized armed militias, such joint operations would be beneficial potentially for both Moscow and Baku. For Azerbaijan, actions against the militias could be used as a front for harassing the Armenians living within its borders, thereby encouraging the inhabitants of the NKAO either to give up all hope of uniting with Armenia or, ultimately, to leave the region for Armenia. For Moscow, legally justifiable military operations along the Armenia-Azerbaijan border and in the NKAO would hold out the promise of dissuading the Armenians from taking further measures regarding independence.[121] Thus, Operation "Ring" was born.

Operation "Ring" began on 30 April 1991, when Azerbaijani militia units and Soviet Army forces attacked the Armenian-inhabited villages of Getashen and Martunashen 25 kilometers north of Nagorno-Karabakh.[122] As its name implies, the venture entailed the surrounding of the villages by Soviet tanks and armored personnel carriers, followed by a sweep through the ringed area by Azerbaijani militia and Soviet Interior Ministry units. Over the course of the next several days, Soviet and Azerbaijani forces combed through both towns in a search for guerrillas and weapons, often interrogating and beating the inhabitants and arresting arbitrarily the male heads of households.[123] Following such actions, the occupants of Getashen and Martunashen were deported forcibly to Stepanakert and replaced by Azeri refugees that had fled Armenia over the previous three years.[124] As agreed to in the apparent *modus vivendi* that led to the operation, the authorities in Moscow and Baku were unified in justifying their actions with the claim that the inhabitants of both towns had been harboring Armenian militias banned by the July Gorbachev decree.[125]

After the initial action against the villages of Getashen and Martunashen in late April and early May 1991, the activities of Operation "Ring" expanded in scope and brutality. On 7 May Soviet and Azerbaijani forces backed by tanks and helicopters entered three towns in Armenia proper, once again under the pretext that illegal militias had been conducting guerrilla operations on Azeri villages from there. More than 20 people were rounded up and arrested in the action, and numerous atrocities were carried out reportedly against the civilian populace.[126]

While Operation "Ring" continued in Armenia, 15 May 1991 saw the onset of Soviet-Azerbaijani military operations in the NKAO. Following the pattern established elsewhere, Armenian villages were ringed by tanks and armored personnel carriers, after which Soviet and Azerbaijani forces entered the area and began harassing the populace. Homes, and in some cases entire villages, were often burned to the ground, and looting was rampant.[127] Moreover, families were "encouraged" to leave their homes for Armenia after being coerced into signing a document stating they had done so of their own volition.[128] Operations continued into the summer, and although the Armenians were forced to abandon several villages, militia and armed bands continued to put up strong resistance.[129]

If the objective of Operation "Ring" from Moscow's point-of-view was to frustrate Armenia's drive for independence, the action was a dismal failure. Armenian leader Levon Ter-Petrosyan termed the Soviet military's actions an "undeclared war" against his republic aimed at punishing it for not taking part in the March all-Union referendum.[130] Other Armenian officials portrayed the operation as an attempt by the Kremlin to neutralize the republic's embryonic self-defense force under the pretext of disbanding illegal armed formations.[131] The effect of this outcry was to widen the split between Yerevan and Moscow, making it less—rather than more—likely for Armenia to return to the Soviet fold.

Operation "Ring" also failed to achieve the objectives of the Azerbaijanis. Rather than breaking the desire of the Karabakh Armenians for union with Armenia, anti-Azeri feelings among the NKAO populace were brought to a new level, virtually precluding the possibility of further coexistence between the two peoples within the borders of Azerbaijan. Relations with Armenia proper also deteriorated significantly as a result of the Soviet-Azerbaijani operations. Viewing Operation "Ring" as a blatant act aimed at ridding Nagorno-Karabakh of its Armenian inhabitants,[132] the government of Armenia threatened to use whatever means necessary to stop the deportations.[133] Thus, full-scale war between the two republics appeared imminent by mid 1991.

Operation "Ring" was a major turning point in the Armenia-Azerbaijan clash. For the first time, clashes between armed units of both republics had broken out with Soviet forces taking part actively on the side of Azerbaijan. Although the campaign's objectives were not met due to stiff Armenian military resistance and political intransigence, Operation "Ring" brought tensions to a level bordering on all-out warfare between Armenia and Azerbaijan. The final catalyst for war came in August 1991, when the failed coup in Moscow led to the dissolution of the Union of Soviet Socialist Republics.

Impact of the August Coup and the Breakup of the USSR

The failed attempt by conservative elements in the Communist Party and the KGB to overthrow Soviet President Mikhail Gorbachev in August 1991 had a momentous impact on the development of the Armenia-Azerbaijan conflict. The months following the attempted coup saw the emergence of the two republics as independent states, the pullout of Soviet forces from Nagorno-Karabakh, and a major escalation in the level of violence in the area. As had been the case in 1918, Armenia and Azerbaijan began their new-found statehood in a *de facto* state of war with one another.

From the onset, the leaderships of Armenia and Azerbaijan took divergent positions toward the August coup attempt. Although the Armenian authorities blamed Gorbachev for many of the developments in the conflict with Azerbaijan in the previous three years, they welcomed the defeat of the conservative coup plotters and the subsequent rout of the Communist Party as a Soviet institution.[134] Yerevan continued with its plans to secede from the USSR, and following a 99.3 percent vote in favor of such a move,[135] Armenia declared its independence as the Republic of Armenia on 23 September.

Contrary to the approach of its Armenian counterpart, the Azerbaijani government took an initial stand of support for the August coup attempt. In neighboring Iran when the putsch occurred, Mutalibov allegedly expressed his satisfaction with Gorbachev's removal from power.[136] When a large rally celebrating the coup's failure was held in front of APF headquarters on 23 August, some 3,000 Azerbaijani militia attacked the demonstrators and ransacked the Front's offices, resulting in more than 50 injuries.[137] Following the suppression of the Popular Front, Mutalibov moved to have himself chosen president in an election in which he was the only candidate.

As had been the case when he was installed as the AzCP First Secretary at the onset of the Soviet intervention in Baku the previous January, Mutalibov once again realized that he would have to cater to nationalist sentiments in Azerbaijan in order to stay in power. As a start, the Azerbaijani government issued a blanket denial of its support for the Moscow putsch,[138] and, in an attempt to preempt a similar Armenian move, the Azerbaijani Supreme Soviet adopted a declaration of independence on 30 August 1991.[139] Finally, in an act most likely to stoke up support for the regime, Mutalibov promised a crackdown on Nagorno-Karabakh separatism.

Despite their failure to achieve the goals of the Soviet and Azerbaijani leadership, military actions associated with Operation "Ring" had continued up through the attempted coup of August 1991.[140] However, the political confusion in Moscow that followed the putsch initiated a period of ambiguity in the role of the

Soviet Army and Interior Ministry in Nagorno-Karabakh. With little or no apparent direction on the matter coming from the central authorities, Soviet forces ceased cooperating with Azerbaijani militia units in their operations against Armenian villages.[141] Nevertheless, the end to direct Soviet participation in combat activities did not mean an end to their role in the Armenia-Azerbaijan conflict. Indeed, the actions of Soviet troops in both republics and in the NKAO remained a factor in the escalation of hostilities through late 1991.

The aftermath of the failed August coup initiated a period of disarray among Soviet military forces stationed in the Transcaucasus. One symptom of such disarray—the breakdown of discipline in the ranks—resulted in the procurement of large amounts of heavy weaponry and ammunition by the Armenians and Azerbaijanis. According to a report by Helsinki Watch, "heavy artillery, rocket-propelled grenades, rocket launchers, tanks, armored personnel carriers, and the like, property of the Soviet Army, were either sold to, loaned to, or otherwise found their way into the hands of combatants on both sides."[142] In addition to obtaining weaponry from Soviet soldiers themselves, Armenian and Azerbaijani fighters often conducted raids on military installations and depots throughout the region.[143] As a result of these phenomena, the two sides came into possession of large numbers of weapons that contributed greatly to an escalation in the level and scope of warfare between Armenia and Azerbaijan in the closing months of 1991.[144] However, before such escalation began in earnest, a major mediation effort was undertaken by the presidents of Russia and Kazakstan in an attempt to head off the outbreak of open hostilities between the two republics.

With the authority of Soviet officials brought to a virtual end by the August coup attempt, Russian Federation President Boris Yeltsin and Kazakstani President Nursultan Nazarbayev—then the two most respected ex-Soviet leaders—tried their hands at finding a solution to the Armenia-Azerbaijan conflict with a burst of shuttle diplomacy in September 1991. After endorsing a key Azerbaijani precondition that the principle of territorial integrity of states would be upheld,[145] Yeltsin and Nazarbayev prompted the leaders of Armenia and Azerbaijan and a bi-ethnic delegation from Nagorno-Karabakh to meet face-to-face for the first time.[146] Unexpectedly, Armenia renounced all claims to Azerbaijani territory on 22 September,[147] allowing a communique to be signed that offered the promise of ending hostilities between the two republics.[148]

The main provisions of the agreement were several. First, a prompt cease-fire was to be followed within two days by the unconditional withdrawal of all armed forces (Soviet Interior and Defense Ministry troops excepted) from the combat zone.[149] Thereafter, a stage-by-stage restoration of the pre-1989 constitutional bodies of administration in the NKAO was to be carried out under Russian and Kazakstani supervision, in tandem also with the release of hostages and the return of deported persons. Finally, both sides were to empower delegations to participate in continuous bilateral talks aimed at achieving a final political resolution of the Nagorno-Karabakh dispute.[150]

The September 1991 communique was a milestone in the conflict between

Armenia and Azerbaijan. For the first time in three years of strife, a compromise acceptable at a minimum to the leaders of both republics and representatives from the NKAO had been found.[151] However, despite the precedent it represented, the pact provided little more than a basis for a settlement to the question of Nagorno-Karabakh. The true test of the agreement's success or failure had to come in the conflict zone.

Despite the Russian- and Kazakstani-mediated negotiations, clashes continued unabated in and around Nagorno-Karabakh. On 24 September, the day after the cease-fire communique was signed, Azerbaijani militia units attacked the village of Chapar in the NKAO, resulting in five Armenian civilian deaths.[152] At the same time, a brutal missile and artillery barrage was unleashed upon the village of Noragyukh from the neighboring Azerbaijani town of Khojaly. Armenian guerillas responded by carrying out a large-scale operation against militia bases in surrounding Azerbaijani villages.[153]

In the midst of continuing and escalating violence in and around Nagorno-Karabakh, negotiations continued between the warring parties as per the terms of the 23 September communique. At the first follow-up meeting of delegates from Armenia, Azerbaijan, and the NKAO held on 25 October, talks termed as "fruitful" resulted in little more than a plea to the combatants to "refrain from violence and voluntarism and to compliment the inter-republican talks with diplomacy by the people."[154] As before, however, fighting went on unabated in the conflict zone. Missile and artillery attacks on Armenian villages in the NKAO were carried out relentlessly from neighboring Azerbaijani towns,[155] while Armenian units in some parts of the oblast evicted Azeris forcibly from their homes.[156]

On 4 November 1991, Azerbaijan shut down a pipeline that supplied Armenia with 1.5 million cubic meters of natural gas per day from Russia.[157] Within two weeks, life in the capital of Yerevan came to a virtual standstill,[158] and Armenian delegates walked out of the ongoing talks mediated by Russian and Kazakstani observers.[159] Thereafter, the pace of military operations by Armenian units in Nagorno-Karabakh accelerated greatly, resulting in the retaking of several dozen villages abandoned by Armenians during Operation "Ring."[160] Amidst heavy fighting on 20 November, an Azerbaijani helicopter was downed over the NKAO in what appeared to be an Armenian rocket attack.[161] Although an event of seemingly little significance on the face of it, the helicopter's loss proved to be a major contributor to the deterioration of the situation in the region.

Among the twenty passengers killed in the 20 November crash of the Azerbaijani Mi-8 helicopter were the Deputy Prime Minister and Interior Minister of Azerbaijan as well as the Russian and Kazakstani observers to the ongoing peace talks.[162] A shocked and outraged Azerbaijani populace demanded retaliation for the apparent Armenian role in the incident, and Mutalibov was able once again to play the nationalist card to his political advantage.

In the opening blow of what Ter-Petrosyan called a "declaration of war" on his republic, the Azerbaijanis recommenced on 25 November the full-scale rail blockade of Armenia that had been carried out sporadically over the prior two years.[163]   Nearly simultaneously, all transportation and communication links between Stepanakert and its environs were cut,[164] and the facilities providing the city with power and water were demolished by Azerbaijani forces.[165]   On 27 November the Azerbaijani Supreme Soviet voted to annul the autonomous legal status of the NKAO and institute direct rule over the oblast via the renamed provincial capital of Hankendi,[166] and 10 days later Mutalibov issued a decree calling up all able-bodied citizens aged 18 or older for active military service.[167] Azerbaijan was thus mobilizing for war by early December 1991.

Just as events in the Transcaucasus were leading Armenia and Azerbaijan to open warfare in late 1991, occurrences elsewhere in the Soviet Union were also taking place that proved to have a major impact on the hostilities. Following the collapse of the August coup in Moscow, Gorbachev's efforts to hold the USSR together by reviving the Union treaty were brushed off by the republics. On 8 December 1991 the leaders of Russia, Ukraine, and Belarus declared that "the USSR, as a subject of international law and geopolitical reality, is ceasing its existence." Together, the three Slavic republics proclaimed the Commonwealth of Independent States open to membership by all the states of the former Soviet Union.[168] The Soviet era came to an end officially on Christmas day with the resignation of Mikhail Gorbachev as president and the lowering of the Soviet flag from atop the Kremlin.

The effects of the breakup of the USSR on the Armenia-Azerbaijan conflict were felt first and foremost on the battlefield. On 23 December USSR Interior Ministry forces based in Nagorno-Karabakh began withdrawing from the oblast under the pretext that the Soviet Union's dissolution had nullified the legal basis for their continued presence there. The troops' egress was followed immediately by an escalation in Azerbaijani attacks on Armenian towns and villages in and around Nagorno-Karabakh. In particular, the NKAO capital became the focus of almost continuous missile and artillery barrages by Azerbaijani forces that had occupied many of the positions vacated by the withdrawing Soviet troops.[169]

The Soviet Union's demise also had a major impact over the longer-term on the military situation in the southern Transcaucasus. In addition to the Interior Ministry military presence in Nagorno-Karabakh, forces of the Soviet Seventh and Fourth Armies were based in Armenia and Azerbaijan, respectively, at the time of the USSR's breakup. According to figures of the International Institute for Strategic Studies, this development left more than 23,000 men, 250 tanks, 350 armored personnel carriers (APCs), 350 artillery pieces, and 7 attack helicopters on the territory of Armenia and 62,000 men, 400 tanks, 720 APCs, 470 artillery pieces, 14 attack helicopters, and 90 fighter-bomber aircraft on the territory of Azerbaijan.[170] As will be noted in chapter four, significant numbers of these forces were nationalized or otherwise found their way into the hands of the Armenians and Azerbaijanis during 1992, with pivotal effects for the course of hostilities between their republics.

The demise of the Soviet Union also had a major impact on the geopolitical landscape of the region. For the first time in more than 70 years, the antagonism between Armenia and Azerbaijan was no longer an internal matter of the USSR; the clash instead became an affair between two ostensibly sovereign members of the international community. Moreover, rivalries among the leading regional powers—Russia, Turkey, and Iran—that had colored the Transcaucasus' history for centuries were awakened once again, bringing new complexities and new dangers to the dispute. From the time of the Soviet Union's breakup onward, the Armenia-Azerbaijan conflict became wrapped up inextricably with the dynamics of regional geopolitical rivalries among the Russians, Turks, and Iranians. The next chapter will examine the effects of the USSR's downfall on the perspectives and interests of both the conflicting parties and the surrounding powers.

NOTES

1. Martin Malia, *The Soviet Tragedy: A History of Socialism in Russia, 1917–1991* (New York: Free Press, 1994): 409–424.

2. Patrick Cockburn, "Dateline USSR: Ethnic Tremors," *Foreign Policy*, no. 74 (Spring 1989): 174.

3. Gail W. Lapidus, "Gorbachev's Nationalities Problem," *Foreign Affairs* 68, no. 4 (Fall 1989): 100–102.

4. Primarily a rural agricultural nation prior to its incorporation into the Soviet Union, Armenia was urbanized and industrialized under Stalin at great cost to the environment. With the onset of *glasnost*, the extent of the ecological disaster that had resulted was exposed in the local press, and numerous grass-roots movements grew up around environmental issues. Ecological themes soon evolved into national ones, with criticism focusing on everything from the meagerness of the land to the lack of autonomy and the corruption of local Communist officials. It was in this environment of national awakening in Armenia that irredentism vis-à-vis Nagorno-Karabakh came once again to the surface. Felicity Barringer and Bill Keller, "A Test of Change Explodes in Soviet," *New York Times* (11 March 1988): A6; and Nadia Diuk and Adrian Karatnycky, *The Hidden Nations: The People Challenge the Soviet Union* (New York: William Morrow & Co., 1990): 157.

5. As per common Soviet practice, it was reported the Aliyev had been granted a request for "retirement on health grounds." *TASS*, 23 October 1987, in Foreign Broadcast Information Service—Soviet Union (hereafter FBIS-SOV), #87–206 (24 October 1987): 30.

6. Cockburn, "Dateline USSR," p. 178.

7. "Petition signed by over 75,000 Armenians from Mountainous Karabagh and Soviet Armenia to General Secretary Gorbachev," in Gerard J. Libaridian, ed., *The Karabakh File: Documents and Facts on the Question of Mountainous Karabakh, 1918–1988* (Cambridge: The Zoryan Institute, March 1988): 88.

8. Claire Mouradian, "The Mountainous Karabagh Question: Inter-Ethnic Conflict or Decolonization Crisis?" *Armenian Review* 43, no. 2–3 (Summer–Autumn 1990): 15.

9. Ronald G. Suny, *Looking Toward Ararat: Armenia in Modern History* (Bloomington: Indiana University Press, 1993): 197–198.

10. Nora Dudwick, "Armenia: The Nation Awakens," in Ian Bremmer and Ray Taras, eds., *Nation and Politics in the Soviet Successor States* (Cambridge: Cambridge University Press, 1993): 275–276.

11. "Response of the Central Committee of the Communist Party of the USSR to the

demand by the government of Mountainous Karabakh," in Libaridian, ed., *The Karabagh File*, p. 98.

12. *Deutsche Presse-Agentur*, 29 February 1988, in FBIS-SOV, #88–039 (29 February 1988): 73.

13. *Agence France Presse*, 29 February 1988, in ibid., p. 67.

14. Igor Nolyain argues provocatively that the Kremlin was behind the Sumgait affair. According to his research, the Azeri mobs that rampaged through Sumgait were criminals released from a prison in nearby Kafan and bussed to the scene by KGB agents. Nolyain alleges that Gorbachev instigated the events in an effort to distract Soviet citizens and the West from his "unfulfilled benevolent perestroika promises." Igor Nolyain, "Moscow's Initiation of the Azeri-Armenian Conflict," *Central Asian Survey* 13, no. 4 (1994): 561.

15. *Agence France Presse*, 1 March 1988, in FBIS-SOV, #88–040 (1 March 1988): 43; and *TASS*, 4 March 1988, in FBIS-SOV, #88–044 (7 March 1988): 44.

16. See, for example, Samvel Shahmuratian, ed., *The Sumgait Tragedy: Pogroms Against Armenians in Soviet Azerbaijan, Volume I: Eyewitness Accounts* (Cambridge: The Zoryan Institute, 1990).

17. Ronald G. Suny, "The Revenge of the Past: Socialism and Ethnic Conflict in Transcaucasia," *New Left Review*, no. 184 (November–December 1990): 29.

18. Audrey L. Altstadt, *The Azerbaijani Turks: Power and Identity Under Russian Rule* (Stanford: Hoover Institution Press, 1992): 197.

19. Ronald G. Suny, *The Revenge of the Past: Nationalism, Revolution, and the Collapse of the Soviet Union* (Stanford: Stanford University Press, 1993): 135–136.

20. Quoted in Francis Field, "Nagorno-Karabakh: A Constitutional Conundrum," *Radio Liberty Research* RL 313/88 (15 July 1988): 3.

21. Richard Pipes, "The Soviet Union Adrift," *Foreign Affairs* 70, no. 1, America and the World (1990/91): 77.

22. Philip Taubman, "Gorbachev Says Ethnic Unrest Could Destroy Restructuring Effort," *New York Times* (28 November 1988): A6.

23. Yuri Rost, *Armenian Tragedy* (New York: St. Martin's Press, 1990): 12.

24. "Party and Government Resolution on Nagorno-Karabakh," *BBC Summary of World Broadcasts* (4 April 1988).

25. Christopher J. Walker, *Armenia and Karabagh: The Struggle for Unity* (London: Minority Rights Publications): 125–126.

26. Suny, *Looking Toward Ararat*, p. 202.

27. Marcus Gee and Anthony Wilson-Smith, "Enraged Republics," *Maclean's* 101, no. 27 (27 June 1988): 28.

28. Quoted in Elizabeth Fuller, "Nagorno-Karabakh: No Closer to Compromise," *Radio Liberty Research* RL 295/88 (30 June 1988): 1.

29. Elizabeth Fuller, "Recent Developments in the Nagorno-Karabakh Dispute," *Radio Liberty Research* RL 312/88 (11 July 1988): 1; and *Pravda*, 6 July 1988, in FBIS-SOV, #88–129 (6 July 1988): 49.

30. *Deutsche Presse-Agentur*, 6 July 1988, and *Agence France Presse*, 6 July 1988, in ibid., p. 50.

31. *Deutsche Presse-Agentur*, 12 July 1988, and *Agence France Presse*, 13 July 1988, in FBIS-SOV, #88–134 (13 July 1988): 55–56.

32. *TASS*, 13 July 1988, in ibid., p. 55; and *Baku Domestic Service*, 14 July 1988, in FBIS-SOV, #88–135 (14 July 1988): 41.

33. Walker, *Armenia and Karabagh*, p. 127.

34. Elizabeth Fuller, "Supreme Soviet Presidium Debates Nagorno-Karabakh," *Radio*

Liberty Research RL 314/88 (20 July 1988): 3; and *TASS*, 18 July 1988, in FBIS-SOV, #88–137 (18 July 1988): 48.

35. *TASS*, 19 July 1988, in FBIS-SOV, #88–138 (19 July 1988): 59–60.

36. Bill Keller, "Soviet Region Hit by New Ethnic Unrest and Strike," *New York Times* (16 September 1988): A8.

37. *Agence France Presse*, 19 September 1988, in FBIS-SOV, #88–182 (20 September 1988): 41.

38. Bill Keller, "Parts of Armenia Are Blocked Off by Soviet Troops," *New York Times* (23 September 1988): A1, A12.

39. Suny, *Looking Toward Ararat*, p. 207.

40. Quoted in Altstadt, *The Azerbaijani Turks*, p. 201.

41. Tadeusz Swietochowski, "Azerbaijan: Between Ethnic Conflict and Irredentism," *Armenian Review* 43, no. 2–3 (Summer–Autumn 1990): 42.

42. *Agence France Presse*, 22 and 23 November 1988, in FBIS-SOV, #88–226 (23 November 1988): 38; and Altstadt, *The Azerbaijani Turks*, pp. 200–201.

43. *Deutsche Presse-Agentur*, 24 November 1988, in FBIS-SOV, #88–227 (25 November 1988): 39.

44. Suny, *Looking Toward Ararat*, p. 210.

45. Bill Keller, "Amid the Rubble, Armenians Express Rage at Gorbachev," *New York Times* (12 December 1988): A1.

46. Mouradian, "The Mountainous Karabagh Question," p. 24.

47. Text of decree printed in *Izvestiya*, 15 January 1989, in FBIS-SOV, #88–010 (17 January 1989): 44.

48. In both republics the Communist authorities were besieged increasingly by the growing nationalist movement in the streets. Therefore, both saw the January decision as a way of calming the populace in order to buy time to conduct internal reforms and reassert party control over the situation. Mark Saroyan, "The 'Karabakh Syndrome' and Azerbaijani Politics," *Problems of Communism*, no. 39 (September–October 1990): 20–21. For the official Azerbaijani response to the decree, see *Baku Domestic Service*, 15 January 1989, in FBIS-SOV, #89–010 (17 January 1989): 52. For the Armenian reply, see *Pravda*, 19 January 1989, in FBIS-SOV, #89–013 (23 January 1989): 66.

49. Niall M. Frasner, Keith W. Hipel, John Jaworsky, and Ralph Zuljian, "A Conflict Analysis of the Armenian-Azerbaijani Dispute," *Journal of Conflict Resolution* 34, no. 4 (December 1990): 668.

50. Mouradian, "The Mountainous Karabagh Question," p. 26.

51. *Yerevan Domestic Service*, 18 August 1989, in FBIS-SOV, #89–167 (30 August 1989): 30–31.

52. Walker, *Armenia and Karabagh*, p. 129.

53. *Armenpress International Service*, 26 September 1989, in FBIS-SOV, #89–189 (2 October 1989): 63–64.

54. Mouradian, "The Mountainous Karabagh Question," pp. 26–27.

55. Saroyan, "The 'Karabakh Syndrome' and Azerbaijani Politics," pp. 22–23.

56. *TASS*, 22 and 23 August 1989, and *Pravda*, 23 August 1989, in FBIS-SOV, #89–162 (23 August 1989): 36–38; and *Agence France Presse*, 3 September 1989, in FBIS-SOV, #88–170 (5 September 1989): 61–62.

57. Altstadt, *The Azerbaijani Turks*, p. 206; and *TASS*, 16 September 1989, in FBIS-SOV, #89–179 (18 September 1989): 45.

58. *Izvestiya*, 2 October 1989, in FBIS-SOV, #89–190 (3 October 1989): 64.

59. *Yerevan Domestic Service*, 25 September 1989, in FBIS-SOV, #89–186 (27

September 1989): 68–69; and Rose Brady, "A Bloody Roadblock for *Perestroika*," *Business Week*, no. 3143 (29 January 1990): 49.

60. *Moscow Domestic Service*, 29 September 1989, in FBIS-SOV, #89–189 (2 October 1989): 58.

61. Elizabeth Fuller, "Nagorno-Karabakh and the Rail Blockade," *Report on the USSR* 1, no. 41 (13 October 1989): 23.

62. Altstadt, *The Azerbaijani Turks*, p. 206.

63. *Pravda*, 6 October 1989, in FBIS-SOV, #88–194 (10 October 1989): 67; and Altstadt, *The Azerbaijani Turks*, p. 206.

64. *Moscow Television Service*, 5 October 1989, in FBIS-SOV, #89–193 (6 October 1989): 42.

65. *Baku Domestic Service*, 29 November 1989, in FBIS-SOV, #89–228 (29 November 1989): 89.

66. *Baku Domestic Service*, 5 December 1989, in FBIS-SOV, #89–233 (6 December 1989): 72–73; and Elizabeth Fuller, "Moscow Attempts New Solution to Nagorno-Karabakh Impasse," *Report on the USSR* 1, no. 49 (8 December 1989): 12.

67. Saroyan, "The 'Karabakh Syndrome' and Azerbaijani Politics," p. 27.

68. *Baku Domestic Service*, 1 December 1989, in FBIS-SOV, #89–230 (1 December 1989): 49.

69. *Agence France Presse*, 30 November 1989, in ibid., p. 48.

70. *Moscow Domestic Service*, 2 December 1989, and *Agence France Presse*, 1 December 1989, in FBIS-SOV, #89–231 (4 December 1989): 112–113.

71. *Baku Domestic Service*, 6 December 1989, in FBIS-SOV, #89–234 (7 December 1989): 86–87.

72. Mouradian, "The Mountainous Karabagh Question," pp. 29–30.

73. Altstadt, *The Azerbaijani Turks*, p. 212.

74. *Baku Domestic Service*, 10 January 1990, in FBIS-SOV, #90–008 (11 January 1990): 97.

75. *TASS*, 10 January 1990, in ibid., p. 97; and *TASS*, 10 January 1990, in FBIS-SOV, #90–009 (12 January 1990): 82.

76. Altstadt, *The Azerbaijani Turks*, p. 212.

77. Mouradian, "The Mountainous Karabagh Question," p. 30.

78. *Moscow Domestic Service*, 11 January 1990, and *Moscow World Service*, 11 January 1990, in FBIS-SOV, #90–009 (12 January 1990): 82.

79. *Moscow Domestic Service*, 14 January 1990, in FBIS-SOV, #90–010 (16 January 1990): 64; and Bill Keller, "Soviet Azerbaijan in Ethnic Turmoil; At Least 25 Dead," *New York Times* (15 January 1990): A8.

80. Bill Keller, "Troops Seek to Calm Azerbaijan; Soviets Debate Cause of Violence," *New York Times* (18 January 1990): A8.

81. According to eyewitness accounts cited by *Helsinki Watch*, the Soviet Interior Ministry troops claimed that they were authorized only to protect Communist Party and government facilities in Baku and had not been given orders to intervene. Other excuses for inaction given by Soviet and local forces ranged from their inability to handle such disturbances to confusion over the chain of command in the midst of the republic's political turmoil. Robert Kushen, *Conflict in the Soviet Union: Black January in Azerbaijan* (New York: Helsinki Watch, May 1991): 7.

82. Mouradian, "The Mountainous Karabagh Question", p. 30.

83. Text of state of emergency declaration printed in *Pravda*, 16 January 1990, in FBIS-SOV, #90–010 (16 January 1990): 77.

84. *TASS*, 20 January 1990, in FBIS-SOV, #90–014 (22 January 1990): 60; and Kushen, *Conflict in the Soviet Union*, p. 8.

85. Bill Keller, "Moscow Dispatches 11,000 Troops to Azerbaijan," *New York Times* (17 January 1990): A1.

86. *Agence France Presse*, 19 January 1990, in FBIS-SOV, #90–014 (22 January 1990): 108; Bill Keller, "Soviet Troops Bogged Down by Azerbaijanis' Blockades of Railroads and Airfields," *New York Times* (19 January 1990): A1; and Francis X. Clines, "Soviet Forces Said to Battle With Azerbaijani Militants; Call-Up of Reserves Halted," *New York Times* (20 January 1990): 1.

87. Kushen, *Conflict in the Soviet Union*, p. 3.

88. *Agence France Presse*, 20 January 1990, in FBIS-SOV, #90–014 (22 January 1990): 108; and Bill Keller, "Soviets Claim Control in Baku; Scores of Azerbaijanis Killed; Coup Averted, Gorbachev Says," *New York Times* (21 January 1990): 1, 12.

89. Francis X. Clines, "Moscow's Troops Consolidate Hold Over Azerbaijan," *New York Times* (22 January 1990): A1, A6.

90. Bill Keller, "Azerbaijan Vows to Secede if Soviet Troops Stay," *New York Times* (23 January 1990): A1.

91. Bill Keller, "Moscow Arrests Azerbaijani Rebels," *New York Times* (25 January 1990): A1, A8.

92. Altstadt, *The Azerbaijani Turks*, pp. 222–223.

93. Ibid., p. 220.

94. Saroyan, "The 'Karabakh Syndrome' and Azerbaijani Politics," p. 29.

95. Anthony Wilson-Smith, "Explosive Protests," *Maclean's* 103, no. 3 (15 January 1990): 22.

96. Altstadt, *The Azerbaijani Turks*, pp. 221–222.

97. *TASS*, 29 May 1990, in FBIS-SOV, #90–103 (29 May 1990): 142; and *Krasnaya Zvezda*, 31 July 1990, in FBIS-SOV, #90–150 (3 August 1990): 70–71.

98. *Komsomolets*, 9 June 1990, in FBIS-SOV, #90–130 (6 July 1990): 72.

99. *TASS*, 26 March 1990, in FBIS-SOV, #90–059 (27 March 1990): 119; *Baku Domestic Service*, 31 March 1990, in FBIS-SOV, #90–063 (2 April 1990): 112; and *TASS*, 11 April 1990, in FBIS-SOV, #90–071 (12 April 1990): 118.

100. The first raid of significant size occurred on 27 May, when Armenian guerrillas attacked a convoy of Soviet Interior Ministry forces on the outskirts of Yerevan. More than 20 people were killed in the clash and 45 were wounded. *Agence France Presse*, 28 May 1990, in FBIS-SOV, #90–103 (29 May 1990): 140–141.

101. *TASS*, 25 July 1990, in FBIS-SOV, #90–143 (25 July 1990): 43.

102. *Moscow Domestic Service*, 30 July 1990, in FBIS-SOV, #90–148 (1 August 1990): 106; and *Pravda*, 4 August 1990, in FBIS-SOV, #90–151 (6 August 1990): 85.

103. The most serious incidents occurred on the night of 2 August, when Armenian militants attacked a police station in the town of Ararat, leaving a senior official dead. From there they proceeded to the local KGB headquarters, which they ransacked and raided for weapons and secret documents. *TASS*, 4 August 1990, in FBIS-SOV, #90–151 (6 August 1990): 85; and Jonas Bernstein, "A Big Brother Turns into a Foe," *Insight on the News* 6, no. 34 (20 August 1990): 29.

104. Ter-Petrosyan's ascension to the chairmanship was made possible, first, by the significant gains of the ANM in the Armenian Supreme Soviet elections in the spring and summer of 1990 and, second, by the resignation of the First Secretary of the Armenian Communist Party on 6 April. After several rounds of voting, the Supreme Soviet chose Ter-Petrosyan over his Communist rival, making him the *de facto* leader of the Armenian SSR.

Suny, *Looking Toward Ararat*, p. 239; and *Yerevan International Service*, 5 August 1990, in FBIS-SOV, #90–152 (7 August 1990): 84.

105. *Moscow Television Service*, 29 August 1990, in FBIS-SOV, #90–170 (31 August 1990): 53.

106. *Krasnaya Zvezda*, 31 August 1990, in ibid., p. 53.

107. For accounts of a number of incidents, see *TASS*, 3 September 1990, in FBIS-SOV, #90–171 (4 September 1990): 110; *TASS*, 13 September 1990, in FBIS-SOV, #90–178 (13 September 1990): 101; *TASS*, 23 October 1990, in FBIS-SOV, #90–206 (24 October 1990): 116–117; and *Moscow Domestic Service*, 3 December 1990, in FBIS-SOV, #90–233 (4 December 1990): 43–44.

108. Although entitled the "Declaration on the Independence of Armenia," the document passed by the Armenian Supreme Soviet declared only "the start of the process of the establishment of statehood." Text of document as read by the *Yerevan Domestic Service*, 24 August 1990, in FBIS-SOV, #90–166 (27 August 1990): 106–107.

109. *Moscow Domestic Service*, 23 August 1990, in FBIS-SOV, #90–165 (24 August 1990): 100.

110. Text of declaration in FBIS-SOV, #90–166 (27 August 1990): 107.

111. Altstadt, *The Azerbaijani Turks*, p. 224.

112. *Izvestiya*, 6 March 1991, in FBIS-SOV, #91–046 (8 March 1991): 83–86.

113. Media reports from the Azerbaijani Supreme Soviet session indicated that attitudes among legislators were not unanimous on the question of holding the referendum. Foremost among the concerns of the dissenters was the view that Moscow had been unwilling or unable to protect the sovereignty and territorial integrity of Azerbaijan against Armenian irredentism vis-à-vis Nagorno-Karabakh, thus calling into question the logic of continued association with the Union. The primary counter-argument used by referendum supporters was that breaking away from the USSR would be suicidal economically in light of the high level of integration between the republic's economy and that of the Union as a whole. In the end, the supporters prevailed by a vote of 254 for, 43 against, with 6 abstentions. *TASS International Service*, 6 March 1991, and *TASS*, 7 March 1991, in FBIS-SOV, #91–046 (8 March 1991): 86; and *Pravda*, 11 March 1991, in FBIS-SOV, #91–049 (13 March 1991): 87.

114. *Yerevan Domestic Service*, 31 January 1991, in FBIS-SOV, #91–022 (1 February 1991): 57–58.

115. *TASS International Service*, 1 March 1991, in FBIS-SOV, #91–042 (4 March 1991): 73.

116. *Yerevan Domestic Service*, 4 March 1991, in FBIS-SOV, #91–044 (6 March 1991): 69–70.

117. Francis X. Clines, "Gorbachev Given a Partial Victory in Voting on Unity," *New York Times* (19 March 1991): A1; and Serge Schmemann, "Gorbachev and the Bear," *New York Times* (30 March 1991): A1.

118. Elizabeth Fuller, "The All-Union Referendum in the Transcaucasus," *Report on the USSR* 3, no. 13 (29 March 1991): 3–4.

119. David E. Murphy, "Operation 'Ring': The Black Berets in Azerbaijan," *Journal of Soviet Military Studies* 5, no. 1 (March 1992): 82–83.

120. Caroline Cox and John Eibner, *Ethnic Cleansing in Progress: War in Nagorno-Karabakh* (London: Institute for Religious Minorities in the Islamic World, 1993): 45.

121. Murphy, "Operation 'Ring,'" p. 84.

122. Michael Dobbs, "Armenia-Azerbaijan Clash Leaves at Least 25 Dead," *Washington Post* (2 May 1991): A26.

123. Helsinki Watch, *Bloodshed in the Caucasus: Escalation of the Armed Conflict in Nagorno-Karabakh* (New York: Helsinki Watch, September 1992): 9.

124. Daniel Sneider, "Armenians and Azerbaijanis Clash in Two Soviet Villages," *Christian Science Monitor* (7 May 1991): 5.

125. Serge Schmemann, "Violence Erupting in Soviet Caucasus," *New York Times* (8 May 1991): A11; and Francis X. Clines, "A Blood Feud Feeds Unrest in Soviet Area," *New York Times* (13 May 1991): A9.

126. John-Thor Dahlburg, "Pro-Moscow Troops Seize 3 Armenian Villages," *Los Angeles Times* (8 May 1991): A8; and David Remnick, "Soviet Troops Tighten Control on Villages Along Armenian Border," *Washington Post* (9 May 1991): A32.

127. Murphy, "Operation 'Ring,'" p. 91.

128. Helsinki Watch, *Bloodshed in the Caucasus*, p. 9.

129. Murphy, "Operation 'Ring'", p. 91.

130. Quoted in Remnick, "Soviet Troops Tighten Control on Villages Along Armenian Border," p. A32.

131. Elizabeth Fuller, "What Lies Behind the Current Armenian-Azerbaijani Tensions?" *Report on the USSR* 3, no. 21 (24 May 1991): 14.

132. *Armenpress International Service*, 4 July 1991, in FBIS-SOV, #91–130 (8 July 1991): 89.

133. In the words of the Armenian Minister of Internal Affairs, "The position of the Armenian Government is simple. If actions to deport the Armenian population in Azerbaijan continue, we will use all our forces to defend our fellow countrymen." Quoted by *TASS International Service*, 14 July 1991, in FBIS-SOV, #91–135 (15 July 1991): 85.

134. The Armenian government's early position vis-à-vis the coup was one of caution and vigilance. Although officials made it clear both that Armenia would not recognize the authority of the coup leaders and that the republic was continuing its drive for secession, evidence suggests that Armenian leaders were worried about the new acting Soviet government's potential policy toward the question of Nagorno-Karabakh. According to Armenian Prime Minister Vazgen Manukyan, setting the clock back on Soviet history would have no serious effect on the republic; "What is most important to us is what attitude the winner will take to the problem of Nagorno-Karabakh." As a further indication of this concern, Armenian Supreme Soviet chairman Levon Ter-Petrosyan phoned the individual coup leaders in the early stages of the putsch to solicit their views on the issue. The apparent response received by Ter-Petrosyan, that direct Soviet rule over the NKAO would be reinstated, was taken with great apprehension among the Armenian leadership. However, the coup's collapse made the issue moot. Armenian prime minister quoted by *Interfax*, 20 August 1991, in FBIS-SOV, #91–162 (21 August 1991): 85; and *Radio Yerevan Network*, 21 August 1991, in FBIS-SOV, #91–163 (22 August 1991): 84–85.

135. Although by the time the referendum was held it was clear that the Soviet Union would probably not emerge from the fall 1991 events in a form similar to that of the past, the Armenians were determined to follow strictly the provisions of Soviet law regarding the process of secession. Shireen T. Hunter, *The Transcaucasus in Transition: Nation-Building and Conflict* (Washington, DC: Center for Strategic and International Studies, 1994): 37; Elizabeth Fuller, "Armenia Votes Overwhelmingly for Secession," *Report on the USSR* 3, no. 39 (27 September 1991): 18.

136. *TASS*, 21 August 1991, in FBIS-SOV, #91–163 (22 August 1991): 85.

137. *Milliyet*, 24 August 1991, *Interfax*, 23 August 1991, and *Izvestiya*, 26 August 1991, in FBIS-SOV, #91–165 (26 August 1991): 105–106.

138. In an attempt to distance himself further from his past affiliation with Moscow and

the CPSU, Mutalibov convened an extraordinary congress of the Azerbaijani Communist Party in September at which the self-liquidation of the party was agreed to. The AzCP's successor was named the Republican Democratic Party, but it retained most elements of the Communist Party program and bureaucracy. *All-Union Radio Mayak Network*, 23 August 1991, in ibid., p. 104; *Radio Baku Network*, 23 August 1991, in FBIS-SOV, #91–166 (27 August 1991): 126; and Elizabeth Fuller, "The Transcaucasus: Real Independence Remains Elusive," *Radio Free Europe/Radio Liberty Research Report* 1, no. 1 (3 January 1992): 48–49.

139. *TASS International Service*, 30 August 1991, in FBIS-SOV, #91–169 (30 August 1991): 123.

140. The final actions of Operation "Ring" were carried out against the Armenian villages of Karachinar and Verishen in a district of Azerbaijan bordering on the NKAO from 24 to 27 August. Five people were killed and many more were injured in the operation, and several dozen Armenian homes were burned to the ground. *TASS International Service*, 24 August 1991, and *TASS*, 27 August 1991, in FBIS-SOV, #91–168 (29 August 1991): 124.

141. *Interfax*, 2 October 1991, in FBIS-SOV, #91–192 (3 October 1991): 73; and Murphy, "Operation 'Ring,'" p. 93.

142. Helsinki Watch, *Bloodshed in the Caucasus*, p. 10.

143. For example, Azerbaijani armed groups took over a major arms depot of the Transcaucasus Military District in the town of Agdam on 21 December, resulting in the acquisition of a large amount of heavy weaponry and ammunition. *TASS International Service*, 21 December 1991, in FBIS-SOV, #91–246 (23 December 1991): 66–67.

144. Paul B. Henze, *The Transcaucasus in Transition* (Santa Monica: RAND Corporation, 1991): 11.

145. Despite having won the uncontested election held weeks earlier, the Azerbaijani leader no doubt felt the need to continue to take a hard line on the question of Nagorno-Karabakh. On 21 September Mutalibov told reporters that he would "under no circumstances agree to hand over Nagorno-Karabakh to the jurisdiction of Armenia, the government of the Union or any other state body." More specifically, the Azerbaijani president claimed that "the restoration of the status quo that existed until the events that began in 1988 is what we seek." First quote by *Radio Rossii Network*, 21 September 1991; second quote by *All-Union Radio Mayak Network*, 21 September, both in FBIS-SOV, #91–184 (23 September 1991): 81.

146. Fred Hiatt, "Armenians, Azerbaijanis Agree to Talks on Disputed Enclave," *Washington Post* (23 September 1991): A13.

147. There are several possible explanations for the Armenian government's decision to give up its claims to Azerbaijani lands. First, it is conceivable that the leadership had come to realize that to continue to insist on unification with Nagorno-Karabakh was utopian and ultimately futile. Thus, searching for a suitable compromise solution was a necessary act in order to avert war. The second possible explanation for Armenia's action, which seems to be confirmed by statements of Levon Ter-Petrosyan, is that the authorities placed a high degree of trust in Boris Yeltsin as an impartial mediator and as a guarantor of any peace agreement. *TASS International Service*, 24 September 1991, in FBIS-SOV, #91–186 (25 September 1991): 74; Bill Keller, "Armenia Yielding Claim on Enclave," *New York Times* (23 September 1991): A12; and Elizabeth Fuller, "El'tsin Brokers Agreement on Nagorno-Karabakh," *Report on the USSR* 3, no. 40 (4 October 1991): 17.

148. Fred Hiatt, "Armenia, Azerbaijan Agree to Cease-Fire," *Washington Post* (25 September 1991): A20.

149. Text of communique in printed by *TASS*, 24 September 1991, in FBIS-SOV, #91–

186 (25 September 1991): 74–75.

150. *TASS International Service*, 24 September 1991, in ibid., p. 73.

151. The Armenian leader made it clear from the start that complete mutual understanding did not exist on all points outlined in the agreement. However, he also stressed the necessity both for compromise and for continued work on the details. See *Radio Rossii Network*, 24 September 1991, in FBIS-SOV, #91–186 (25 September 1991): 71; and Bill Keller, "Armenia and Azerbaijan Sign a Peace Agreement," *New York Times* (24 September 1991): A12.

152. *Radio Rossii Network*, 24 September 1991, in FBIS-SOV, #91–186 (25 September 1991): 77.

153. *Interfax*, 24 September 1991, in ibid., p. 76.

154. Quoted by *TASS International Service*, 25 October 1991, in FBIS-SOV, #91–208 (28 October 1991): 81.

155. *TASS*, 31 October 1991, in FBIS-SOV, #91–212 (1 November 1991): 69; and *Interfax*, 15 November 1991, in FBIS-SOV, #91–222 (18 November 1991): 69.

156. *All-Union Radio First Program Radio-1 Network*, 1 November 1991, in FBIS-SOV, #91–213 (4 November 1991): 76.

157. *Interfax*, 13 November 1991, in FBIS-SOV, #91–220 (14 November 1991): 77.

158. *Komsomolskaya*, 13 November 1991, in ibid., p. 77.

159. A third round in the talks had begun on 18 November, with agreement in principle being reached on a cease-fire, withdrawal of forces from the conflict zone, and the exchange of prisoners. The Armenians walked out two days later, declaring they would return only after the pipeline's reopening. *Interfax*, 18 November 1991, in FBIS-SOV, #91–223 (19 November 1991): 82; and *Radio Yerevan Network*, 20 November 1991, in FBIS-SOV, #91–225 (21 November 1991): 80.

160. *Armenpress International Service*, 19 November 1991, in FBIS-SOV, #91–224 (20 November 1991): 81; and *Interfax*, 20 November 1991, in FBIS-SOV, #91–225 (21 November 1991): 84.

161. It was believed initially that the helicopter had crashed into a mountain and exploded as a result of foggy flying conditions. However, an investigation found holes in the fuselage consistent with the explosion of a rocket. Although the Armenians denied any involvement, they were blamed immediately for the incident. *TASS International Service*, 20 November 1991, in ibid., p. 83; and *Interfax*, 21 November 1991, in FBIS-SOV, #91–226 (22 November 1991): 78.

162. *Radio Baku Network*, 21 November 1991, in FBIS-SOV, #91–225 (21 November 1991): 83.

163. Quoted by the *Radio Moscow World Service*, 25 November 1991, in FBIS-SOV, #91–227 (25 November 1991): 93.

164. *Central Television First Program Network*, 25 November 1991, in ibid., p. 94.

165. *TASS International Service*, 24 November 1991, and *Armenpress International Service*, 22 November 1991, in ibid., pp. 93–94.

166. *Radio Baku Network*, 27 November 1991, and *TASS International Service*, 26 November 1991, in FBIS-SOV, #91–229 (27 November 1991): 63–64.

167. Text of decree read by the *Radio Baku Network*, 5 December 1991, in FBIS-SOV, #91–235 (6 December 1991): 81.

168. Serge Schmemann, "Declaring Death of Soviet Union, Russia and 2 Republics Form New Commonwealth," *New York Times* (9 December 1991): A1, A4.

169. *TASS*, 30 December 1991, in FBIS-SOV, #91–250 (30 December 1991): 53.

170. International Institute for Strategic Studies, *The Military Balance, 1992–1993* (London: Brassey's, 1992): 100.

3

Changing Regional Dynamics in the Post-Soviet Period

The Caucasus region is a traditional sphere of Russian interests, and we do not intend to abandon it.

—Russian Foreign Minister Andrei Kozyrev,
September 1992

The demise of the USSR altered greatly the geopolitical realities of the Trans-caucasus and its surroundings. On the one hand, Armenia and Azerbaijan emerged from the shadow of the Soviet empire as independent actors on the international stage for the first time in more than seven decades. On the other hand, the major surrounding powers—Turkey, Iran, and Russia—scrambled to assert their geopolitical interests in the region after the retreat of Soviet power. An examination of each side's reaction to the new geopolitical dynamics of the Transcaucasus is crucial to understanding the sources of their conduct since 1992.

PERSPECTIVES AND INTERESTS OF EXTERNAL POWERS

Turkey

Of all the countries bordering on the former Soviet periphery, few showed more interest in the USSR's demise than Turkey. With the disappearance of the Soviet monolith and the subsequent emergence of independent states, Turkish policy-makers looked to the southern regions of the former Soviet Union (FSU) as a source of potential opportunity as well as risk.[1] Over the course of the post-Soviet period, Ankara's interests in the southern FSU, and in the Transcaucasus in particular, have been driven by the dual desires to spread Turkish influence while maintaining Turkish security.

Turkey's attraction to the Muslim republics of the former Soviet Union is rooted, first and foremost, in common historical and linguistic ties. With the exception of Tajikistan, whose population is predominantly Farsi-speaking, each of the Muslim republics of the FSU boasts a population whose titular nationality speaks a Turkic language as its native tongue. Added to the substantial historical links between the Turks and the peoples of Central Asia and Azerbaijan, which developed over centuries of migration and intermingling, the basis for a close identification between Turkey and the Muslim former Soviet republics exists.[2]

With the breakup of the Soviet empire, Turkey looked to Central Asia and the Transcaucasus as areas into which it could spread its influence. Turkey stressed not only its close historical and linguistic ties to the Turkic peoples of the southern FSU, but also its standing as a model of a Westernized, secular, market-oriented democracy upon which the newly independent Muslim states could pattern their transition from Soviet rule.[3] In essence, Ankara sought to portray itself as a "big brother" to the Turkic republics.

Although power and prestige no doubt figured into Turkish calculations in its quest to strengthen ties with the southern former Soviet states, there were other elements at play. With the decline of the Soviet Union in the late 1980s and early 1990s, Ankara came to feel increasingly that its geostrategic value as an ally of the West was dissipating. Primary among the concerns of Turkish policy-makers was that, with the end of the Cold War, Turkey would become increasingly irrelevant to the West, thereby foreclosing upon its long-standing dream of full integration with a "united" Europe.[4] Thus, "finding a new role for Turkey within the overall Western strategy that would guarantee Turkey's continued importance" became a central occupation of Ankara.[5] With the redrawing of the geopolitical map of Eurasia spawned by the Soviet demise, the most logical option to Turkey for doing so would be to offer itself as a "bridge" between the West and the Turkic former Soviet republics. Thus, Ankara's move to expand its influence in the region was likely attributable at least partly to the perceived need to heighten its own importance in the eyes of the West.[6]

Perhaps the final element driving Turkey to look to the east was an economic one. On the one hand, the six Muslim former Soviet republics represented new potential markets for Turkish goods. More importantly, on the other hand, the three republics bordering upon the Caspian Sea—Azerbaijan, Kazakstan, and Turkmenistan—were known to possess large reserves of oil and natural gas waiting to be tapped. Through its ties to the West, Turkey sought to offer the littoral states access to European and American investment possibilities for the development of their energy resources.[7] Moreover, Ankara eyed Caspian oil and gas with the desire not only to attain lucrative transit revenues for their shipment to the Mediterranean Sea via Turkish pipelines, but also to meet expanding domestic demand for energy.[8] In short, Turkey sought to make itself the hub of a regional economic network to complement the strong political ties it desired of the newly independent republics.

Importantly, the key to Turkey's ambitions as a power-broker in the southern

FSU was recognized to be the Transcaucasus—specifically, Azerbaijan and, to a lesser extent, Armenia. As a crossroads among landmasses, Transcaucasia offers Turkey access to the republics of Central Asia. Serving as a bridgehead to the east is Azerbaijan, important to Turkey in its own right due to its vast oil reserves and its 7.5 million population of Azerbaijani Turks—the closest relatives to the Anatolian Turks of all the Turkic peoples of the FSU.[9] However, due to geographical reality, Turkey is kept separate from Azerbaijan proper by the Republic of Armenia.[10]

Armenia's location situates it as either a bridge or a barrier between Turkey and its eastern Turkic neighbors. In light of the strained relations between the Turks and Armenians throughout history, Armenia has traditionally been a barrier. However, with the breakup of the Soviet Union and the reassertion of Turkish interest in the Muslim republics, rapprochement with Yerevan was made a necessity if Turkey wished to realize fully its goal of becoming a regional great power—a fact due precisely to Armenia's geographic position separating Turkey from Azerbaijan and Central Asia.[11] Nonetheless, historical memory and more recent events have made a *modus vivendi* difficult for either side to undertake.

Just as Turkey's designs in the post-Soviet states were limited at least in theory by geographic reality, further potential barriers to the expansion of Turkish leverage were extended by Russia and Iran. For reasons of influence, neither power wished to see an increase in Turkish engagement along Russia's Muslim periphery, and both sought actively to exclude the Turks by various means.

Although Ankara's geopolitical interests in the post-Soviet republics were framed primarily in terms of its desire to expand Turkish influence, a strong security element also pervaded Ankara's thinking. In the words of one Turkish official, "Before all else, the Caucasus and its extensions in Asia constitute a very important security region for Turkey. Therefore, the protection of political stability in these republics is a basic element of Turkey's policy regarding the Caucasus and the Central Asian republics."[12] Central to Turkish concerns was the prospect of nationalist strife in areas adjacent to its borders.[13]

Already battling a major internal insurgency by Kurdish terrorists in the southeast, Turkey feared the spillover of further violence into its territory or the development of a situation in which Ankara would be prompted to become involved in fighting outside its borders. To the dismay of Turkish policy-makers, the Armenia-Azerbaijan conflict represents exactly such a threat: "Turkey is concerned that a clash between Azerbaijan and Armenia could turn into a 'spreading wave of fire,' engulfing the Caucasus region and other Soviet republics. It is feared that this could eventually force Turkey to become a direct partner to the problem, and could undermine regional peace and development."[14] Ankara's attempts to reconcile its desire to expand its influence in the Transcaucasus with the necessity of meeting the security challenges of the Armenia-Azerbaijan conflict will be assessed in chapter four.

Iran

Like Turkey, Iran viewed the breakup of the USSR with both optimism and apprehension. Seeing a golden opportunity to expand its influence in the newly independent republics of the Transcaucasus and Central Asia, Iran set out to fulfill "what it sees as its natural geopolitical role of providing a bridge between the outside world and landlocked Central Asia."[15] Situated as a land bridge between the Transcaucasus and Central Asia on the one hand and the Middle East and the Persian Gulf on the other hand, Iran was poised to play an important role in the region. However, Tehran was also forced to take into account the potential security problems posed by the Soviet breakup.

Iran's attraction to the southern regions of the FSU is rooted in a number of factors. As Turkey, Iran has desired to use the demise of the Soviet Union to its advantage by building new political and economic relationships with the Trans-caucasian and Central Asian states. In offering the republics potential access to the Persian Gulf via the extensive Iranian transportation network, Tehran sought to break out of its international isolation and become the transit point for their large energy resources.[16] Moreover—although apparently of less importance to Tehran—the Islamic Republic also portrayed itself as a model upon which the Muslim states of the FSU could pattern their political and religious development after the Soviet breakup.

While Iranian interests in the Transcaucasus and Central Asia have largely been a result of Tehran's desire to expand its leverage in the two regions, a notable corollary to its ambitions has been the need to exclude—or at least limit—the spread of Turkish and Russian influence there.[17] In the calculations of Iranian policy-makers, excessive vigor in making overtures to the Muslim republics is to be avoided lest Tehran risk raising the ire of Russia. Any backlash from Moscow sparked by suspicion of Iranian motives would not only threaten to bring a resurgence of Russian dominance in the region at Iran's expense but also have negative effects on the *modus vivendi* desired by Tehran for the receipt of Russian military hardware and technology.[18] Thus, Iran viewed it necessary to put on the appearance of a cautious and not overly active policy in Central Asia and the Transcaucasus.

While Tehran perceived the need to show a modicum of restraint in its dealings with the newly independent states in order to appease Russia, it was also faced with the perception that Turkey has been determined to fill the post-Soviet geopolitical vacuum in Central Asia and Transcaucasia at Iran's expense. Central to Iranian concerns was not only that Turkey might upstage Iran and deny it the potential benefits of being the leading power-broker in the region but also that Ankara might open the door to Western involvement in the Muslim states of the FSU. Indeed, in light of post-revolutionary Iran's deeply seated hostility toward the West and the United States in particular, Tehran at times concocted images of a great Western conspiracy to use Turkey as its agent of influence in the Transcaucasus and Central Asia to undermine Iran's geopolitical position, if not its very security. According to one Iranian commentary, "the objective of the coordinated Washington-Ankara move appears at first glance to be to fill the region's political vacuum, and to violate the security of Iran's boundaries in the long term."[19] Over time, such fears led Iran to view Turkey as its primary competitor for influence in the newly independent states.

Just as the key to Turkey's geopolitical designs in the southern FSU has been the Transcaucasus, Iran, too, accorded Armenia and Azerbaijan with special emphasis. Whereas Transcaucasia represents Ankara's bridge to Central Asia, the strategic crossroads represents also a region in which Tehran could potentially block Turkey's eastern objectives.[20] In light of the fact that Armenia is located between Turkey and the Muslim former Soviet republics, Iran recognized that, were it to establish an axis with Armenia at Ankara's expense, it would be in a position to keep Turkey geographically separated from Azerbaijan and Central Asia.[21] If successful, Iran would then be in a better position to increase and consolidate its own influence in the Muslim republics.

While Iran felt a geopolitical attraction to Armenia after the breakup of the Soviet Union, Tehran also looked to Azerbaijan with keen interest. Despite their close linguistic identification with the Turks, the Azeris hold strong cultural and religious ties with Iran. Indeed, Azerbaijan is the only Muslim former Soviet republic in which Shi'a Islam is practiced by a majority (some 70 percent) of the populace. As such, Azerbaijan is perceived to present potentially fertile ground for the expansion of Iranian influence in the Transcaucasus.[22] However, a major source of concern among Iranian officials in their approach to relations with Baku has been the existence of irredentist claims by the Azerbaijanis on large parts of northwestern Iran.

As a result of the Russo-Iranian War of 1826–1828, the border between what is now Azerbaijan and Iran was established. Importantly, although there was no historical Azerbaijani state to speak of, the demarcation left significant numbers of ethnic Azeris on each side of the frontier; those to the north were integrated into the Russian and later the Soviet empire, while those to the south remained within Iran. Due to Soviet-era historical revisionism and myth-building intended to denounce imperialism, the notion of a "northern" and "southern" Azerbaijan was created and propagated throughout the USSR. It was charged that the "two Azerbaijans," once united, were separated artificially by a conspiracy between imperial Russia and Iran.[23] While such revisionism suited Soviet purposes well, it became the basis for irredentism among Azeri nationalists in the closing years of Soviet rule.

Although Iran's fifteen-million Azeri population is well integrated into Iranian society and has shown little desire to secede,[24] Tehran has nonetheless shown extreme concern with prospects for the rise of sentiments calling for union between the "two Azerbaijans." Were separatist stirrings to rise among Iranian Azeris, Iran could see its territorial integrity violated, perhaps encouraging more of its numerous ethnic minorities also to break away.[25] Thus, it has remained strongly in the interests of the Iranian government to ensure that the rise of such sentiments among Iranian Azeris is avoided.

Iran's need to balance its desire for closer ties to Azerbaijan and its necessity for maintaining domestic tranquility likely made for substantial policy debates within the Iranian government. It also demonstrated, at a more fundamental level, the interaction between considerations of spreading Iranian influence and those of maintaining Iran's security in the post-Soviet Transcaucasus. Like those of the Turks, Iranian geopolitical interests in the FSU contain a legitimate security component. According to a commentary in the *Tehran Times* (which is regarded as the mouthpiece of the Iranian Foreign Ministry), "the first ground for concern from the point of view in Tehran is the lack of political stability in the newly independent republics. The unstable conditions in those republics could be serious causes of insecurity along the lengthy borders [over 2000 kilometers] Iran shares with those countries."[26] Clearly, Iran is apprehensive at the prospect of the rise of instability and conflict along its former Soviet borders. Unfortunately for Iranian policy-makers, the Armenia-Azerbaijan dispute represents just such a prospect.

Russia

Russian perspectives and interests in the Transcausus are the product of a complex set of geopolitical calculations that have evolved since the breakup of the Soviet Union. On the one hand, Russia's interests in the area have been framed in terms of the potential threats to the security and territorial integrity of the Russian Federation that may arise there; on the other hand, Moscow has viewed the Transcaucasus as a key region in which to forward its strategic goals at the expense of other international actors. Before delving into the nature and sources of those perspectives and interests, however, it is necessary first to lay the proper background by probing briefly the evolution of Russian foreign and security policy vis-à-vis the former Soviet states as a whole. Such a discussion will provide critical insights into the development of Russian policies vis-à-vis the Armenia-Azerbaijan conflict between 1992 and 1995.

The events of December 1991 marked not only the breakup of the Soviet Union, but also the dismantling of the Russian empire as it had existed as a geopolitical entity for more than two hundred years. Among the challenges faced by the leaders of the empire's self-proclaimed successor state—the Russian Federation—was to formulate a new concept of foreign and security policy toward the post-Soviet states based on an as yet undefined set of Russian national interests.

The two key players early on in this process were President Boris Yeltsin and Foreign Minister Andrei Kozyrev, whose approaches to foreign policy were said to be underpinned at the time by the belief that, in order for Russia to complete its transformation into a democratic, market-oriented country, Moscow would have to jettison the inherently aggressive and imperialistic aspects of Soviet foreign policy.[27] Then, and only then, would Russia be able to enter truly the club of Western nations.

In an effort to effect Russia's transformation, Yeltsin and Kozyrev spent most of 1992 trying to dissociate the country from its imperial past. As a consequence, relations with the West were given high priority in Russian foreign policy, and establishing a stable partnership with the world's democracies became a leading goal of Moscow.[28] Whether intentional or not, the pursuit of such a goal left Yeltsin and Kozyrev open to substantial criticism at home for having neglected relations with the former Soviet states.

Moscow's perceived slight of the newly independent states in its external relations hastened the rise in late 1992 of a strong and highly vocal opposition calling for a reappraisal of Russia's foreign policy orientation and a more precise definition of its national interests. This broadly based opposition, which included Vice President Alexander Rutskoi, Supreme Soviet Speaker Ruslan Khasbulatov, and groups such as the center-right Civic Union and the military, chided Yeltsin and Kozyrev openly and vocally for their over-emphasis on ties with the West and their corresponding neglect of relations with immediate neighbors, especially the former Soviet republics.[29]

Central to the opposition's argument was the view that Moscow's course of partnership with the West was not congruent with Russia's interests and that Russian policies should focus on relations with the former Soviet states (which were referred collectively to by this group as the "Near Abroad").[30] Indeed, these critics viewed the entire post-Soviet space as a sphere of vital Russian interests in which, by right of historical, military, political, and economic realities, Russia has special rights and responsibilities to uphold peace and stability. In pursuing an overly pro-Western foreign policy, it was argued, Russia was ignoring these rights and responsibilities to the detriment of its continued status as a great power.

In late 1992 and early 1993, a distinct shift in Russian foreign policy priorities emerged as first Yeltsin and then Kozyrev began to move closer to the position of their opponents.[31] This shift became evident initially in increasingly assertive statements toward Russia's neighbors by members of the government and Foreign Ministry, but it was more substantive actions such as the adoption of a new foreign policy concept and a new military doctrine that offered greater evidence of the emergence and makeup of Russian foreign and security policy.

On 25 January 1993, the Russian Foreign Ministry outlined its general foreign policy agenda with the adoption of a document entitled "Concept of Foreign Policy of the Russian Federation." Some of the key concepts outlined were the need to protect "the external borders of the Commonwealth," the assumption of responsibility by Russia "for ensuring stability and human rights and freedoms in the space of the former USSR," and the need to guarantee "the protection of the rights of Russian citizens living outside the limits of the Federation."[32] In contrast to an earlier document that defined Russian national interests in terms of the achievement of democracy, concern for human rights, and integration into the world economy, the new concept of foreign policy marked a major reorientation of the Foreign Ministry's priorities in the "Near Abroad."

Further evidence of Moscow's transition to an activist role in the post-Soviet space was provided by Russia's new military doctrine, approved on 2 November 1993. According to the doctrine's basic provisions, the main potential threats to Russian interests include, *inter alia*, the suppression of the rights and freedoms of ethnic Russians in the "Near Abroad," the expansion of military blocs to the detriment of Russian security, attacks on Russian military facilities in foreign states, and the deployment of foreign troops on the territory of states adjacent to Russia without Moscow's approval or the endorsement of the United Nations Security Council or some other relevant international mechanism.[33] Furthermore, the doctrine recognizes the possibility of the use of military force not only to repel aggression against Russia proper but also to protect "the vital interests of Russia," which are not defined explicitly.[34] These characteristics of Russia's new military doctrine marked an activist view in Moscow vis-à-vis the "Near Abroad" in that they, in the words of Mary FitzGerald, gave Russia "any number of excuses for intervention" there.[35]

The transformation of Russian foreign and security policy since 1992 has been attributed to many causes, ranging from the rise of Russian nationalism to the often cited claim in the Russian press of Moscow's treatment as a "junior partner" by the West.[36] Though the true causes are beyond the scope of this book, it is unmistakable that a broad consensus has emerged in Russia around the concept of the FSU as a sphere of vital Russian interests within which Moscow has special rights and responsibilities to act to maintain peace and security.[37]

Most Russian political and military leaders view the Transcaucasus as a key region of the "Near Abroad" due to its position both as a key land bridge among Europe, Central Asia, and the Middle East and as a crucial border area along Russia's Caucasian underbelly.[38] What follows from this perception are two primary Russian geostrategic interests in the Transcaucasus: The maintenance of stability on the Russian Federation's southern flank and the expansion and con-solidation of Russian influence in the Transcaucasus at the expense of other international actors.

Excluding the brief period of Armenian, Azerbaijani, and Georgian independ-ence from 1918 to 1920, more than two centuries of Russian rule of the Trans-caucasus was ended by the breakup of the USSR. Thus, among the first and most evident results of the Soviet breakup was the alteration of Russia's southern frontier between the Black and Caspian Seas: No longer sharing a common border with Iran and Turkey along the Aras River and the Pontus Mountains, respectively, post-Soviet Russia drew its boundary at the Caucasus mountain chain, north of which lay the volatile region of the North Caucasus.

Prior to the onset of imperial Russian expansion into Transcaucasia in the eighteenth and nineteenth centuries, the North Caucasus was regarded as a region of substantial geostrategic importance to Russia, serving alternately as a buffer zone against Muslim expansionism from the south and as a forward base for the advancement of Russia's own imperial designs in the Near East.[39] Although the spread of Russian rule into the Transcaucasus had shifted those roles away from the North Caucasus by the end of the last century, the latter region again became crucial in the geostrategic calculations of Moscow following the Soviet demise for many of the same reasons that it had been previously: As the southernmost territory of the Russian Federation between the Black and Caspian Seas, the North Caucasus represents the region of Russia closest geographically to the Middle East.[40] Thus, as the critical anchor of Russia's southern flank in a key area of the world, Moscow has perceived a vested interest in the stability and integrity of the North Caucasus region. However, to the chagrin of Russian leaders, the North Caucasus is not an area of inherent stability.

A region of greater ethnic heterogeneity than even Transcaucasia, the North Caucasus has been a frequent source of instability and conflict along Russia's southern frontier over the past two centuries, earning it the occasional depiction as Russia's "Achilles' heel."[41] According to Uwe Halbach and Heinrich Tiller, "In the North Caucasus, what is probably the greatest ethnic diversity in Eurasia goes hand in hand with a political territorial demarcation from the Soviet era which in no way does justice to this structure."[42] Such ethno-territorial complexity is complicated further by the overlap of many ethnic groups among the republics of the North Caucasus and Transcaucasia, thus linking the two regions in the minds of Russian policy-makers.

Since the breakup of the Soviet Union, Russian leaders have shown intense concern at times over the potential for ethnic conflict in the Transcaucasus spreading into the North Caucasus region. A primary focus of anxiety has been Georgia, which is home to a handful of peoples that share close ethnic ties to inhabitants of the North Caucasus republics. In the spring of 1989, one such group, the Ossetians, began an armed campaign to break away from Georgia and reunite with the North Ossetian region of Russia. Moscow was concerned with the chances of violence spreading into Russia, and in July 1992 it dispatched troops to the area to police a cease-fire between the combatants. Similarly, Russian leaders became concerned in 1993 that separatist acts by the Abkhazians of western Georgia would incite comparable actions by the North Caucasian peoples, and Russian troops were again sent to enforce a cease-fire.[43]

Russia's concern with the security of its southern flank has also focused on the potential rise of Islamic extremism in areas adjacent to its soil. Russia has shown substantial worry that Islam will grow as a radical political force in Central Asia and the Transcaucasus, thus holding out the possibility of the rise of a group of potentially hostile states along the Russian underbelly. Moscow has also feared that Islamic extremism, once rooted in the southern states of the FSU, could gain a foothold among Russia's own sizable Muslim population, thereby threatening potentially the territorial integrity of the country. Although there is little evidence that Islam is on the rise as a political force along Russia's southern flank,[44] Moscow continues to be highly sensitive to the possibility.[45]

While Russia's concerns for the stability of its southern flank imply that its geopolitical interests in the Caucasus are primarily defensive in nature, such is not altogether the case. A strong element of Russian interests in the region is derived from the central tenet of Moscow's "Near Abroad" policy: The perception of the former Soviet space as an exclusive sphere of Russian influence in which Moscow has the right and responsibility to uphold peace and stability.

Underlying Russia's approach to relations with states of the "Near Abroad" is the perceived need to maintain Russian predominance across the territory of the FSU. In order to achieve this goal, a number of conditions have to be met. First, Russia has to become the chief intermediary between the post-Soviet states and the outside world. Second, no other country or international organization can be allowed to gain a foothold in the "Near Abroad" that could rival the influence of Moscow. Next, the rise of potential threats to Russian security or ascendancy in the region have to be prevented.[46] Fourth, Moscow has to establish itself as the sole peacemaker and peacekeeper in the former Soviet space. Lastly, the "Near Abroad" has to be maintained as a sphere of economic influence for Russia, but without the necessity for Moscow to provide the assistance to the republics that it did under Soviet rule.[47] Taken together, these measures aim to provide for the resurgence and consolidation of Russia's influence in the FSU.

As applied to the Transcaucasus, these conditions have dictated that Russia must be engaged vigorously in the region. First, Moscow must seek a place of prominence both in the foreign policies of the Transcaucasian states and in attempts to resolve regional conflicts. Second, Russia must constrain the growth of foreign influence in the region while preventing the rise of threats to Russian security. Finally, Moscow must build favorable economic links with regional states and assert proprietary rights over Azerbaijan's energy reserves. The means through which Russia pursued each of these goals will be made clear in ensuing chapters.

Turkey, Iran, and Russia entered the post-Soviet period with considerable geopolitical interests in the Transcaucasus. Each looked at the region first and foremost in terms of the potential security challenges that might arise there, such as the possible spread of ethnic conflict beyond Transcaucasia's borders. While the interests of the three regional powers were congruent in their need to avoid such challenges, their interests also clashed to a large extent. Russia, Turkey, and Iran each sought to expand its influence in the post-Soviet Transcaucasus at the expense of the others, and each was deeply suspicious of the others' motives. This element of competition proved to be a major factor influencing the course of the Armenia-Azerbaijan conflict after the Soviet breakup.

PERSPECTIVES AND INTERESTS OF THE CONFLICTING PARTIES

The breakup of the USSR transformed the Armenia-Azerbaijan conflict from an internal matter of the Soviet Union into an inter-state clash almost overnight. After four years of bitter dispute under the Soviet system, the two republics had to adjust their perspectives on the Nagorno-Karabakh question to account for the realities of independent statehood. At the same time, consideration also had to be given to foreign policy matters, including how to approach relations with Russia, Turkey, and Iran. Thus, the evolution and content of Armenian and Azerbaijani perspectives on foreign policy and the Nagorno-Karabakh dispute must be traced briefly in order to provide necessary insight into the sources of the two republics' conduct in the years since independence.

Azerbaijan

In most respects, Azerbaijani perspectives on the Nagorno-Karabakh question changed little in substance following the breakup of the Soviet Union. Karabakh continued to be viewed as an historically vital and inseparable part of Azerbaijan, and any measure with the potential of diluting Azerbaijani sovereignty over it was treated with disfavor. Issues relating to the region's administrative status— including the question of greater self-rule for the Armenian population—were viewed as an internal matter of Azerbaijan. It was alleged that Armenia escalated the dispute into an inter-republican war by becoming involved in domestic Baku's affairs—that is, by trying to annex Azerbaijani land. Thus, central to the Azer-baijanis' perspective on the Nagorno-Karabakh question since independence has been the view that a foreign power, Armenia, has illicit designs on the territorial integrity and sovereignty of Azerbaijan—designs that must be repelled by any means necessary.

While the perceived challenge to Azerbaijani territorial integrity from without was largely a holdover from the late Soviet period, by independence the possibil-ity of such a challenge from within was brought to heightened recognition. Unlike Armenia, which is the most ethnically homogenous of the states of the FSU,[48] Azerbaijan is a patchwork of peoples of varying ethnicity, language, and religion. The Armenian population of Nagorno-Karabakh aside, Azerbaijan is home to three major non-titular ethnic groups. In the north are the Lezgin, a Sunni Muslim people who speak an Ibero-Caucasian language and numbered close to 200,000 in the 1989 Soviet census.[49] To the southeast are more than 20,000 Talysh, an Iranian people whose language belongs to the northwest Iranian language group. Finally, in southwestern Azerbaijan are some 12,000 Kurds that share close ties to the Kurdish populations of Armenia, Turkey, and Iran.[50]

Azerbaijan's ethno-linguistic heterogeneity posed a number of potential problems for post-Soviet Azerbaijani leaders. Whereas the Azeri people them-selves have a mixed cultural and ethnic identity, the presence of other diverse ethnic groups further complicated the development of a coherent sense of national identity for the newly independent republic.[51] Also, territorial gerrymandering from the imperial Russian and Soviet periods left open the possibility of future irredentism on the part of each of the major non-Azeri ethnic groups.

The historical homeland of the Talysh was divided between Russia and Iran in 1813,[52] while the Lezgin people were left on each side of the Russian-Azerbaijani frontier with the drawing of Soviet borders in the region in 1922.[53] As regards the Kurds, the current Armenian-Azerbaijani border divides the area of "Red Kurdistan" that existed as an autonomous region from 1923 to 1929.[54] Although not a problem during the Soviet period, the potential for irredentism among the Talysh, Kurdish, and Lezgin peoples of Azerbaijan is regarded as a real and dangerous prospect because it could—under the right circumstances—threaten to fragment the republic.

In light of the perceived dangers to Azerbaijan's territorial integrity posed by the republic's non-titular, non-Armenian minorities, the Nagorno-Karabakh problem heightened the sense of vulnerability of post-Soviet Azerbaijani leaders. With the Karabakh Armenians engaged in an active campaign to break away from Azerbaijan and join Armenia, the precedent was set for similar movements to arise among the Talysh, Lezgin, and Kurdish peoples. Thus, any type of bargain on the Karabakh issue that would entail a decrease in Baku's sovereignty over the region was seen as giving potential encouragement to the rise of separatism among Azerbaijan's other minorities. In the years following the Soviet breakup, this perception played an important, though not often clearly apparent, role in Azerbaijan's approach to the Nagorno-Karabakh dispute.

Baku's liberation from the grip of Soviet rule also left Azerbaijani leaders with the need to formulate a foreign policy concept. Yet, in light of the republic's mixed ethnic and historical legacy, no consensus existed on where Azerbaijani foreign policy priorities should reside.

Numerous dynamics have impacted upon the articulation of Baku's policy toward Iran. While strong religious and cultural links are held with the Iranians, the Azerbaijani people have been prone toward secularism throughout their history, thus limiting in some circles the desirability of close ties with the Islamic Republic of Iran.[55] At the same time, however, Iran's long common border with Azerbaijan and its extensive transportation infrastructure have offered potential economic benefits to Baku through trade opportunities and possible access to Iranian ports on the Persian Gulf. Moreover, Iran also represents the only overland link, other than Armenia, between Azerbaijan and the autonomous Azerbaijani republic of Nakhichevan. Finally, northwestern Iran holds what many Azerbaijani nationalists covet: So-called "Southern Azerbaijan" and its population of fifteen million Azeris.[56] Throughout the post-Soviet period, each of these factors have impacted heavily upon the formulation of Azerbaijani policy toward Iran.

In light of the close historical and linguistic ties between the Azeris and the Turks, Turkey held strong appeal for Azerbaijani policy-makers in the wake of the Soviet breakup. Such appeal was strengthened by Turkey's model as a secular, democratic, free-market-oriented state with close links to Europe and the United States. However, geographic reality and domestic political constraints within both Turkey and Azerbaijan have placed limits on the practicality and advantageousness of a close Azerbaijani-Turkish relationship. Consequently, the perceived value of Turkey as a partner has fluctuated among various post-Soviet Azerbaijani leaders, although all have recognized the necessity of maintaining good relations with Ankara.

A variety of factors have also impacted on Baku's approach to relations with

Russia. Although large segments of the Azerbaijani populace were embittered by their experience with rule from Moscow during the closing years of the USSR, ties with the former center had to be reconciled with the new realities of statehood. Among the more important factors guiding the articulation of Azerbaijani policy toward Russia have been lingering Soviet-era economic ties and questions relating to Moscow's strategic objectives in the FSU. Moreover, the importance of Baku's relations with Moscow have tended to depend greatly on the personal preferences of various post-Soviet Azerbaijani leaders.

The formulation of Azerbaijani foreign policy—already a complicated matter considering the multiplicity of factors at play—was complicated further by the nature of Transcaucasia's post-Soviet geopolitics. Because the strategic agendas of Turkey, Iran, and Russia often conflicted with one another, Azerbaijan became the subject of efforts by each of the three powers to gain influence in the region at the expense of the others. As Shireen Hunter notes, "these rivalries have focused on determining the direction of Azerbaijan's internal evolution and its external orientation."[57]

Armenia

Like Azerbaijan, Armenia was forced by the realities of independence to reconsider its perspectives on the Nagorno-Karabakh question and to formulate a concept of foreign relations. In emotional and nationalistic terms, the Armenians' view of the dispute with Azerbaijan changed little with the breakup of the USSR: As the only part of historical Armenia where a tradition of national sovereignty was preserved nearly unbroken, Nagorno-Karabakh represents a stronghold whose defense is perceived as vital to the survival of all Armenians. According to one Armenian fighter, "if we lose Karabakh, we will be turning the last page of Armenian history."[58]

However, the official Armenian position on the Karabakh matter underwent a noteworthy change with the passing of the USSR. Whereas substantial effort was dedicated to achieving political union between the Armenian SSR and the NKAO beginning in 1988, Armenian endeavors focused after late 1991 on the more ambiguous goal of obtaining self-determination for the Armenian population of Nagorno-Karabakh. The first step in this process was taken on 18 January 1992, when, in keeping with a 99 percent popular vote in favor of independence, the Supreme Soviet of the former NKAO proclaimed an independent "Nagorno-Karabakh Republic" (NKR).[59]

In an apparent continuation of its policy from the previous September, when all claims to Azerbaijani territory were renounced officially, Armenia refused to be the first state to recognize the "Nagorno-Karabakh Republic" as an independent state, declaring that such an act would appear to the world as an encroachment upon the territorial integrity of Azerbaijan.[60] This policy had one apparent objective, an understanding of which is crucial.

The Armenian government's stance on the issue of Karabakh independence aimed ostensibly to alter international perceptions of the Armenia-Azerbaijan conflict. By refusing to be the first state to recognize the "Nagorno-Karabakh Republic," Yerevan sought to avoid creating the impression that Armenia had designs on the territory of Azerbaijan, designs that would have made it a direct party to the Karabakh dispute. According to President Ter-Petrosyan, "We want to make every effort to ensure that the problem of Nagorno-Karabakh is not regarded as a conflict between Armenia and Azerbaijan. It is wrong to say that Armenia has territorial claims on Azerbaijan. But if we officially recognize the 'Republic of Nagorno-Karabakh,' we could be accused of interference or even provocation."[61]   By renouncing their claims to the region while refusing to recognize its independence, Armenian officials sought to deny Baku its strongest argument for justifying suppression of Karabakh separatism, that Armenia was trying to annex Azerbaijani land, while at the same time gaining a powerful argument of their own, that Azerbaijan was forcibly denying the right of self-determination to its own constituents.[62]

Yerevan's move allowed the Armenian government to take a number of key policy positions. First, in all but a handful of occasions, Armenia was able to deny that it was involved directly in hostilities with Azerbaijan. Rather, all fighting was attributed to "the self-defense forces of Nagorno-Karabakh, who are ethnically Armenian, and the Azerbaijani army."[63]   Second, Yerevan was able to maintain as a consequence that the Karabakh Armenians should be allowed to represent themselves in any negotiations on the future administrative status of the former NKAO. In the words of President Ter-Petrosyan, "any talks on Nagorno-Karabakh will be doomed if representatives of the legitimate authorities in Nagorno-Karabakh do not take part."[64]

Self-styled NKR leaders followed Yerevan's lead in their portrayal of the conflict as the result of Azerbaijan's forceful denial of the Karabakh Armenians' right of self-determination. Forgoing (at least officially) the possibility of a union with Armenia, the "Nagorno-Karabakh Republic" began to form the trappings of an independent state in 1992; regular elections have been held for the office of president and for the national assembly, and organs of government including ministries of foreign affairs, defense, agriculture, health, and economics have been formed.[65]   Karabakh authorities have also insisted on their participation in peace talks at the same level as delegates from Armenia and Azerbaijan. Yet, no single state has recognized Nagorno-Karabakh's independence.

In addition to formulating an official stance on the question of Nagorno-Karabakh, the Armenian government was forced to come up with a foreign policy strategy to correspond with the realities of the post-Soviet era. Embracing aspects of the Armenian historical experience as well as Transcaucasia's post-Soviet geo-politics, Armenia's foreign relations became an important factor impacting upon the course of the Karabakh conflict.

The smallest of the former Soviet republics, Armenia emerged from the breakup of the USSR nestled between Azerbaijan and Turkey. Although the Armenians' attitudes toward Turkey have been driven for nearly three-quarters of a century by the genocide of 1915–1916 and the nostalgic but unrealistic yearning to recover the lands of historical Armenia in eastern Anatolia, the advent to power of the Armenian National Movement in mid 1990 brought a fundamental change in Armenian policy toward Turkey.[66] Under the leadership of Ter-Petrosyan, who argued that Turkey had been transformed over the past 70 years and no longer posed a threat to the Armenian people, Yerevan set out to pursue improved relations with Ankara.[67]

The path to a rapprochement with Turkey has not been an easy one for Armenia. The nationalist Dashnak Party has been a vehement opponent of closer ties with Turkey, arguing that Ankara must first issue a formal apology for the genocide.[68] Moreover, the deep psychological wounds of the Armenians' abuse at the hands of the Turks have created a general apprehension toward Turkish intentions, and Ankara's support for Azerbaijan in the Karabakh conflict has added to these fears.[69] Indeed, the Nagorno-Karabakh dispute has been the dominant factor working against the improvement of ties between Armenia and Turkey.

As the leadership of independent Armenia sought to better its relations with Turkey, Yerevan also set out to bolster ties with its other large neighbor, Iran. From the viewpoint of Armenian authorities, Iran has much to offer the fledgling republic. With Armenia landlocked and under blockade, Iran offers potential trade opportunities and access to much needed energy resources.[70] Moreover, Tehran shares Armenia's opposition to the expansion of Turkish influence in the FSU, and close ties with the Islamic Republic have been viewed as a potential means through which to offset a Turkish-Azerbaijani axis.[71] However, while geopolitical necessity has driven Yerevan to pursue strengthened relations with Tehran, the course of the Karabakh conflict has made Armenia's task a difficult one.

Although isolated geographically from Russia, relations with Moscow have been the centerpiece of Armenia's foreign policy since independence. Despite sometimes strained ties with the Russian people under both the czars and the Communists, Armenia has regarded post-Soviet Russia as a fellow Christian state with the ability—via its status as a great power—to protect the Armenian people from the potentially hostile designs of its neighbors. The warm relations with Moscow cultivated by Yerevan have played a significant role in the course of Armenian-Azerbaijani hostilities since 1992.

In the aftermath of the Soviet Union's dissolution, Armenian and Azerbaijani perspectives on the Nagorno-Karabakh dispute held a number of similarities as well as a number of differences. The primary divergence between the positions of both sides existed in each republic's portrayal of the Karabakh conflict. Whereas Armenia depicted the dispute as a struggle for self-determination by the majority Armenian population of Nagorno-Karabakh, Azerbaijan portrayed the clash as an undeclared inter-republican war provoked by Armenia with the intent of dismembering the country. However, in emotional and nationalistic terms, both sides viewed the Karabakh issue with similarly uncompromising tenacity:

Each viewed Karabakh as an historically vital piece of territory that must be liberated at all costs. The stage was therefore set for a bloody war and a terrible human tragedy.

NOTES

1. Stephen J. Blank, "Turkey's Strategic Engagement in the Former USSR and U.S. Interests," in Stephen J. Blank, Stephen C. Pelletiere, and William T. Johnsen, eds., *Turkey's Strategic Position at the Crossroads of World Affairs* (Carlisle Barracks, PA: Strategic Studies Institute, 3 December 1993): 55.

2. Graham E. Fuller, "Turkey's New Eastern Orientation," in Graham E. Fuller and Ian O. Lesser, eds., *Turkey's New Geopolitics: From the Balkans to Western China* (Boulder: Westview Press, 1993): 67, 84.

3. Andrew Apostolou, "New Players in an Old Game," *The Middle East*, no. 213 (July 1992): 5.

4. While it was feared among Turkish officials that the relevance of the NATO alliance itself would decline with the end of the Cold War, Ankara's primary concern was that Turkey's importance within the alliance would deteriorate. At the heart of this anxiety was the belief that, with the revolutionary changes in East-West relations and the decline of a Soviet threat to Western Europe, the *raison d'être* of Turkey's membership in NATO was dissipating largely. After all, Turkey's role in NATO had long been seen in terms of its contribution to the deterrence of a Soviet attack on Western Europe. With that threat largely gone, many Turkish officials feared that their country would be seen increasingly with less importance to NATO. Michael P. Croissant, "Turkey and NATO After the Cold War," *Strategic Review* 23, no. 4 (Fall 1995): 67.

5. Shireen T. Hunter, *The Transcaucasus in Transition: Nation-Building and Conflict* (Washington, DC: Center for Strategic and International Studies, 1994): 162.

6. Bulent Aras, "The Importance of Turkey to Relations Between Europe and the Turkic Republics of the Former Soviet Union," *UCLA Journal of International Law and Foreign Affairs* 2, no. 1 (Spring–Summer 1997): 111.

7. Colin Barraclough, "Asian Republics a Turkish Delight," *Insight on the News* 8, no. 47 (23 November 1993): 15.

8. Gareth M. Winrow, "Turkey's Role in Asian Pipeline Politics," *Jane's Intelligence Review* 9, no. 2, (February 1997).

9. Kenneth Mackenzie, "Azerbaijan and the Neighbors," *World Today* 48, no. 1 (January 1992): 2; and Philip Robins, "Between Sentiment and Self-Interest: Turkey's Policy Toward Azerbaijan and the Central Asian States," *Middle East Journal* 47, no. 4 (Autumn 1993): 597.

10. Turkey shares a nine kilometer border with Nakhichevan, an autonomous republic of Azerbaijan separated from it physically by Armenia. Central Intelligence Agency, *The World Factbook: 1993–1994* (New York: Brassey's, 1993): 24.

11. Hunter, *The Transcaucasus in Transition*, p. 165.

12. Unnamed Turkish "government official" quoted in *Milliyet*, 14 November 1991, in Foreign Broadcast Information Service—Western Europe (hereafter FBIS-WEU), #91–224 (20 November 1991): 60.

13. Duygu Bozoglu Sezer, "Turkey's Grand Strategy Facing a Dilemma," *International Spectator* 27, no. 1 (January–March 1992): 26.

14. *Milliyet*, 26 November 1991, in FBIS-WEU, #91–231 (2 December 1991): 39.

15. Peter Feuilherade, "Searching for Economic Synergy," *The Middle East*, no. 209 (March 1992): 33.

16. Theodore Karasik, *Azerbaijan, Central Asia, and Future Persian Gulf Security* (Santa Monica: RAND Corporation, 1992): 46.

17. Bulent Aras, "Iran'in Orta Asya ve Kafkasya ile Iliskileri," *Avrasya Dosyasi* 3, no. 3 (Fall 1996): 169.

18. Robert O. Freedman, "Russia and Iran: A Tactical Alliance," *SAIS Review* 17, no. 2 (1997): 108.

19. *Salam*, 15 February 1992, in Foreign Broadcast Information Service—Near East and South Asia (hereafter FBIS-NES), #92–043 (4 March 1992): 39.

20. Shahram Chubin, "The Geopolitics of the Southern Republics of the CIS," *Iranian Journal of International Affairs* 4, no. 2 (Summer 1992): 317.

21. One Iranian commentary pointed out the virtues of an axis with Yerevan in noting that "regardless of its cultural activities, one major geopolitical object exists between Turkey and the six Muslim republics—Armenia. An age old hostility exists between the Turks and Armenians because of the massacre of Armenians in 1915 by the Turks. Thus it is very unlikely at least in the near future that the Republic of Armenia will allow the Turks to have land access to Azerbaijan and consequently other Central Asian states. In comparison to Ankara, Tehran's position is better." *Kayhan International*, 22 April 1992, in FBIS-NES, #92–103 (28 May 1992): 50.

22. R. K. Ramazani, "Iran's Foreign Policy: Both North and South," *Middle East Journal* 46, no. 3 (Summer 1992): 405; and Shireen T. Hunter, "The Emergence of Soviet Muslims: Impact on the Middle East," *Middle East Insight* 8, no. 5 (May–June 1992): 36.

23. Hunter, *The Transcaucasus in Transition*, p. 15.

24. Richard W. Cottam, *Nationalism in Iran* (Pittsburgh: University of Pittsburg Press, 1964): 131.

25. Iran would also be averse to a unity scheme joining the "two Azerbaijans" within the Iranian state. The addition of Azerbaijan's 7.5 million population to the 15 million of Iranian Azerbaijan would upset sharply the demographic balance in Iran, "making the Azeri Turks the dominant political and economic force within the Iranian state." Graham E. Fuller, *The "Center of the Universe": The Geopolitics of Iran* (Boulder: Westview Press, 1991): 174.

26. *Tehran Times*, 30 December 1991, in FBIS-NES, #92–005 (8 January 1992): 56.

27. Jeff Checkel, "Russian Foreign Policy: Back to the Future?" *Radio Free Europe/ Radio Liberty* (hereafter RFE/RL) *Research Report* 1, no. 41 (16 October 1992): 18–19; and Milton Kovner, "Russia in Search of a Foreign Policy," *Comparative Strategy* 12, no. 3 (July–September 1993): 308–309.

28. Vera Tolz, "The Burden of the Imperial Legacy," *RFE/RL Research Report* 2, no. 20 (14 May 1993): 45.

29. Mohiaddin Mesbahi, "Russian Foreign Policy and Security in Central Asia and the Caucasus," *Central Asian Survey* 12, no. 2 (1993): 181, 185.

30. John Lough, "The Place of the 'Near Abroad' in Russian Foreign Policy," *RFE/RL Research Report* 2, no. 11 (12 March 1993): 27.

31. Yeltsin attacked Kozyrev in a speech in October 1992 in which, according to *ITAR-TASS*, he "expressed his dissatisfaction with Russia's frequently spineless conduct on the international arena, her defensive tactics, and her imitation of others." Quoted in William C. Bodie, "Anarchy and Cold War in Moscow's 'Near Abroad,'" *Strategic Review* 21, no. 1 (Winter 1993): 48.

32. Quoted in Alvin Z. Rubinstein, "The Geopolitical Pull on Russia," *Orbis* 38, no. 4 (Fall 1994): 575.

33. "Basic Provisions of the Military Doctrine of the Russian Federation," *Jane's Intelligence Review* Special Report, 6, no. 1 (January 1994): 7.

34. Quoted by Sergey Rogov, Deputy Director of the USA and Canada Institute, in *Ssha: Ekonomika, Politika, Ideologiya*, No. 4, April 1994, in Joint Publications Research Service—Military Affairs, #94–033 (17 August 1994): 58.

35. Mary C. FitzGerald, "The Russian Military's Strategy For 'Sixth Generation' Warfare," *Orbis* 38, no. 3 (Summer 1994): 475.

36. Suzanne Crow, "Why Has Russian Foreign Policy Changed?" *RFE/RL Research Report* 3, no. 18 (6 May 1994): 3–5.

37. Suzanne Crow, "Russia Asserts Its Strategic Agenda," *RFE/RL Research Report* 2, no. 50 (17 December 1993): 1–2, 6–7.

38. Hunter, *The Transcaucasus in Transition*, p. 19.

39. Marie Bennigsen Broxup, "Russia and the North Caucasus," in Marie Bennigsen Broxup, ed., *The North Caucasus Barrier: The Russian Advance Towards the Muslim World* (New York: St. Martin's Press, 1992): 11.

40. Daniel Sneider, "Russia and the Caucasus: Empire in Transition," *Christian Science Monitor* (13 December 1993): 11.

41. Ann Sheehy, "Russia's Republics: A Threat to Its Territorial Integrity?" *RFE/RL Research Report* 2, no. 20 (14 May 1993): 37.

42. Uwe Halbach and Heinrich Tiller, "Russia and Its Southern Flank," *Aussenpolitik* 45, no. 2 (1994): 158.

43. Catherine Dale, "Turmoil in Abkhazia: Russian Responses," *RFE/RL Research Report* 2, no. 34 (27 August 1993): 49.

44. Shirin Akiner, "Melting Pot, Salad Bowl—Cauldron? Manipulation and Mobilization of Ethnic and Religious Identities in Central Asia," *Ethnic and Racial Studies* 20, no. 2 (April 1997): 390–391.

45. See, for example, Igor Lipovsky, "The Awakening of Central Asian Islam," *Middle Eastern Studies* 32, no. 3 (July 1996): 1–21.

46. Crow, "Russia Asserts its Strategic Agenda," p. 2.

47. Hunter, *The Transcaucasus in Transition*, p. 155.

48. According to figures of the Central Intelligence Agency, Armenia's population breaks down as follows: 93.3% Armenian, 1.5% Russian, 1.7% Kurd, 3.5% other. Central Intelligence Agency, *The World Factbook*, p. 17.

49. Elizabeth Fuller, "Caucasus: The Lezgin Campaign of Autonomy," *RFE/RL Research Report* 1, no. 41 (16 October 1992): 30.

50. Elizabeth Fuller, "Azerbaijan Rediscovers Its 'Vanished' Minorities," *Report on the USSR* 2, no. 52 (28 December 1990): 20.

51. Hunter, *The Transcaucasus in Transition*, p. 64.

52. Elizabeth Fuller, "Azerbaijan Rediscovers Its 'Vanished' Minorities," p. 20.

53. Elizabeth Fuller, "Caucasus," p. 30.

54. Elizabeth Fuller, "Kurdish Demands for Autonomy Complicate Karabakh Equation," *RFE/RL Research Report* 1, no. 23 (5 June 1992): 12.

55. Besik Urigashvili, "The Transcaucasus: Blood Ties," *Bulletin of the Atomic Scientists* 50, no. 1 (January–February 1994): 19.

56. Paul B. Henze, *The Transcaucasus in Transition* (Santa Monica: RAND Corporation, 1991): 16.

57. Hunter, *The Transcaucasus in Transition*, p. 64.

58. Quoted in Philip Marsden, "Winning a War on a Wing and a Prayer," *New Statesman Society* 6, no. 282 (10 December 1993): 23.

59. Because the Azeri inhabitants of the NKAO boycotted the referendum, the vote was not entirely reflective of the whole Karabakh population. *Interfax*, 19 January 1992, in FBIS-SOV, #92–013 (21 January 1992): 90–91.

60. *ITAR-TASS World Service*, 30 June 1992, in FBIS-SOV, #92–126 (30 June 1992): 52.

61. Quoted by *Le Figaro*, 25 February 1992, in FBIS-SOV, #92–039 (27 February 1992): 74.

62. In the words of Armenian Foreign Minister Raffi Hovannisian, "This is not a territorial issue, and Armenia does not have any territorial claims." Instead, "the problem of Nagorno-Karabakh is one of human rights and the right of citizens to self-determination." Quoted by *TASS International Service*, 30 January 1992, in FBIS-SOV, #92–022 (3 February 1992): 72.

63. Alexander Arzoumanian, "Armenia Has No Forces in Azerbaijan," *New York Times* (24 April 1993): 22.

64. Quoted by *Teleradiokompaniya Ostankino Television First Program Network*, 9 May 1992, in FBIS-SOV, #92–091 (11 May 1992): 70.

65. Rouben P. Adalian, ed., *Armenia and Karabagh Factbook* (Washington, DC: Armenian Assembly of America, 1996): 109.

66. Elizabeth Fuller, "The Armenian-Turkish Rapprochement," *Soviet Analyst*, no. 10 (15 May 1991): 4.

67. Hunter, *The Transcaucasus in Transition*, p. 30.

68. Ibid., pp. 32–33.

69. Elizabeth Fuller, "The Thorny Path to an Armenian-Turkish Rapprochement," *RFE/RL Research Report* 2, no. 12 (19 March 1993): 47.

70. "Armenia and Iran Walking the Tightrope," *Armenian International Magazine*, no. 5 (May 1994): 46; and Felix Corley, "Armenia and Iran: Balancing Act," *Middle East International* (28 August 1993): 15.

71. James M. Dorsey, "The Growing Entente Between Armenia and Iran," *Middle East International* (4 December 1992): 18.

4

The Armenia-Azerbaijan Conflict, 1992–1994

War is on in Karabakh. Previously a local conflict, it is escalating into a full-fledged war.

—Azerbaijani President Ayaz Mutalibov,
January 1992

The conflict between Armenia and Azerbaijan entered a new, more deadly phase with the breakup of the Soviet Union. Gone with the demise of Soviet rule was any restraining effect that Moscow may have had on the escalating violence between the two republics, and Armenia and Azerbaijan began their newfound independence in a *de facto* state of war with one another, much as they had in 1918. With substantial stocks of modern former Soviet weaponry in hand, the Armenians and Azerbaijanis set out to resolve the Nagorno-Karabakh question by force of arms. Meanwhile, Turkey, Russia, and Iran watched matters in the Transcaucasus closely, seeing prospective opportunities as well as potential dangers in the course of events.

THE MILITARY AND POLITICAL DEVELOPMENTS OF 1992

Armenian Victory in Nagorno-Karabakh, January–May 1992

The opening months of 1992 were marked by the explosion of full-scale war in and around Nagorno-Karabakh between forces of the fledgling Azerbaijani national army and locally raised units of the so-called Karabakh army, both of whom had acquired substantial amounts of weaponry from withdrawing Soviet Interior Ministry troops and from Soviet military facilities. While Baku had begun mobilizing for war in December 1991, the ostensible catalyst for an early 1992 Azerbaijani offensive was the 18 January proclamation of an independent

"Nagorno-Karabakh Republic" (NKR) by the Supreme Soviet of the former NKAO.

In response to the declaration of independence by Nagorno-Karabakh, the Azerbaijanis launched a major military operation against Stepanakert from the nearby town of Agdam on 31 January. Intended apparently to drive Armenian forces out of the area,[1] the offensive included several thousand Azerbaijani soldiers backed by armored vehicles and rocket and artillery fire.[2] However, in what emerged as a pattern common to most of Baku's military operations over the next two years, Azerbaijani forces carried out their attacks in a haphazard and uncoordinated way and were beaten back in rapid fashion by Stepanakert's Armenian defenders.[3] Thereafter, Azerbaijani troops resorted to seemingly indiscriminate rocket and artillery attacks on the Karabakh capital and nearby villages from nearby heights in an attempt to break the will of the Armenian populace.[4] Such attacks, however, failed to achieve their goal, and Armenian efforts to silence the sources of Azerbaijani fire became a major factor in the escalation of hostilities through early 1992.

Following the collapse of the large-scale Azerbaijani ground assault against Stepanakert by the first week of February, ethnic Armenian forces went on the offensive in areas to the north and southwest of the Karabakh capital. With the stated objective of "suppress[ing] Azeri fire emplacements,"[5] Armenian forces took the village of Malybeyli on 11 February and began a major assault towards Khojaly, a town with both strategic and symbolic value several kilometers north of Stepanakert.

After several days of fierce fighting, which was accompanied according to some reports by the slaying of up to 1,000 Azebaijani civilians,[6] ethnic Armenian forces took Khojaly on 25 February. The town's seizure not only silenced the nearly unending missile and artillery barrages against Stepanakert that had been originating from there since January, but it also brought into Armenian control the only airstrip in Nagorno-Karabakh suited for use by large fixed-wing aircraft, thus making possible an air bridge between Armenia and Karabakh.[7]

For the Azerbaijanis, who once again showed great ineptitude on the battlefield, the fall of Khojaly was a tremendous psychological and military defeat. As the second largest Azeri-inhabited enclave remaining in Nagorno-Karabakh prior to its capture, Khojaly was of major symbolic and strategic significance to Azerbaijan in its quest to retain control over the territory of the former NKAO. Its loss, combined with the allegations of massacre by Armenian forces, spawned a period of political upheaval in Baku.

The fall of Khojaly proved to be the last straw for the regime of President Ayaz Mutalibov. With popular anger building over the government's failure to bring the situation in Nagorno-Karabakh under control and protect the region's remaining Azeri population, more than 80,000 angry demonstrators calling for Mutalibov's resignation gathered outside the parliament building, and police refused to obey orders to disperse the crowd.[8] Mutalibov agreed to step down on 5 March, and parliament speaker Yaqub Mamedov was made acting president until elections could be held on 7 June.[9] Although Mutalibov's ouster was enough to placate the populace, the political upheaval in Baku set the stage both for a power struggle within Azerbaijan and a renewed Armenian offensive in Nagorno-Karabakh. Before such events could be realized fully, however, Iran entered the arena as a mediator of the Armenia-Azerbaijan conflict.

Viewed by both sides as an honest broker on the Karabakh question,[10] Iran began its mediation efforts in early February 1992 at the behest of the Armenian and Azerbaijani foreign ministers. From the Iranian perspective, the possibility of becoming the chief peacemaker in the Armenia-Azerbaijan conflict was a golden opportunity to gain influence in the region at the expense of Turkey.[11]

Tehran was awakened immediately to the difficulties of brokering even a temporary break in the hostilities between Armenian and Azerbaijani forces when two Iranian-mediated cease-fires were ignored on the battlefield.[12] Despite its early failures, an Iranian diplomatic offensive prompted a tripartite meeting among representatives of the Baku and Yerevan governments and the Iranian Foreign Ministry in Tehran from 14 to 16 March. The result was an agreement in principle on a draft plan for resolution of the Nagorno-Karabakh dispute.[13]

Although a cease-fire was observed generally by the warring sides for more than a week,[14] Azerbaijani units resumed their relentless shelling of Stepanakert on 29 March, and Karabakh Armenian fighters were again forced to take action against the sources of the attacks.[15] As conditions in Stepanakert became desperate with the mounting death toll and dwindling supplies of fuel and electricity,[16] Karabakh Armenian military leaders elected to take decisive action to suppress Azerbaijani rocket and artillery positions surrounding the city on 8 May 1992. The focus of Armenian operations was the city of Shusha, the last remaining Azeri stronghold in Nagorno-Karabakh and the staging point for Azerbaijani military operations against Stepanakert.[17] After two days of fierce fighting, local Armenian units took the city, forcing their opponents to flee in disarray toward the town of Lachin.[18]

The fall of Shusha—which coincided with another failed Iranian mediation effort—[19] was a major blow to Azerbaijan in both psychological and strategic terms. Not only was the city one of the historic centers of Azeri culture and nationalism in Nagorno-Karabakh, but it was also the last remaining Azeri-inhabited area in the region. As had been the case following the loss of Khojaly, Shusha's downfall to Armenian forces sparked political upheaval in Azerbaijan. In the space of 24 hours from 14 to 15 May, the government changed hands twice,[20] and the Karabakh Armenians took advantage of the disarray in Baku to press further gains on the battlefield.

In the midst of the political fracas in Azerbaijan, local Armenian forces launched an assault on Lachin, a town situated strategically at the narrowest strip of Azerbaijani land separating Nagorno-Karabakh from Armenia. Azerbaijani forces had concentrated in Lachin since the fall of Shusha out of realization that the town's capture by the Armenians would allow the formation of a vital land link between the Armenia and Karabakh.[21] Nonetheless, the army again proved unable to stand up to the better motivated Armenian fighters, and Lachin fell on 18 May.[22]

The fall of Lachin altered the course of the Armenia-Azerbaijan conflict. Not only did the town's capture consolidate the ouster of Azerbaijani forces from Nagorno-Karabakh that had begun at Khojaly, but it also allowed the creation of the so-called Lachin corridor—a physical link between the Republic of Armenia and Nagorno-Karabakh. The corridor *de facto* ended the isolation of Karabakh from Armenia that had been imposed by Stalin in 1923, but it necessitated the occupation of Azerbaijani land outside of Nagorno-Karabakh by Armenian forces. Over time, the status of Lachin would become a central issue in efforts to achieve a political settlement to the Armenia-Azerbaijan conflict.

With the fall of Lachin in May 1992, the first phase of the newly escalated war in the Transcaucasus came to a close with an Armenian military victory in Nagorno-Karabakh. The Azerbaijani army had been routed wherever it had come into contact with Karabakh Armenian forces, and political instability in Baku had encouraged further Armenian advances. By the end of May, nearly all of Nagorno-Karabakh was in the firm control of Armenian fighters, and the prospects for a comeback by Azerbaijan seemed bleak.

While the string of Armenian military victories in Nagorno-Karabakh, the political unrest in Azerbaijan, and the failed Iranian mediation efforts were the distinguishing events of the first phase of the Karabakh war, other aspects of early 1992 are also worthy of note. First was the glaring absence of Russia as an active player in the Transcaucasus. Following the collapse of joint Russian-Kazakstani efforts to achieve a peaceful resolution of the Nagorno-Karabakh dispute in late 1991, Russia withdrew from its active peacemaking role in the Transcaucasus. Aside from a fleeting and unsuccessful attempt to achieve a cease-fire in the combat zone in late February,[23] Moscow's position on the Armenia-Azerbaijan conflict in early 1992 was characterized more by inaction than action. One critic of the Russian government wrote that such behavior had made Moscow "an outside observer of what is happening in the Transcaucasus."[24]

Although Russia's political inactivity vis-à-vis the Armenia-Azerbaijan conflict was clear in the opening months of 1992, less clear was the role of Russian military forces in the Transcaucasus. As Azerbaijani defeats piled up in February and March, Azerbaijan began to accuse locally based Russian troops of involvement in the fighting on the side of Armenia. While denying Baku's accusations of participation by Russia's 366th Motorized Rifle Regiment in the alleged massacre at Khojaly,[25] Moscow acknowledged the possibility that some Russian soldiers could have been fighting on one side or the other as volunteers or mercenaries.[26] Despite the 366th Regiment's withdrawal from Nagorno-Karabakh in late February and early March,[27] claims of Russian involvement in the fighting continued to surface over the next two years.

Early 1992 also saw the onset of a heated internal debate in Ankara on the question of Turkish policy toward the Armenia-Azerbaijan conflict. Fearing that heightened Turkish support for Azerbaijan would not only increase the risk of creating the perception of a newly aggressive pan-Turkic policy in Ankara but also run the danger of estranging Turkey from its North Atlantic Treaty Organization (NATO) allies,[28] Prime Minister Suleyman Demirel pursued a cautious policy aimed primarily at finding a peaceful solution to the dispute while "prevent[ing] the clashes from spreading further and involving the entire region."[29] However, because such a policy necessitated a somewhat even-handed approach to the problem, Demirel left himself open to substantial criticism at home for not taking a hard enough stand vis-à-vis the Armenians' actions in Azerbaijan.

Detractors of Demirel's policies toward the Armenia-Azerbaijan conflict argued that Ankara was remaining shamefully passive in the face of large-scale violence against the Turks' "cousins" in Azerbaijan.[30] These critics feared that Turkey's failure to support Azerbaijan unambiguously would undermine the confidence of the Muslim states of the FSU in the Turkish "model," possibly leaving the door open to the growth of Iranian influence.[31] Another—perhaps exaggerated—argument charged that Turkish acquiescence in Armenian acts in the Transcaucasus encouraged the renewal of Armenian irredentist claims on eastern Turkey.[32]

The domestic political debate in Turkey on the question of the Armenia-Azerbaijan conflict was brought to a head in May 1992, when Armenian forces attacked Nakhichevan, the autonomous republic of Azerbaijan separated from it physically by Armenia. While the Turks were dismayed with the outbreak of violence, the assault on Nakhichevan was cause for concern primarily because the enclave represents the only portion of a Muslim state of the FSU with which Turkey is geographically contiguous.[33] Fearing the loss of its physical link with Azerbaijan by an Armenian military victory in Nakhichevan, Turkey was faced with a serious dilemma.

In the face of a deteriorating situation in Nakhichevan and amid growing pleas for humanitarian and military-technical assistance from the enclave's leadership,[34] the Turkish government faced a political crisis in the third week of May. With all of the major opposition parties and President Turgut Ozal himself calling for action, Prime Minister Demirel was forced to take a tougher stand vis-à-vis Armenia. On 18 May Demirel pledged unspecified aid to Nakhichevan,[35] and the Turkish Foreign Ministry issued a statement warning Armenia that "*faits accomplis* created through the use of force cannot be accepted."[36] Although there was little indication that Turkey was preparing for military intervention in Nakhichevan,[37] Turkish sabre-rattling prompted a provocative response from Russia.

In a clear reference to Turkey, Marshal Shaposhnikov of the CIS Joint Armed Forces warned on 20 May that "third party intervention in the dispute [between Armenia and Azerbaijan] could trigger a Third World War."[38] The presumable basis for the comment was the Treaty on Collective Security concluded in Tashkent on 15 May among Russia, Armenia, and four of the former Soviet Central

Asian republics. According to Article Four of the treaty:

If one of the participating states is subjected to aggression by any state or group of states, this will be perceived as aggression against all participating states to this treaty.

In the event of an act of aggression being committed against any of the participating states, all the other participating states will give it the necessary assistance, including military assistance, and will also give support with the means at their disposal by way of exercising the right to collective defense in accordance with Article 51 of the UN Charter.[39]

As a consequence of the above provisions, a Turkish attack on Armenia would have been treated as an attack on Russia,[40] and since Turkey is bound to the United States and Western Europe by similar terms under the North Atlantic Treaty,[41] the stage would have been set theoretically for a conflict between NATO and Russia.

Although the situation in Nakhichevan calmed down substantially after the Turkish government's warning to Armenia, the unease shown by Moscow and Ankara during the crisis was demonstrative of each side's perception of the new geopolitics of the Transcaucasus. In the eyes of the Turks, the Armenian action against Nakhichevan was not just an attack on ethnic kinsmen in Azerbaijan, but it was also a challenge to Turkey's ability to project influence in the Muslim states of the FSU. For the Russians, the situation held out the possibility of inter-vention in the Transcaucasus by a third party, which entailed the inherent risk not only of a wider regional war but also of the loss of Moscow's own future ability to hold sway in a region of major geostrategic importance to Russia. When Iran's efforts to build its prestige as the primary peacemaker between Armenia and Azerbaijan in early 1992 are considered in tandem with the actions of Russia and Turkey, it is clear that the first phase of the newly intensified conflict in the Transcaucasus saw the reawakening of old geopolitical rivalries buried by de-cades of Soviet rule. In the subsequent stages of the war, the three major external powers continued to view regional events as potential sources of opportunity as well as risk.

Shifting Fortunes, June–December 1992

Following the rout of the Azerbaijani army by Karabakh Armenian forces and corresponding political upheaval in Baku during the first half of 1992, it seemed that Azerbaijan had lost the armed struggle for Nagorno-Karabakh. However, new circumstances arose in June that caused the military situation to shift back in Azerbaijan's favor, albeit temporarily. Additionally, the latter part of 1992 also witnessed the commencement of an active mediatory role in the Transcaucasus both by Russia and by the Conference on Security and Cooperation in Europe (CSCE).

The first event that had a major impact on the situation in the Transcaucasus was the election of Abulfaz Elchibey as president of Azerbaijan on 7 June.[42] An ardent nationalist and head of the Azerbaijani Popular Front (APF), Elchibey set out immediately to reverse many of the policies of the Mutalibov regime. First and most notably, the new head of state launched a major reorientation in the republic's foreign policy direction. Starting with the removal from consideration of the agreement affirming Azerbaijan's membership in the Commonwealth of Independent States (CIS), which had been signed by Mutalibov but never ratified by the Azerbaijani parliament, Elchibey sought to steer the republic's external alignment away from Russia and the CIS.[43]

Eschewing Mutalibov's policy of cultivating close ties with the former center in Moscow, Elchibey strove to make Turkey the primary focus of Azerbaijani foreign relations. There were a handful of reasons for this shift. First, the APF and Elchibey in particular held ardently pro-Turkish and, in some respects, pan-Turkic views, believing that the Azerbaijanis' ethno-linguistic heritage made Turkey a natural choice as Baku's main external partner. Second, Turkey represented the model of a secular, democratic, market-oriented state to which Azerbaijan could aspire. Finally, Turkey—through its ties to NATO and the West—offered Azerbaijan a potential means through which to offset what was viewed as biased Russian support for Armenia in the Karabakh struggle.[44]

The new APF-led government's foreign policy was also colored by an anti-Iranian bias. Driven by the long-term nationalist goal of achieving the union of "Northern" and "Southern" Azerbaijan, Elchibey called upon the Azeris of north-western Iran to break away from the Islamic Republic and join their brethren to the north in the formation of a "Greater" Azerbaijan.[45] Because such a move represented a clear challenge to the territorial integrity of Iran, relations between Baku and Tehran cooled substantially under the Elchibey regime.

While implementing its new foreign policy, the Elchibey government also set out to regain the initiative in the conflict zone. An ardent proponent of military action to liberate the "Turkic homeland" of Karabakh,[46] Elchibey gave priority to increasing the effectiveness of the fledgling national army that had been brutalized by the Armenians over the previous months. Emergency measures were enacted immediately to begin the process, including a decree requiring the disbandment and disarmament of all informal military formations in Azerbaijan, whose often independent and uncoordinated operations in Nagorno-Karabakh had resulted in much of the gains by ethnic Armenian forces.[47] Elchibey's reform efforts were undertaken in tandem with the launching of a large-scale Azerbaijani offensive in Nagorno-Karabakh on 12 June, scarcely five days after his election.

The assault, involving some 100 tanks and armored personnel carriers backed by artillery and close air support, was directed at the Mardakert and Askeran districts in northern and central Nagorno-Karabakh, respectively.[48] Initial operations appeared to be aimed at cleaving the region in two,[49] and Azerbaijani units made significant headway toward such a goal during the opening days of the offensive. Taken by surprise by the tenacity of the attack, Karabakh Armenian troops were forced to abandon several of the villages they had gained in earlier fighting.[50]

Although Azerbaijan opened a front in southern Nagorno-Karabakh on 28 June 1992 with limited success,[51] the greatest gains came in the north. A large-scale assault by some 10,000 soldiers and 100 armored vehicles against the town of Mardakert succeeded in expelling Karabakh units and Armenian civilians from the area on 5–6 July.[52] The fall of Mardakert and surrounding towns left virtually all of northern Nagorno-Karabakh in Azerbaijani hands for the first time since the beginning of the year,[53] thus signaling a shift in the fortunes of war in favor of Azerbaijan.

In light of the disastrous performance of Azerbaijani forces between January and May 1992, the sudden turn-around in the military situation in the region following Elchibey's election raises important questions. Without detracting from the efforts of the Elchibey regime to increase the effectiveness of the Azerbaijani army, it is highly unlikely that the President's reforms could have been a prominent factor responsible for the sudden success of Azerbaijani forces during the offensive that began a mere five days after the elections that brought him to power. What is both more likely and sustainable by evidence is that Azerbaijan received the tacit support of Russia in its June offensive.

Prior to mid 1992, whatever combat equipment possessed by Armenia and Azerbaijan had been acquired either from raids on ex-Soviet military facilities or through the shady activities of former Soviet personnel.[54] While accurate figures for the relative numbers of assorted weaponry in the possession of the warring parties during the first half of 1992 are unavailable, by all accounts the Karabakh Armenians held superiority over the Azerbaijanis as indicated by their string of victories through late May.

However, under the pretext of implementing a follow-on agreement to the 1990 Conventional Forces in Europe (CFE) Treaty, which accorded 220 tanks, 220 combat vehicles, 285 artillery pieces, 100 combat aircraft, and 50 attack helicopters each to Armenia and Azerbaijan,[55] Moscow handed over unilaterally a large cache of weapons to Baku in the days leading up to the June offensive. According to several news agencies citing Armenian Defense Ministry officials, the transfer included some one hundred tanks, two hundred armored personnel carriers, and several dozen attack aircraft.[56] Although these figures were not confirmed by Azerbaijan, an official reply to the charges—corroborated later by Russia—[57] acknowledged that an equipment transfer had indeed taken place under the terms of the 15 May Tashkent agreement apportioning conventional forces among the former Soviet republics.[58] Importantly, this transfer was not followed immediately by a similar distribution of weaponry to Armenia;[59] thus, Azerbaijan was empowered with a temporary superiority in armaments that was put to effective use in the June offensive.

In mid September 1992, Azerbaijani troops pressed their continued advantage to strike at the strategic Lachin corridor linking Armenia and the former NKAO. The capture of commanding heights in the Lachin and Shusha districts on 18–19

September gave Azerbaijani forces the ability to interdict traffic through the corridor with artillery.[60] With their lifeline to Armenia in grave danger, Karabakh forces launched a counter-offensive aimed at retaking the heights around Lachin. After intense fighting from 7 to 11 October, the Armenians succeeded in pushing their opponents off the heights and retaking nearby villages.[61] While the immediate danger to the Lachin corridor was relieved by the operation, the region continued to come under periodic Azerbaijani military pressure over the next several months.

Although the second half of 1992 witnessed a significant upsurge in fighting in the Transcaucasus, it also saw the commencement of often overlapping mediation efforts by two international actors, Russia and the Conference on Security and Cooperation in Europe (CSCE). With Iranian engagement in the peace process brought to an end by Tehran following the fall of Shusha, Moscow and the CSCE stepped in to try to find a settlement to the Nagorno-Karabakh dispute.

The Conference on Security and Cooperation in Europe was formed in 1973 to promote dialogue between East and West on the issues of military security, economics, and human rights. With the breakup of the USSR and the subsequent ascension of the former Soviet republics as members, the CSCE took on a role not intended for it originally: Conflict prevention and resolution. In this new role the conference continued to be guided by its founding principles as spelled out in the 1975 Helsinki Final Act: The inviolability of international borders, the right to self-determination, and universal respect for human rights.[62] (See Appendix D.)

The CSCE convened multilateral talks in June 1992 for the purpose of preparing for a formal peace conference to be held in Minsk on the Nagorno-Karabakh question. At preliminary discussions in Rome, which were attended by delegates of a core group of CSCE member states that came to be known as the Minsk Group—Russia, Sweden, Turkey, Italy, Germany, France, Czechoslovakia, Belarus, and the United States—Armenian and Azerbaijani delegates were pressed to hammer out negotiating positions acceptable at a minimum to each other.[63] However, talks broke down almost immediately over two main stumbling blocks.

In keeping with its policy that Armenia is not a party to the Karabakh dispute, Yerevan insisted that the Karabakh Armenians be recognized as a separate negotiating entity at the Minsk conference.[64] Azerbaijani officials rejected this position out of hand, claiming that any such recognition would strike a blow at the republic's sovereignty. Instead, according to Baku, Armenia and Azerbaijan should have been acknowledged as the sole parties to the conflict, with Armenian and Azeri officials representing both communities of Nagorno-Karabakh within Azerbaijan's delegation.[65]

The second major obstacle to progress in establishing a framework for talks was the timetable for discussions of the final status of Nagorno-Karabakh. According to Armenia's position, the future legal status of Karabakh should have been discussed only after the achievement of a permanent cessation of hostilities and the deployment of international peacekeeping forces to the conflict zone. In the eyes of Baku, however, the dispatch of peacekeepers to Nagorno-Karabakh would have diminished Azerbaijani sovereignty over the region, thereby biasing talks on the region's final disposition. Thus, Azerbaijani delegates to the CSCE discussions argued that the status of Nagorno-Karabakh must be defined as a prerequisite to formal peace talks in Minsk.[66]

The seemingly irreconcilable positions of the Armenian and Azerbaijani contingents led to an almost immediate breakdown in the CSCE-sponsored talks in Rome. With common ground present on little more than the need to see a prompt end to the fighting, the parties withdrew from the discussions on 21 June as each side accused the other of having created the impasse.[67] Over the course of the next several months, repeated efforts by the CSCE to convene a Minsk peace conference were struck dead by the Armenians' and Azerbaijanis' unwillingness to alter their respective pre-conditions for further negotiations.

With the CSCE mediation effort a virtual non-starter from the outset, Russia stepped in to try its hand at resolving the Armenia-Azerbaijan dispute for the first time since September 1991. However, Moscow elected to limit its goals to the achievement of a cease-fire in the conflict zone while leaving the thorniest issues aside.[68] After a marathon negotiating session carried out in secret with the active participation of Russian Defense Minister Pavel Grachev, the defense chiefs of Armenia and Azerbaijan signed a detailed agreement on 19 September calling for a five-month cease-fire and a phased withdrawal of the warring parties' armed formations from Nagorno-Karabakh.[69]

As had been the case with most other negotiated cease-fires, the warring parties continued their military operations without pause. The closing month of 1992 was marked by heavy fighting along the border between Armenia and Azerbaijan.[70] After being confined generally to the region of Nagorno-Karabakh and immediately surrounding areas, the conflict was at last threatening to take on the character of a full-scale war between the two Transcaucasian republics. Indeed, 1993 witnessed a major escalation in the hostilities between Armenia and Azerbaijan, an escalation that nearly resulted in international crises on two separate occasions.

THE MELTDOWN OF 1993–1994

The Year of Crisis, 1993

The fifth year of the Armenia-Azerbaijan conflict opened with the onset of a large-scale military operation by Karabakh Armenian forces aimed ostensibly at regaining ground lost to Azerbaijan over the prior six months. Reeling from heavy personnel losses and a steep drop in morale that had been the price of its earlier successes,[71] Baku's army found itself unable to stop the Armenian assault. By the end of March, local Armenian forces had succeeded in retaking most of northern Nagorno-Karabakh, including a strategic road junction linking the area with the Lachin corridor.[72]

Following their victories in the north, Karabakh Armenian forces turned to the west and attacked the Kelbajar district of Azerbaijan. Spokesmen of the self-styled NKR administration claimed the offensive was necessary to relieve Azer-baijani military pressure on the Lachin corridor,[73] but the unmistakable strategic objective behind the assault was the opening of a new land link between Armenia and Nagorno-Karabakh. After heavy fighting from 31 March to 3 April, local Armenian troops succeeded in capturing the regional center of Kelbajar and numerous surrounding villages.

The attack on Kelbajar prompted a humanitarian crisis in western Azerbaijan. As local Armenian troops advanced on the city, a frantic effort was made to remove women, children, and the elderly from the city's population of 62,000 by helicopter, but artillery attacks on landing facilities made the operation untenable before it could be completed.[74] As a result, tens of thousands of Azeris fled into the snow-bound mountain passes surrounding Kelbajar, and President Elchibey was forced to declare a state of emergency across the republic.[75]

In the midst of the chaotic situation in Kelbajar and environs, local Armenian forces opened a further offensive to the south of Nagorno-Karabakh on 4 April. Within a week, Karabakh Armenian units seized 18 villages and began a siege of Fizuli, the district capital situated a mere 20 kilometers from the Iranian border.[76] An Armenian victory in the area threatened to cut off the entire southwestern corner of Azerbaijan from Baku's control, thus ushering in a new stage in the five-year war.

The expansion of military operations significantly beyond the borders of Nagorno-Karabakh by local Armenian forces sparked a major outcry by a host of international actors. The UN Security Council released a statement on 6 April expressing "serious concern" with the capture of Kelbajar and calling for an immediate cessation of the hostilities.[77] Similarly, the United States made known its "deep concern" with the offensive and called for "the prompt and complete withdrawal of all ethnic Armenian forces from the Kelbajar district."[78] However, the most serious reactions came from Turkey and Iran.

Under increasing pressure to take action in support of Baku, the government of Turkish Prime Minister Demirel adopted a number of steps to demonstrate its disapproval with the seemingly imminent Armenian victory over Azerbaijan. On 3 April, Ankara decided to exploit the virtually desperate living conditions in Armenia imposed by the Azerbaijani blockade by announcing that humanitarian and other aid would no longer be allowed to transit Turkish territory on the way to Armenia.[79] Four days later, the Turkish Third Army in eastern Anatolia was put on alert and moved into positions along the Armenian border.[80]

As military forces were massing on the border, Turkish officials were sound-ing stern warnings to Yerevan. At the United Nations, Turkey's envoy noted that "the Turkish government will take every measure, up to and including military measures, to repulse Armenian aggression."[81] Turkey's chief NATO diplomat warned while in Brussels that his country was reassessing its policy of neutrality vis-à-vis the Armenia-Azerbaijan conflict,[82] and President Ozal claimed before the Azerbaijani parliament that Turkey might consider a military alliance with Baku.[83]

Although Turkey's sabre-rattling seemed to suggest that the Turks were entertaining the possibility of armed intervention in the Karabakh clash, Prime Minister Demirel continued to show reluctance to become involved directly in the conflict. Rather than choosing the path of intervention, Demirel argued for a cautious approach to developments in the Transcaucasus: "We, as a requisite of a coolheaded policy, are trying to pursue a path that will minimize and not maximize the problem, although we are following [developments] very closely. We are seeking peace."[84] However, despite the prime minister's well-known anxiety with the prospect of military involvement in the Nagorno-Karabakh dispute, such ambiguous statements were likely intended to create uncertainty in the minds of Armenian policy-makers vis-à-vis Turkish intentions. With a large armed force taking up positions along its border and Turkish officials refusing to rule out intervention, Yerevan would have been remiss to rule out the possibility of an invasion from the west. No doubt recognizing this, Ankara was in all likelihood attempting to intimidate the Armenians into halting their advance into Azerbaijani territory.

Whatever the motives behind Turkey's actions in the spring of 1993, the heightened tensions in the Transcaucasus following the fall of Kelbajar held out the real possibility of a wider regional conflict. Anticipating a Turkish attack, Armenia reinforced its border areas with elements of the Seventh Army—still controlled ostensibly by Moscow and staffed partly with Russian soldiers.[85] With Turkish troops facing off across the frontier with Armenian and Russian forces, the danger of a larger regional clash was heightened greatly.

While the Turkish government's actions in April 1993 reflected clearly its displeasure and unease with the course of events between Armenia and Azerbaijan, Iran also looked to the fighting to the north with dismay. For the first time in five years of the Armenia-Azerbaijan conflict, the incursion by local Armenian forces into the Fizuli district of Azerbaijan in April 1993 brought warfare to the vicinity of Iran's northern border.

Viewing the possibility of the descent of thousands of Azerbaijani refugees onto the Iranian side of the frontier, Tehran feared the rise of nationalist, and perhaps separatist, sentiments among its own ethnic Azeri population.[86] Thus, President Rafsanjani noted on 12 April that "the fighting close to the Iranian border is now affecting Iran's security" and claimed that "a more serious stance" would have to be adopted should the situation continue.[87] Abandoning its past tone of neutrality, the Iranian Foreign Ministry expressed "deep concern about the recent intensification of the clashes and the massacre of innocent people" and called on "the Armenian forces to withdraw from the areas of Azerbaijan it has occupied."[88]

As international tensions increased in the Transcaucasus, the UN Security Council passed Resolution 822 on 30 April 1993. (See Appendix E.) The first Security Council resolution concerning the Armenia-Azerbaijan conflict, 822 called for an immediate cease-fire and the prompt withdrawal of "all occupying forces from the Kelbadjar district and other recently occupied areas of Azerbaijan."[89] Additionally, the resolution upheld the principle of the inviolability of international borders and designated the CSCE as the primary forum through which the parties were encouraged to seek peace.

Significantly, all sides in the dispute welcomed Resolution 822. Both the Armenian government and the self-styled NKR administration greeted the act favorably due to a phrase portraying the recent hostilities as a clash between "the Republic of Azerbaijan" and "local Armenian forces." Yerevan took the wording as recognition of its claims of non-involvement in the dispute, while the Karabakh Armenians interpreted it as acknowledgment of their status as a party to the conflict.[90] Azerbaijan, on the other hand, supported 822 for its provision rejecting the forceful alteration of existing borders.[91]

In the wake of the passage of Resolution 822, an effort was made to jumpstart the stalled CSCE mediation effort. A tripartite peace plan prepared by Turkey, Russia, and the United States was presented to the warring parties in late April; the document called for a cease-fire, the withdrawal of Armenian forces from occupied territories outside of Nagorno-Karabakh, and the preparation of a plan for a comprehensive peace settlement.[92] Rejected initially by the Armenians, a modified proposal was accepted by Baku, Yerevan, and—as a result of pressure from Moscow—Stepanakert.[93] While the adoption of the Russian-Turkish-American plan held out promise for a peaceful resolution of the Karabakh clash, events in the Transcaucasus in June 1993 once again outpaced the efforts of mediators and leaders alike as political instability returned to Baku.

The popularity of President Elchibey and the Azerbaijani Popular Front among the Azerbaijani populace began to decline substantially in the first half of 1993. As discontent with the slow pace of economic reforms, the failure to achieve a military victory in Nagorno-Karabakh, and the continued presence of corrupt former Communist *nomenklatura* at high levels of the government grew among the populace,[94] the APF came to realize that its declining popularity threatened increasingly its hold on power.

In early 1993, the APF began to view Colonel Surat Huseinov as the greatest potential danger to its position. As the most successful of all Azerbaijani military commanders in Nagorno-Karabakh,[95] Huseinov built up a popular following in a number of towns near the conflict zone. When Huseinov pulled his forces out of Mardakert in February and redeployed them in the Azerbaijani town of Ganja, the APF-led Elchibey government dismissed the commander in disgrace and expelled him from the Popular Front.[96]

Despite his ouster, Huseinov and his 709th Brigade remained in Ganja, where they enjoyed great popularity as opponents of the Elchibey regime.[97] On 28 May 1993, by prior agreement with the Baku authorities, Russian forces based in Ganja began their pullout from Azerbaijan, leaving behind substantial quantities of arms, ammunition, and equipment. When Huseinov's men attempted to seize the weaponry on 4 June, Azerbaijani government forces stepped in, and a major clash ensued.[98]   Infuriated by the attack, Huseinov and his supporters seized control of Ganja and several surrounding villages and demanded the immediate resignation of Elchibey and two other high officials.[99]   With a mutiny in the making, Elchibey elected to open negotiations with the rebels.

Huseinov and his supporters rejected quickly the president's offer to negotiate and reiterated their demands for the resignation of the top authorities. Although the prime minister and parliament speaker agreed to step down, Huseinov's forces began to march on Baku, and President Elchibey was forced to summon a figure from Azerbaijan's past to the capital in an effort to avert civil war.

Heydar Aliyev had a long and distinguished past in the Communist Party of the Soviet Union. In the 1960s, he served as head of the Azerbaijani KGB before being elected as first secretary of the republic's Communist Party in 1969. Aliyev was made deputy chairman of the USSR Council of Ministers in 1982, only to be sacked from the Politburo by Gorbachev five years later. The Azerbaijani official returned to his native Nakhichevan in 1990, and in September 1991 he was elected chairman of the autonomous region's parliament. Following the breakup of the USSR, Aliyev ruled Nakhichevan as his own private fiefdom, cultivating commercial ties with Turkey and Iran. Isolated from the post-Soviet political intrigues in Baku, Aliyev became one of Azerbaijan's most popular politicians.[100]

Hoping perhaps to strengthen his regime's sagging favor, President Elchibey held talks with Aliyev in Baku during the second week of June on a possible power-sharing arrangement. After declining the post of prime minister, Aliyev agreed to accept nomination as chairman of the Supreme Soviet—a position that would have given him broad powers over the government.[101]   Aliyev was voted to the post on 15 June, and he made an immediate appeal to Huseinov and his supporters to end their revolt peacefully so the process of national reconciliation could begin. The rebels pressed forward toward the capital, however, and Elchibey chose to flee after being informed that the military would not intervene to stop them.

Elchibey's departure from Baku left an opening for Aliyev to seize the reins of power in Azerbaijan, and he was made acting president on 19 June. Having no quarrel with each other, Aliyev and Huseinov commenced negotiations on a power-sharing arrangement, and it was agreed that the latter would become prime minister and head of the military and the internal security ministry.[102] Thus, what began as a revolt by a local warlord ended with a *coup d'etat* and a major realignment of the political forces in Azerbaijan.[103]

Supporters of the Azerbaijani Popular Front, as well as many observers in the West, alleged that Russia had a hand in the events of June 1993. Proceeding from the highly plausible assumption that Elchibey's openly pro-Turkish, anti-Russian/CIS orientation was a source of annoyance to circles in Moscow that wished to see the reassertion of Russian influence in the region, circumstantial evidence exists to suggest that Russia offered at least tacit support to the rebels.

The first clue that raised the possibility of Russian involvement was the timing of the coup. Elchibey had been poised to sign a multibillion dollar accord in late June with a group of Western oil companies providing for the exploitation of three Azerbaijani oilfields offshore in the Caspian Sea and the construction of a pipeline to carry the oil to the Mediterranean via Turkey.[104] While it may be mere coincidence that Elchibey was ousted before the contract could be closed, it would not be unreasonable to suggest that those responsible for the coup— whether directly or indirectly—wished to thwart the oil deal from coming to fruition.

Because the agreement created a precedent for the establishment of an economic foothold in a part of the FSU by Western oil companies with the implicit promise of further Azerbaijani ties to Turkey and the West, it would be logical to finger Russia as the party most likely to desire Elchibey's ouster. The oil deal was the greatest manifestation of the Azerbaijani chief's pro-Turkish and anti-Russian foreign policy, and it promised to challenge Moscow's self-perceived zone of exclusive influence in the so-called "Near Abroad." Such a view of the "Near Abroad"—already prevalent in some circles by late 1992—was dominant among the makers of Russian foreign policy by the middle of 1993.

If the desire to oust the Elchibey regime and its policies that ran contrary to Moscow's interests was the motive for possible Russian support of the June 1993 coup, a further circumstance that suggested a covert Russian role was the conduct of Russian military forces upon their pullout from Ganja. As noted, the withdrawing units left behind large quantities of arms, ammunition, and equipment, no doubt with the full knowledge that a popular, anti-Elchibey military leader and his restive supporters were encamped nearby in the same city. Thus, it cannot be ruled out that circles in Moscow were offering tacit encouragement to Huseinov and his men by making weapons available to them. Incidentally, the same arms left behind by departing Russian forces at the end of May were used by the rebels in their revolt, which began just days later.

While it is less clear how Moscow may have been linked to Heydar Aliyev, the former Communist official's rise to power in Azerbaijan proved initially to be beneficial to Russian interests. Among the first changes enacted by Aliyev upon his ascension to the presidency was a major reorientation of Azerbaijani foreign policy. No doubt to Moscow's approval, Elchibey's priority on relations with Turkey was abandoned by Aliyev,[105] and among the new president's first policy decisions in June 1993 was to postpone indefinitely the signing of the proposed oil deal with Western companies.[106] In lieu of Turkey, Aliyev sought initially to make ties with Russia the focus of Azerbaijan's external relations. This newfound orientation was manifest in a major policy directive by Aliyev in the first months of his presidency.

Declaring that "all our relations [with Russia], not only economic, must be consolidated, and the ones lost must be restored," President Aliyev announced his country's intention to join the Russian-dominated Commonwealth of Independent States on 7 September 1993.[107] After pledging to see to it personally that Azerbaijan's independence and sovereignty would be not be compromised,[108]

Aliyev lobbied the Azerbaijani parliament to approve CIS membership two weeks later. Russian Foreign Minister Andrei Kozyrev welcomed the decision as "very timely and good,"[109] no doubt because it signaled the return of Azerbaijan to the Russian fold.

The ascension to power of Heydar Aliyev was also felt on the battlefield. The Karabakh Armenians took advantage of the June disarray in Baku to expand the scope of their military operations with a 12 June attack on Agdam, a large Azerbaijani city to the east of Nagorno-Karabakh. With the stated aim of silencing the artillery and missile positions from which Stepanakert and surrounding towns had been shelled,[110] ethnic Armenian forces sought, in effect, to establish a security zone by capturing Agdam and other towns ringing the eastern border of the former NKAO. After five weeks of fierce fighting, Agdam fell to Armenian troops on 23 July, thus marking the seizure of additional Azerbaijani territory outside of Nagorno-Karabakh.[111]

The new gains by local Armenian forces in the Agdam district of Azerbaijan sparked a renewed volley of international criticism aimed at Yerevan and Stepanakert. Iran's Foreign Minister Ali Akbar Velayati and spiritual leader Ayatollah Ali Khamenei both decried the attacks as "aggression" against the territorial integrity of Azerbaijan, and the former called for an immediate halt to the hostilities.[112] Officials in Ankara expressed similar sentiments, and a Turkish diplomatic initiative at the United Nations resulted in UN Security Council Resolution 853 adopted on 29 July 1993. Similar to Resolution 822 of the previous April, 853 upheld the principle of the inviolability of international borders, condemned the fighting, and called for an immediate cease-fire and withdrawal of "occupying forces" from Azerbaijani territory. (See Appendix F.) Moreover, 853 appeared to add further legitimacy to the view of the Karabakh Armenians as a separate party to the conflict implied in Resolution 822; it called on "the Government of the Republic of Armenia to continue to exert its influence to achieve compliance [with the resolution] by *the Armenians of the Nagorny-Karabakh region*" (emphasis added).[113]

With the international community's attention focused on events in the Agdam district, ethnic Armenian forces renewed their offensive in the southwest of Azerbaijan. On 23 July, Fizuli came under heavy attack after being the scene of intermittent fighting since the second week of April.[114] As the Azerbaijani army fled in the face of the assault, local Armenian troops turned south to blitz the town of Jebrail, a mere 14 kilometers from the Iranian border. Jebrail and Fizuli fell on 20 and 24 August, respectively,[115] thus solidifying Armenian control over most of southwestern Azerbaijan.[116] Perhaps more important in the near term, however, was the fact that the assault drove much of the region's 250,000-strong Azeri populace from its homes.

With Armenian-controlled territories to the north, west, and, to a lesser extent, east, most of the Azeri refugees chose to flee south toward the Iranian frontier. Iran, which had already shown uneasiness with the proximity of clashes to its border, viewed with extreme concern the prospect of several thousand Azeri refugees descending upon its border. When warnings to the Armenians to cease their activities were ignored,[117] Tehran was forced to take greater action to deal with the perceived threat to its border security.

As the first groups of displaced persons reached the Aras River separating Azerbaijan from Iran on 27 August, Iranian authorities moved to head off an impending refugee problem on its northern frontier. In cooperation with the UN High Commissioner for Refugees, Iran set up a number of temporary camps on its side of the border to which children and the elderly were evacuated. Within a matter of days, as many as 20,000 refugees were housed in the camps, with many more awaiting evacuation.[118]

Already unhappy with the prospect of a deluge of Azerbaijani war refugees, Iran viewed events with increasing concern when ethnic Armenian forces seized the town of Kubatly and threatened to take Goradiz in late August and early September. The possible capture of Goradiz was viewed with particular disfavor not only because of the town's close proximity to the Iranian border,[119] but also because it was the last remaining exit route to eastern Azerbaijan for the fleeing populace. With nowhere else to go but Iran, some 200,000 refugees began to head south.

Faced with a potentially overwhelming flood of displaced persons onto its side of the border, Tehran took action to preempt the approaching tide. Under the pretext of an agreement between local Azerbaijani and Iranian officials, armed Iranian military units crossed over into Azerbaijan on 2 September and set up a 3–4 kilometer buffer zone aimed ostensibly at creating a safe environment for the provision of humanitarian relief to the refugees while preventing them from advancing into northwest Iran.[120] The move, which amounted to a *de facto* incursion by Iran into the territory of Azerbaijan, sparked considerable alarm among the regional states. Indeed, Tehran's actions seemed to indicate to many that the internationalization of the Armenia-Azerbaijan conflict was at hand.

Incensed by the continuation of Armenian attacks in southwestern Azerbaijan and alarmed by Iranian troop movements, Turkey reinforced its military units along the frontier with Armenia, claiming the measure was necessary "for the protection of the security of Turkey and of the independence and territorial integrity of Azerbaijan."[121] However, Ankara charted a cautious diplomatic course toward the Iranian incursion, noting that ". . . it must be viewed as natural for regional countries, which are directly or indirectly affected by the Armenian attacks, to adopt the measures they deem necessary to protect their own and the region's security, as long as they respect Azerbaijan's unity, sovereignty, and territorial integrity."[122] Thus, Turkey acquiesced in the Iranian border operation, though its concern with the prospects for the conflict's regionalization continued.

Russia's diplomatic response to developments along the Azerbaijani-Iranian frontier reflected the concern showed by Turkey. A Foreign Ministry statement of 8 September expressed anxiety with the "dangerous spread of the zone of the Karabakh conflict" and called for maximum restraint on the part of all regional states.[123] However, unlike Ankara, Moscow showed veiled disapproval with

Iran's troop dispatch.

In the words of a Russian Foreign Ministry spokesman:

In connection with the new development of the situation in the Armenian-Azerbaijani conflict, we have made it clear that, *whatever their motivation, we cannot show any understanding or support for the actions of the Iranian side. The fact that Iranian armed groups have crossed the border into Azerbaijan will not only lead to a further escalation of the conflict, but also pushes it dangerously close to the verge of internationalization* [emphasis added].[124]

Such rhetoric was a clear reflection of one of the central tenets of Russia's emerging policy vis-à-vis the "Near Abroad": The desire to exclude intervention in the post-Soviet states by a foreign power. However, Moscow offered no serious diplomatic or other resistance to the Iranian action, suggesting that it was viewed as a benign, legitimate, and above all temporary operation.

Despite the caution demonstrated by Turkey, Russia, and Iran during the events of early September 1993, tensions remained high in the Transcaucasus. On the one hand, Iran's maintenance of a security zone on the Azerbaijani side of the border put its troops in close proximity to Armenian forces that were undertaking active combat operations—thus making an armed encounter between the two sides a potentially dangerous possibility. Turkey, on the other hand, faced off once again with Russian and Armenian border guards as a 50,000-strong Turkish force took up positions along the frontier with Armenia.[125] Under such conditions, despite the caution with which the three powers approached the emerging developments, the very real potential lingered for the explosion of a major regional war in the Transcaucasus.

An emerging international awareness of the possible dangers of expanded warfare in Transcaucasia was enshrined in UN Security Council Resolution 874 adopted on 14 October 1993. (See Appendix G.) Similar to the previous two Security Council resolutions in its affirmation of the principle of the inviolability of international borders, condemnation of continued fighting, and call for an immediate cease fire, 874 differed in that it "urge[d] all States in the region to refrain from any hostile acts and from any interference or intervention which would lead to the widening of the conflict and undermine peace and security in the region."[126] The Security Council's plea was put to the test shortly thereafter, when a new round of fighting broke out along the Azerbaijani-Iranian border in late October.

Perhaps unexpectedly, Azerbaijani forces launched a sudden attack in the Jebrail region on 21 October. Spearheading the raid was a group of about three hundred Afghan *mujaheddin* fighters, part of a 1,000- to 1,500-strong force hired by the Azerbaijani government in a last-ditch effort to reverse the tide of battle.[127] Although an interesting new element in the Armenia-Azerbaijan clash, the Afghan fighters made little difference on the battlefield, and local Armenian forces went on the counter-offensive after repulsing the assault.[128] The town of

Goradiz fell on 25 October, and Armenian troops occupied a 40-kilometer stretch of land on the north bank of the Aras River.[129]

After severing completely the southwestern corner of Azerbaijan from the rest of the country, ethnic Armenian units attacked Zangelan, the last Baku-controlled town in the area. On 28 October, the last remaining Azerbaijani forces in the region fled in disarray toward Iran along with the town's population of 60,000, thus leaving Zangelan and all of southwest Azerbaijan to the Armenians.[130] By the end of November, local Armenian units controlled a 160-kilometer expanse of the Azerbaijani-Iranian frontier.

Iran was alarmed demonstrably by the latest developments along its northern border. Two army divisions were sent to the vicinity of a strategic bridge across the Aras River seized by the Armenians on 11 November, and President Rafsanjani declared that Iran would not allow the escalation of military operations on its border.[131] The UN Security Council responded the next day with Resolution 884, which reiterated its prior call for all states in the region to refrain from acts that could lead to a widening of the conflict.[132] (See Appendix H.) Although the feared expansion of the war never came, tensions in the Transcaucasus remained high nonetheless.

End Game? December 1993–May 1994

As the situation on the battlefield stood near the end of 1993, the Karabakh Armenians appeared to have achieved the long-standing goal of ensuring the security and viability of Nagorno-Karabakh. The Azeri population had been driven out of the region along with the Azerbaijani army, and two land corridors had been opened with neighboring Armenia. Moreover, a buffer zone had been created around Nagorno-Karabakh to place its population centers largely out of the reach of Azerbaijani missiles and artillery. With 20 percent of Azerbaijani territory under their control and Baku's army routed at nearly every turn, the Karabakh Armenians appeared in a position to dictate terms for peace.[133]

The Karabakh Armenians' runaway victories through late 1993 faced the regime of Heydar Aliyev with a dire situation. Recognizing the need to bolster his position both at home and at the negotiating table, Aliyev launched a large-scale offensive along several fronts in the conflict zone on 10 December 1993. Much to the surprise of many who had counted Azerbaijan out, the operation experienced some small but noteworthy gains.

The opening blows of Azerbaijan's winter offensive centered on the southeastern sector of Nagorno-Karabakh. Infantry and armored units backed by artillery succeeded in penetrating three to four kilometers into Armenian-held territory near Fizuli,[134] and Armenian settlements in eastern Karabakh again came under intense shelling.[135] Following these gains, a major attack was launched near Agdam on 28 December, and, in their first major setback in almost a year, local Armenian troops were forced to abandon a number of strategic heights near the Azerbaijani city.[136] With much of eastern Nagorno-Karabakh now within range of Azerbaijani guns, an assault was launched into the former NKAO itself.

Azerbaijani units struck into the Mardakert and Askeran districts of Nagorno-Karabakh on 9 January 1994. Small gains were made, and Azerbaijani forces were reported to have penetrated to within 18 kilometers of the capital of Stepanakert.[137] Meanwhile, advances were made on two other fronts. The city of Goradiz and a 40-kilometer stretch of the Azerbaijani-Iranian border were re-taken between 6 and 12 January,[138] and a vigorous push was made into the Kelbajar district in the northwest. Baku's forces also came into temporary possession of the strategic Omar pass linking northern Nagorno-Karabakh with Armenia, but they were repulsed in heavy fighting by the end of the month.[139]

Azerbaijan's winter offensive began to stall in early February 1994. While the heavy snowfall that blanketed the region may have been partly to blame,[140] the most likely reason for the declining pace of military operations was the enormous cost in manpower and equipment imposed by the offensive. According to several sources, Azerbaijan lost as many as 5,000 troops and 60 armored vehicles in the two-month operation that was characterized often by "human wave" assaults reminiscent of the Iran-Iraq War.[141] Nonetheless, the human and material toll paid off to the extent that it resulted in some notable territorial gains for Azerbaijan.

Considering that the Azerbaijani army had been all but defeated by late 1993, questions arise as to the sources of the sudden and modest success of the Azerbaijani winter offensive. Evidence suggests that at least some of the credit must go to President Aliyev's military policies. Upon taking power, the former KGB leader moved to subordinate the often independently acting field chiefs to a single commander,[142] and all deserters were pardoned and ordered to return to their units.[143]

Notwithstanding these moves to improve the army's strength and coordination, the war-fighting capability of the Azerbaijani military did not improve noticeably in the short term, as demonstrated by the defeats of late 1993. With desertion a leading problem among the ranks, Aliyev introduced an ominous measure to heighten discipline in the front-line units: All servicemen attempting to flee the fighting were to be shot on the spot.[144] According to one report, special "deterrent detachments" were formed to roam behind the lines and carry out the order.[145] Thus, fear in the ranks may have been a factor motivating Azerbaijani soldiers to participate in the "human wave" assaults that characterized much of the winter offensive.

An additional, and perhaps more important, factor behind the success of Azerbaijani military operations in late 1993 and early 1994 was the role of foreign mercenaries and advisors. To supplement the force of 1,000–1,500 Afghan *mujaheddin* fighters acquired in the fall of 1993, Baku went to great lengths to recruit combat veterans from other CIS states, offering by one account to pay them as much as 500,000 rubles per month each.[146] Additionally, in late 1993 Turkey agreed to return the 150 military experts it had withdrawn from Azerbaijan following Elchibey's ouster, claiming its differences with the Aliyev regime had been resolved.[147] Together with the two hundred advisors dispatched reportedly by Russia in the fall of 1993,[148] Turkey's experts were credited with training elements of the Azerbaijani army in the months leading up to the winter assault.[149]

While the real reasons for the sudden turnaround in the performance of Baku's army can only be a matter of speculation, the modest Azerbaijani successes in late 1993 and early 1994 had a significant impact on the hostilities. After a brief April offensive by local Armenian forces intended ostensibly to regain lost territory,[150] the warring parties agreed to a termination of military operations on 12 May 1994. Aside from a handful of relatively minor violations, the cease-fire has held to the present.

With the establishment of a viable cease-fire in the conflict zone, the business of negotiation began in earnest. However, the peace process, like the Armenia-Azerbaijan conflict itself, became more than just an affair among the warring parties. External actors with their own geopolitical agenda became involved, and each attempted to influence the process according to that agenda.

NOTES

I have attempted painstakingly to sort through often conflicting accounts to reconstruct objectively the historical developments depicted above. The interpretation in this chapter is my own, and I take full responsibility for it.

1. According to President Mutalibov, "The only way to achieve peace is for the [Armenian] terrorists and mercenaries to be moved away. Then we will sit down and make peace with the remaining Armenians, with whom we have always lived in peace." Quoted by *Agence France Presse*, 1 February 1992, in Foreign Broadcast Information Service—Central Eurasia (hereafter FBIS-SOV), #92–023 (4 February 1992): 77.

2. *Agence France Presse*, 31 January 1992, in FBIS-SOV, #92–021 (31 January 1992): 73.

3. Pavel Felgengauer, "Prospects for a War of Attrition," *Current Digest of the Post-Soviet Press* 44, no. 8 (25 March 1992): 11.

4. Mark Urban, "Nagorno-Karabakh: Beleaguered Enclave in the Caucasus," *International Defense Review* 25, no. 6 (June 1992): 504.

5. Press service of the Karabakh Armenian Operational Headquarters as quoted by *Interfax*, 10 February 1992, in FBIS-SOV, #92–028 (11 February 1992): 91.

6. The Azerinform Information Agency cited eyewitness reports on 29 February to the effect that over 1,000 civilians were killed in cold blood by advancing Armenian forces during the assault on Khojaly, while scores of others were wounded or left stranded in the snow-bound mountain passes nearby. The report was later substantiated by the Azerbaijani Interior Ministry and by President Mutalibov himself, but Karabakh Armenian officials refuted the charges of massacre, claiming that Armenian forces had entered the town with little resistance and found it nearly empty of inhabitants. However, one Armenian combatant pointed out to a Western journalist not only that the Khojaly assault coincided with the fourth anniversary of the anti-Armenian pogroms in the Azerbaijani city of Sumgait, but also that many of the Armenian fighters that took part in the attack had been former residents of that city. Thus, revenge may have played a part in the actions of

Armenian forces.   For the Azerbaijani account of the Khojaly violence, see *TASS International Service*, 29 February 1992, and *Interfax*, 1 March 1992, in FBIS-SOV, #92–041 (2 March 1992): 64. For the Armenian response, see *Interfax*, 26 February 1992, in FBIS-SOV, #92–039 (27 February 1992): 77. For the account of the Armenian fighter to the Western journalist, see Paul Quinn-Judge, "Stepanakert Postcard: Revenge Tragedy," *The New Republic* 206, no. 14 (6 April 1992): 12.

7. Quinn-Judge, "Stepanakert Postcard," p. 11.

8. *Interfax*, 6 March 1992, in FBIS-SOV, #92–045 (6 March 1992): 64.

9. Francis X. Clines, "Angry Azerbaijanis Impel Chief to Quit," *New York Times* (7 March 1992):   3; and Elizabeth Fuller, "The Ongoing Political Power Struggle in Azerbaijan," *Radio Free Europe/Radio Liberty (*hereafter RFE/RL) *Research Report* 1, no. 18 (1 May 1992): 13.

10. For Yerevan, Iran was preferable as a mediator to all other regional states at the time, for strengthened ties with the Islamic Republic offered a potential hedge against the increase of Turkish influence in the Transcaucasus as well as a possible way out of Armenia's economic and political isolation after the Soviet breakup. For the Azerbaijanis, Iran was less attractive as a mediator than the Turks, but Tehran was nonetheless viewed as an honest and credible broker on the question of Nagorno-Karabakh. James M. Dorsey, "The Growing Entente Between Armenia and Iran," *Middle East International* (4 December 1992):   17; and Konsantin Eggert, "Velayati's Mission to Nagorno-Karabakh," *Current Digest of the Post-Soviet Press* 44, no. 8 (25 March 1992): 12.

11. Commentaries in the Iranian media and statements by Iranian officials indicate that Iran was not concerned greatly with the potential for the Armenia-Azerbaijan conflict spilling over into its borders at this early stage of the hostilities. Indeed, it seems that Iranian leaders were interested primarily at the time with forestalling the growth of U.S. and Turkish influence in the Transcaucasus by preempting Western mediation efforts. See, for example, *Agence France Presse*, 13 February 1992, in Foreign Broadcast Information Service—Near East and South Asia (hereafter FBIS-NES), #92–030 (13 February 1992): 41–42; and *Islamic Republic News Agency*, 10 March 1992, in FBIS-NES, #92–048 (11 March 1992): 26.

12. *Voice of the Islamic Republic of Iran First Program Network*, 24 February 1992, in FBIS-NES, #92–037 (25 February 1992): 51; *TASS*, 26 February 1992, in FBIS-SOV, #92–038 (26 February 1992): 62; and *TASS*, 27 February 1992, in FBIS-SOV, #92–039 (27 February 1992): 77.

13. An early component of the draft plan envisaged the deployment of "multinational peacemaking forces," dominated not surprisingly by Iran, to the conflict zone following a cease-fire. Although Armenia welcomed the proposal, the issue of peacekeeping forces was not included in the final draft plan for reasons not given. *TASS*, 11 March 1992, in FBIS-SOV, #92–049 (12 March 1992): 69; *Islamic Republic News Agency*, 15 March 1992, in FBIS-NES, #92–051 (16 March 1992): 50–51; and *Izvestiya*, 17 March 1992, in FBIS-SOV, #92–053 (18 March 1992): 4.

14. *Voice of the Islamic Republic of Iran First Program Network*, 27 March 1992, in FBIS-SOV, #92–060 (27 March 1992): 66.

15. *Teleradiokompaniya Ostankino Television First Program Network*, 31 March 1992, and *Interfax*, 1 April 1992, in FBIS-SOV, #92–063 (1 April 1992): 62, 64.

16. Quinn-Judge, "Stepanakert Postcard," p. 11.

17. *ITAR-TASS*, 10 May 1992, in FBIS-SOV, #92–091 (11 May 1992): 80.

18. *Armenia's Radio First Program Network*, 9 May 1992, in ibid., p. 72.

19. At the invitation of Iranian President Hashemi Rafsanjani, the leaders of Armenia

and Azerbaijan were brought together in Tehran on 6 May for bilateral talks on the Nagorno-Karabakh dispute. Several days of negotiations produced a document that envisioned the establishment of a permanent cease-fire, the deployment of international observers to the conflict zone, the lifting of the economic blockade against Armenia and Nagorno-Karabakh, and the exchange of prisoners and war dead, all of which were to be followed by measures to achieve a final solution to the Karabakh dispute. *Islamic Republic News Agency*, 8 May 1992, in FBIS-NES, #92–091 (11 May 1992): 46.

20. The Azerbaijani Supreme Soviet restored Ayaz Mutalibov as president by special decree on 14 May, after which Mutalibov declared a state of emergency in Baku for a period of 60 days. The Popular Front, still the most powerful opposition group in parliament, deemed Mutalibov's reinstatement illegal and took control of important facilities throughout the city with the backing of the army. On 15 May, Popular Front supporters entered the parliament building without violence and forced Mutalibov to flee. A coalition government was set up subsequently to rule Azerbaijan until elections could be held on 7 June. *Radio Baku Network*, 14 May 1992, and *ITAR-TASS World Service*, 14 May 1992, in FBIS-SOV, #92–095 (15 May 1992): 67; and *ITAR-TASS*, 15 May 1992, *Programma Radio Odin Network*, 15 May 1992, *TRT Television Network*, 15 May 1992, and *Russian Television Network*, 17 May 1992, in FBIS-SOV, #92–096 (18 May 1992): 54–56, 62.

21. Urban, "Nagorno-Karabakh," p. 504.

22. *Postfactum*, 18 May 1992, in FBIS-SOV, #92–096 (18 May 1992): 68–69.

23. A meeting of the Russian, Armenian, and Azerbaijani foreign ministers in Moscow on 20 February resulted in the adoption of a communique calling for an immediate cease-fire in the conflict zone, the lifting of energy and communications blockades, the delivery of humanitarian aid, and the commencement of negotiations for a comprehensive political settlement. The plan drew support from Turkey and the West primarily because it excluded Iran as a partner. However, the communique came to naught with the Armenian capture of Khojaly five days later. *Mayak Radio Network*, 20 February 1992, in FBIS-SOV, #92–035 (21 February 1992): 22; and *TRT Television Network*, 22 February 1992, in Foreign Broadcast Information Service—Western Europe (hereafter FBIS-WEU), #92–036 (24 February 1992): 41.

24. *Izvestiya*, 17 March 1992, in FBIS-SOV, #92–053 (18 March 1992): 5.

25. *Interfax*, 27 February 1992, in FBIS-SOV, #92–040 (28 February 1992): 61.

26. For example, the Russian ambassador to Turkey noted in an interview that "we reject rumors that our military units have taken part in the incidents. However, we have to consider the armed men who have deserted their units. They are paid large sums of money. *There are Slavic troops on both sides, either as volunteers or as mercenaries*" (emphasis added). Quoted by *Milliyet*, 13 April 1993, in FBIS-WEU, #93–079 (27 April 1993): 60.

27. Shaposhnikov ordered the 366th Regiment out of the region ostensibly because of the repeated attacks upon its personnel and military facilities carried out by armed units of both Azerbaijan and Nagorno-Karabakh in January and February 1992. Although the withdrawing forces destroyed a battalion's worth of equipment in order to prevent it from falling into the hands of the warring parties, some weaponry was known to have been sold or given to Karabakh forces. *Mayak Radio Network*, 28 February 1992, in FBIS-SOV, #92–040 (28 February 1992): 60–61; *Postfactum*, 9 March 1992, in FBIS-SOV, #92–047 (10 March 1992): 7; and Viktor Litovkin, "The 366th Regiment is Leaving Nagorno-Karabakh," *Current Digest of the Post-Soviet Press* 44, no. 8 (25 March 1992): 14.

28. Elizabeth Fuller, "Nagorno-Karabakh: Can Turkey Remain Neutral?" *RFE/RL Research Report* 1, no. 14 (3 April 1992): 37.

29. Statement of Prime Minister Suleyman Demirel as read by *TRT Television Network*, 1 March 1992, in FBIS-WEU, #92–041 (2 March 1992): 28.

30. *Turkiye*, 14 March 1992, in FBIS-WEU, #92–053 (18 March 1992): 43.

31. *TRT Television Network*, 9 May 1992, in FBIS-WEU, #92–091 (11 May 1992): 54.

32. Fuller, "Nagorno-Karabakh: Can Turkey Remain Neutral?" p. 37; and *Anatolia*, 14 May 1992, in FBIS-WEU, #92–095 (15 May 1992): 29.

33. Although Turkey's border with Nakhichevan spans a mere nine kilometers, the link is nonetheless significant in the eyes of both the Turks and the Azerbaijanis.

34. Heydar Aliyev, then chairman of the parliament of Nakhichevan, made it clear from the beginning of the crisis that he neither wanted nor needed Turkey to intervene militarily against Armenia. Instead, he asked for humanitarian aid and modern weaponry with which to deal with the Armenian attack. *Turkiye Radyolari Network*, 19 May 1992, and *Radio Baku Network*, 19 May 1992, in FBIS-SOV, #92–098 (20 May 1992): 65.

35. *Radio Baku Network*, 20 May 1992, in FBIS-SOV, #92–099 (21 May 1992): 96.

36. *Anatolia*, 18 May 1992, in FBIS-WEU, #92–097 (19 May 1992): 37–38.

37. Throughout the crisis in Nakhichevan and the Armenian victories in Nagorno-Karabakh that preceded it, Demirel remained a fervent opponent of military intervention. On 20 May, two days after Turkey's warning to Armenia, Demirel again rejected the use of force, claiming that "Turkish intervention could spiral into a Muslim-Christian conflict and it would take Turkey 20 years or more to get back out of the region." Quoted by *Agence France Presse*, 20 May 1992, in FBIS-WEU, #92–099 (21 May 1992): 53.

38. Quoted in Amberin Zaman, "Azerbaijan Looks to Ankara," *The Middle East*, no. 213 (July 1992): 8.

39. Text of treaty printed in *Rossiyskaya Gazeta*, 23 May 1992, in FBIS-SOV, #92–101 (26 May 1992): 8–9.

40. When it appeared that Turkish policy was beginning to take a harder line against Armenia during its attack on Nakhichevan in May, the Armenian Foreign Minister made it clear that his country would not hesitate to invoke the Tashkent Treaty on collective security in case of Turkish military intervention. Russia's Foreign Minister concurred, warning Turkey that Moscow would come to Armenia's aid in the event of an attack. *Interfax*, 22 May 1992, in FBIS-SOV, #92–100 (22 May 1992): 54; and *RDP Commercial Radio Network*, 22 May 1992, in FBIS-SOV, #92–101 (26 May 1992): 5.

41. Article Five of the North Atlantic Treaty stipulates that NATO members "agree that an armed attack against one or more of them in Europe or North America shall be considered an attack against them all and consequently they agree that, if such an attack occurs, each of them, in exercise of the right of individual or collective self-defense recognized by Article 51 of the Charter of the United Nations, will assist the Party or Parties [to the Treaty] so attacked by taking forthwith, individually, and in concert with the other Parties, such action as it deems necessary, including the use of armed force, to restore and maintain the security of the North Atlantic area." North Atlantic Treaty Organization, *NATO Handbook* (Brussels: NATO Office of Information and Press, 1992): 144.

42. According to *Komsomolskaya Pravda*, the election was a fairly free and open one. Of the 73 percent of the electorate that participated, some 64 percent voted for Elchibey, while between 20 and 30 percent voted for his chief rival. *Komsomolskaya Pravda*, 9 June 1992, in FBIS-SOV, #92–112 (10 June 1992): 68.

43. Elizabeth Fuller, "Azerbaijan's Relations With Russia and the CIS," *RFE/RL Research Report* 1, no. 43 (30 October 1992): 54.

44. Shireen T. Hunter, *The Transcaucasus in Transition: Nation-Building and Conflict* (Washington, DC: Praeger, 1994): 83–84.

45. David Nissman, "The National Reawakening of Azerbaijan," *World and I* 7 (February 1992): 81–82.

46. Quoted by *Terkumen*, 29 February 1992, in FBIS-SOV, #92–048 (11 March 1992): 66.

47. Elizabeth Fuller, "Paramilitary Forces Dominate Fighting in Transcaucasus," *RFE/RL Research Report* 2, no. 25 (18 June 1993): 79.

48. *ITAR-TASS World Service*, 12 June 1992, in FBIS-SOV, #92–115 (15 June 1992): 51.

49. *ITAR-TASS*, 13 June 1992, in ibid., p. 53.

50. *Interfax*, 14 June 1992, in ibid., p. 54; and *Russian Television Network*, 15 June 1992, in FBIS-SOV, #92–116 (16 June 1992): 64.

51. *Teleradiokompaniya Ostankino Television First Program Network*, 28 June 1992, in FBIS-SOV, #92–125 (29 June 1992): 65.

52. *ITAR-TASS World Service*, 6 July 1992, and *Interfax*, 5 July 1992, in FBIS-SOV, #92–129 (6 July 1992): 76, 78.

53. Serge Schmemann, "In the Caucasus, Ancient Blood Feuds Threaten to Engulf 2 New Republics," *New York Times* (8 July 1992): A3.

54. *Postfactum*, 23 June 1992, in FBIS-SOV, #92–122 (24 June 1992): 75–76.

55. Congressional Research Service, "Armenia-Azerbaijan Conflict," *Congressional Research Service Issue Brief* IB92109 (31 January 1995): 3.

56. *ITAR-TASS World Service*, 12 June 1992, in FBIS-SOV, #92–115 (15 June 1992): 51; and *Russian Television Network*, 27 June 1992, in FBIS-SOV, #92–125 (29 June 1992): 64.

57. The Russian Television Network, citing "sources close to the Russian Defense Ministry," claimed on 6 August 1992 that the June offensive had in fact been "preceded by the transfer to Azerbaijan of the equipment and weapons of three divisions from the Caucasus military district," amounting to "more than 250 tanks, 300 infantry fighting vehicles and armored personnel carriers, 170 artillery pieces, and 14 helicopters." *Russian Television Network*, 6 August 1992, in FBIS-SOV, #92–153 (7 August 1992): 18.

58. *Mayak Radio Network*, 22 June 1992, in FBIS-SOV, #92–121 (23 June 1992): 70.

59. Russia dispensed the equipment of two motorized infantry divisions from the Seventh Army to Armenia on 8 July, more than a month after having transferred weaponry to Azerbaijan. *Russian Television Network*, 8 July 1992, in FBIS-SOV, #92–132 (9 July 1992): 75.

60. *Mayak Radio Network*, 19 September 1992, and *ITAR-TASS*, 19 September 1992, in FBIS-SOV, #92–183 (21 September 1992): 65.

61. *Assa-Irada*, 7 October 1992, in FBIS-SOV, #92–196 (8 October 1992): 51; and *Interfax*, 11 October 1992, in FBIS-SOV, #92–198 (13 October 1992): 38.

62. Richard Weitz, "The CSCE's New Look," *RFE/RL Research Report* 1, no. 6 (7 February 1992): 27, 29.

63. *Agence France Presse*, 20 June 1992, in FBIS-WEU, #92–120 (22 June 1992): 2; and *ITAR-TASS*, 18 June 1992, in FBIS-SOV, #92–120 (22 June 1992): 4.

64. *ANSA*, 20 June 1992, in FBIS-WEU, #92–120 (22 June 1992): 2.

65. *Nezavisimaya Gazeta*, 15 September 1992, in FBIS-SOV, #92–180 (16 September 1992): 51.

66. *Izvestiya*, 19 June 1992, in FBIS-SOV, #92–120 (22 June 1992): 4.

67. *Turkiye Radyolari Network*, 21 June 1992, in ibid., p. 5.

68. *Nezavisimaya Gazeta*, 25 September 1992, in FBIS-SOV, #92–187 (25 September 1992): 50.

69. *Krasnaya Zvezda*, 23 September 1992, in FBIS-SOV, #92–185 (23 September 1992): 3–5.

70. Armed formations reportedly entered the Zangelan district of Azerbaijan from Armenia proper on 17 December and penetrated some 15 kilometers into Azerbaijani territory. Six days later, armored units from Azerbaijan advanced several kilometers into Armenia, ostensibly to strike at the military base at Krasnoselsk. However, neither side proved able to consolidate its gains. *Radio Rossii Network*, 17 December 1992, in FBIS-SOV, #92–243 (17 December 1992): 64; and *Interfax*, 23 December 1992, in FBIS-SOV, #92–248 (24 December 1992): 40.

71. According to one report, Azerbaijan's gains during the summer 1992 offensive may have come at the cost of 10,000 casualties, though other estimates are much lower. Nonetheless, mass desertions became a common occurence among Azerbaijani units, and Azeri youths became less willing to go to the front to fight. Fuller, "Paramilitary Forces Dominate Fighting in Transcausus," p. 79.

72. *Snark*, 6 February 1993, and *Agence France Presse*, 6 February 1993, in FBIS-SOV, #93–024 (8 February 1993): 48.

73. *Interfax*, 29 March 1993, in FBIS-SOV, #93–059 (30 March 1993): 76; *Turan*, 30 March 1993, in FBIS-SOV, #93–060 (31 March 1993): 79; and Elizabeth Fuller, "Nagorno-Karabakh Roundup," *RFE/RL News Briefs* 2, no. 15 (29 March–2 April 1993): 9.

74. *ITAR-TASS World Service*, 1 April 1993, in FBIS-SOV, #93–061 (1 April 1993): 72–73.

75. Text of state of emergency decree as read by *Radio Baku Network*, 2 April 1993, in FBIS-SOV, #93–063 (5 April 1993): 80.

76. "Southern Strategic Positions Taken," *Facts on File* 53, no. 2734 (22 April 1993): 293.

77. Quoted in Elizabeth Fuller, "International Diplomatic Reaction to Fighting in Azerbaijan," *RFE/RL News Briefs* 2, no. 16 (5–8 April 1993): 8.

78. United States Department of State, "Offensive in Azerbaijan's Kelbajar District," *U.S. Department of State Dispatch* 4, no. 15 (12 April 1993): 229.

79. *TRT Television Network*, 3 April 1993, in FBIS-WEU, #93–063 (5 April 1993): 71.

80. *Kanal-6 Television*, 8 April 1993, in FBIS-WEU, #93–067 (9 April 1993): 51.

81. Quoted in Aidyn Mekhtiyev, "The Karabakh Problem Has Finally Been Internationalized," *Current Digest of the Post-Soviet Press* 45, no. 14 (5 May 1993): 23.

82. *Anatolia*, 6 April 1993, in FBIS-WEU, #93–066 (8 April 1993): 2.

83. Elizabeth Fuller, "Ozal Raises Possibility of Turkish-Azerbaijani Military Alliance," *RFE/RL News Briefs* 2, no. 17 (13–16 April 1993): 8.

84. *TRT Television Network*, 13 April 1993, in FBIS-WEU, #93–070 (14 April 1993): 45.

85. *Hurriyet*, 12 April 1993, in FBIS-WEU, #93–070 (14 April 1993): 44.

86. *Islamic Republic News Agency*, 12 April 1993, in FBIS-NES, #93–069 (13 April 1993): 44.

87. Quoted in "Iranians Deliver a Warning to Azerbaijan and Armenia," *New York Times* (13 April 1993): A5.

88. Excerpt of statement as read by *IRIB Television First Program Network*, 5 April 1993, in FBIS-NES, #93–064 (6 April 1993): 48.

89. United Nations Security Council, S/RES/822 [1993] (30 April 1993): 2.

90. *ITAR-TASS*, 6 May 1993, in FBIS-SOV, #93–086 (6 May 1993): 54.

91. *Azertac*, 2 May 1993, in FBIS-SOV, #93–083 (3 May 1993): 55.

92. *Izvestiya*, 5 May 1993, in FBIS-SOV, #93–086 (6 May 1993): 55.

93. *Izvestiya*, 16 June 1993, in FBIS-SOV, #93–116 (18 June 1993): 14.

94. Mekhman Gafarly, "The People Like the President, But Not the President's Team," *Current Digest of the Post-Soviet Press* 45, no. 24 (14 July 1993): 4.

95. Huseinov had been hand-picked by Elchibey in 1992 to command the Azerbaijani force that led the successful assault on Armenian-controlled northern Nagorno-Karabakh. For his efforts, he was awarded the republic's highest award, that of National Hero of Azerbaijan. Sokhbet Mamedov, "Geidar Aliyev Urges That the Threat of Civil War Be Eliminated," *Current Digest of the Post-Soviet Press* 45, no. 24 (14 July 1993): 2.

96. *Radio Rossii Network*, 23 February 1993, in FBIS-SOV, #93–034 (23 February 1993): 58.

97. *Agence France Presse*, 18 June 1993, in FBIS-SOV, #93–118 (22 June 1993): 49.

98. Elizabeth Fuller, "Military Revolt in Azerbaijan," *RFE/RL News Briefs* 2, no. 25 (7–11 June 1993): 6–7.

99. *Russian Television Network*, 7 June 1993, in FBIS-SOV, #93–107 (7 June 1993): 82.

100. Elizabeth Fuller, "Azerbaijan: Geidar Aliev's Political Comeback," *RFE/RL Research Report* 2, no. 5 (29 January 1993): 6, 9.

101. Georgy Ivanov-Smolensky and Sokhbet Mamedov, "G. Aliyev Promises Azerbaijan Civil Peace," *Current Digest of the Post-Soviet Press* 45, no. 24 (14 July 1993): 3.

102. "Veteran Communist Crowns a Comeback in Azerbaijan," *New York Times* (1 July 1993): A2.

103. Soon after coming to power, Aliyev began a major crackdown against the APF. The Front's offices were raided on 17 July, and dozens of its supporters were arrested. "Azerbaijan Crackdown Widens," *New York Times* (18 July 1993): 10.

104. Amalia van Gent, "Azerbaijan: Oil, Armenians, Russians and Refugees," *Swiss Review of World Affairs*, no. 2 (February 1994): 22.

105. Ankara's strong initial support for Elchibey in the first days of the June rebellion may have damaged its credibility among the new Azerbaijani administration. Although Turkish officials toned down their remarks from statements of personal support for Elchibey to vague calls for the continuance of democratic processes in Azerbaijan as the June crisis wore on, their early solidarity with the ousted president was criticized by the new Azerbaijani leaders. *TRT Television Network*, 20 June 1993, in FBIS-SOV, #93–117 (21 June 1993): 81; and *TRT Television Network*, 18 July 1993, in FBIS-WEU, #93–136 (19 July 1993): 46.

106. *Mayak Radio Network*, 29 June 1993, in FBIS-SOV, #93–124 (30 June 1993): 71.

107. Quoted by *ITAR-TASS*, 7 September 1993, in FBIS-SOV, #93–172 (8 September 1993): 7.

108. Aliyev went so far as to argue that "I am positive that [by] being a member of the Commonwealth of Independent States, Azerbaijan will not only preserve its independence but strengthen it." Quoted by *ITAR-TASS*, 29 September 1993, in FBIS-SOV, #93–188 (30 September 1993): 45.

109. Quoted by *ITAR-TASS World Service*, 21 September 1993, in FBIS-SOV, #93–182 (22 September 1993): 6.

110. Elizabeth Fuller, "Refugees Flee Agdam as Armenian Advance," *RFE/RL News Briefs* 2, no. 29 (5–9 July 1993): 7; and *Snark*, 23 July 1993, in FBIS-SOV, #93–141 (26

July 1993): 72.

111. Elizabeth Fuller, "Armenian Forces Take Agdam, Azerbaijan, Karabakh Agree on 3-Day Ceasefire," *RFE/RL News Briefs* 2, no. 32 (26 July–6 August 1993): 7.

112. *Voice of the Islamic Republic of Iran First Program Network*, 24 July 1993, in FBIS-NES, #93–141 (26 July 1993): 63; and Joseph de Courcy, "It Looks As If Iran is Coming Off the Fence On the Question of Nagorno-Karabakh," *Intelligence Digest* (6–27 August 1993): 8.

113. United Nations Security Council, S/RES/853 [1993] (29 July 1993).

114. *Turan*, 23 July 1993, in FBIS-SOV, #93–141 (26 July 1993): 76; and *Agence France Presse*, 15 August 1993, in FBIS-SOV, #93–156 (16 August 1993): 63.

115. Elizabeth Fuller, "Armenia-Azerbaijan Update," *RFE/RL News Briefs* 2, no. 34 (16–20 August 1993): 8.

116. Jebrail was the location of a key national highway that linked the three southwestern districts of Azerbaijan with the eastern two-thirds of the country. *Agence France Presse*, 24 August 1993, in FBIS-SOV, #93–162 (24 August 1993): 55.

117. The Iranian Foreign Ministry issued a strongly worded statement on 12 August "seriously warning the Armenian forces" that Iran "cannot remain indifferent to these aggressions" against the territory of Azerbaijan. Press release of the Permanent Mission of the Islamic Republic of Iran to the United Nations, 16 August 1993.

118. *Islamic Republic News Agency*, 27 August 1993, in FBIS-NES, #93–170 (3 September 1993): 36; and *Rossiyskaya Gazeta*, 31 August 1993, in FBIS-SOV, #93–168 (1 September 1993): 57.

119. On several occasions Armenian forces were reported to have fired into Iranian territory with small arms as well as artillery. However, the actions seemed to be unintentional, and no injury or loss of life was reported. *Islamic Republic News Agency*, 24 August 1993, in FBIS-NES, #93–163 (25 August 1993): 48–49.

120. Tehran never admitted explicitly that it had sent troops across the border, and Aliyev, too, was ambiguous on the matter, claiming that Iranian troops "might have entered" Azerbaijani territory. However, both sides conceded that they were working together to set up temporary camps on the Azerbaijani side of the border to house the refugees. Construction began on 7 September for a camp intended to house 100,000 refugees four kilometers inside of Azerbaijan, and a total of four temporary facilities were eventually erected through late October. Nonetheless, numerous sources in the Turkish and Russian media confirmed that Iranian-flagged vehicles and Persian-speaking troops had been observed north of the Aras River in early September. *Islamic Republic News Agency*, 31 August 1993, in FBIS-NES, #93–170 (3 September 1993): 36; *Turkiye Radyolari Network*, 3 September 1993, in FBIS-SOV, #93–171 (7 September 1993): 95; *ITAR- TASS*, 2 September 1993, in FBIS-SOV, #93–170 (3 September 1993): 53; *TRT Television Network*, 3 September 1993, in FBIS-WEU, #93–171 (7 September 1993): 47–48; *Voice of the Islamic Republic of Iran First Program Network*, 7 September 1993, in FBIS-NES, #93–172 (8 September 1993): 33; and *IRIB Television First Program Network*, 23 October 1993, in FBIS-NES, #93–204 (25 October 1993): 63.

121. Excerpt of 2 September Turkish Security Council communique as read by *Agence France Presse*, 3 September 1993, in FBIS-WEU, #93–170 (3 September 1993): 56.

122. Turkish government spokesman quoted in *Anatolia*, 3 September 1993, in FBIS-WEU, #93–171 (7 September 1993): 45.

123. Excerpts of statement as read by *ITAR-TASS World Service*, 8 September 1993, in FBIS-SOV, #93–173 (9 September 1993): 14.

124. Quoted by *ITAR-TASS World Service*, 10 September 1993, in FBIS-SOV, #93–

175 (13 September 1993): 15.

125. *Anatolia*, 3 September 1993, and *Hurriyet*, 4 September 1993, in FBIS-WEU, #93–171 (7 September 1993): 45–46.

126. United Nations Security Council, S/RES/874 [1993] (14 October 1993): 2.

127. Daniel Sneider, "Afghan Fighters Join Azeri-Armenian War," *Christian Science Monitor* (16 November 1993): 7.

128. Steve Le Vine, "Afghan Fighters Aiding Azerbaijan in Civil War," *Washington Post* (8 November 1993): A14.

129. *Interfax*, 25 October 1993, and *Azertac*, 25 October 1993, in FBIS-SOV, #93–205 (26 October 1993): 76.

130. Colin Barraclough, "Azeri-Armenian Clashes Force Thousands Into Iran," *Christian Science Monitor* (1 November 1993): 3; and *Turan*, 29 October 1993, in FBIS-SOV, #93–208 (29 October 1993): 81.

131. *Snark*, 11 November 1993, in FBIS-SOV, #93–217 (12 November 1993): 72.

132. United Nations Security Council, S/RES/884 [1993] (12 November 1993): 2.

133. Anthony Hyman, "War Draws to a Close," *The Middle East*, no. 228 (October 1993): 24.

134. *Radio Yerevan*, 14 December 1993, in FBIS-SOV, #93–239 (15 December 1993): 96; and *Radio Yerevan*, 20 December 1993, in FBIS-SOV, #93–243 (21 December 1993): 64.

135. *Mayak Radio Network*, 17 December 1993, in FBIS-SOV, #93–241 (17 December 1993): 85.

136. *Agence France Presse*, 28 December 1993, in FBIS-SOV, #93–247 (28 December 1993): 45.

137. *Agence France Presse*, 9 January 1994, in FBIS-SOV, #94–006 (10 January 1994): 76.

138. *Azerbaycan Radio Televiziyasi Television Network*, 6 January 1994, in FBIS-SOV, #94–005 (7 January 1994): 53; and *Nezavisimaya Gazeta*, 13 January 1994, in FBIS-SOV, #94–010 (14 January 1994): 38.

139. *Armenpress International Service*, 31 January 1994, and *ITAR-TASS*, 31 January 1994, in FBIS-SOV, #94–021 (1 February 1994): 49–50.

140. *Armenia's Radio First Program Network*, 7 February 1994, in FBIS-SOV, #94–026 (8 February 1994): 51.

141. *Interfax*, 8 February 1994, in FBIS-SOV, #94–026 (8 February 1994): 53.

142. "Rebel Leader Named Premier," *Facts on File* 53, no. 2745 (8 July 1993): 507.

143. *Radio Baku Network*, 5 July 1993, in FBIS-SOV, #93–127 (6 July 1993): 70.

144. Mekhman Gafarly, "Big Changes in Store for Azerbaijan," *Current Digest of the Post-Soviet Press* 46, no. 10 (6 April 1994): 24.

145. *Armenia's Radio First Program Network*, 28 December 1993, in FBIS-SOV, #93–248 (29 December 1993): 49.

146. *Mayak Radio Network*, 8 January 1994, in FBIS-SOV, #94–007 (11 January 1994): 72–73.

147. *Hurriyet*, 23 December 1993, in FBIS-WEU, #93–249 (30 December 1993): 28.

148. *Hurriyet*, 1 October 1993, in FBIS-SOV, #93–190 (4 October 1993): 21.

149. *Turkish Daily News*, 28 January 1994, in FBIS-WEU, #94–021 (1 February 1994): 38–39.

150. *Interfax*, 19 April 1994, in FBIS-SOV, #94–076 (20 April 1994): 76.

5

The Armenia-Azerbaijan Conflict Since 1994

To my great regret, the war between Armenia and Azerbaijan long ago ceased to be a war between two rivals from the Caucasus. This is a war in which the combating peoples have become the pawns of mightier powers.

—Azerbaijani President Abulfaz Elchibey,
May 1993

The achievement of a cease-fire in the Nagorno-Karabakh conflict zone in May 1994 set the stage for difficult negotiations mediated by a host of global actors. Claiming the right to self-determination, the Armenians of Nagorno-Karabakh sought to separate from Azerbaijan and thus to change the latter's borders. The Azerbaijanis, however, claimed the right of inviolability of frontiers to rebuff the perceived challenge to their republic's territorial integrity. With these two internationally recognized principles at loggerheads, the setting was created for immediate deadlock in the peace talks.

This already difficult basis for peace talks was complicated further by the competing agendas of the mediating parties, who looked to the Transcaucasus with great interest, particularly with the opening of Azerbaijan to international oil companies in 1994. Meanwhile, the warring parties jockeyed to find ways to use the international community's newfound interest in the region to their advantage.

INTERNATIONAL MEDIATION EFFORTS

Although the Karabakh mediation process began essentially in September 1991 with the failed Russian-Kazakstani peace plan, efforts to bring a peaceful settlement to the Nagorno-Karabakh question were given new impetus in mid-

1993 by Russia and the CSCE's Minsk Group. While Russia is a member of the body, Moscow pursued initially an independent track in the peace process in an effort to exclude foreign influence in the region. This approach succeeded in producing the May 1994 cease-fire, but Russia proved unable to dictate a peace in Nagorno-Karabakh. By early 1997, the United States had entered the scene as a counterbalance to Russia in the Karabakh mediation process.

Background on the May 1994 Cease-Fire

The May 1994 cease-fire had its origins in a Russian drive to become the chief mediator of the Nagorno-Karabakh dispute beginning in mid 1993. With a disastrous situation unfolding on the battlefield, Heydar Aliyev sought a mediator that could induce the Armenians to halt their march into Azerbaijani territory. Due to its lack of both a mandate and experience with either peacekeeping or peacemaking,[1] the CSCE was not a forum that promised to offer such inducement in time to save southwestern Azerbaijan. Russia was able to seize upon the Azerbaijani leader's discontent with the Minsk Group by offering itself as the chief mediator and enforcer of a peace settlement between Armenia and Azerbaijan in exchange for the right to base military forces on the latter's territory.

At the behest of Moscow, Baku opened direct Russian-mediated talks with representatives of the Karabakh Armenian leadership in July 1993.[2] Importantly, the negotiations did not entail formal recognition of the so-called "Nagorno-Karabakh Republic" by Azerbaijan. On the contrary, Aliyev continued to insist that such recognition would not be forthcoming. However, Baku adopted—again at Russia's suggestion—the view of the Karabakh Armenians as an armed, but not a political, party to the conflict.[3]

This change in outlook by the Azerbaijani administration made possible a three-day cease-fire beginning on 24 July,[4] and although restricted solely to the area of Nagorno-Karabakh itself, its success led to several further extensions.[5] Thus, for the first time in years of warfare, agreement on the suspension of hostilities extended beyond the negotiating table to the battlefield itself, and it was achieved by Russia in total disregard for its "partners" in the Minsk Group.

The price for Russia's mediation efforts was soon made clear to the warring parties. At the 8 October Moscow summit between President Boris Yeltsin and the three Transcaucasian heads of state, the Russian side proposed the signing of a communique envisioning "a significant strengthening of Russia's position and role in the Transcaucasus region."[6] As regards Azerbaijan, the proposal sought the return of a Russian paratroop division to the country along with the dispatch of Russian border guards along the Azerbaijani-Iranian frontier.[7] Although under growing pressure at home to take action to arrest the Armenian advances in the southwest, Aliyev rejected Russia's overture and its accompanying offer to deploy peacekeeping forces in the conflict zone.

Aliyev's reluctance to accede to the Russian demand was rooted in several factors. While the notion of peacekeepers in general became more acceptable to the Baku as military defeats piled up throughout 1993, Aliyev was concerned that, in light of the fact that Russia had at no point argued for an immediate and unconditional Armenian withdrawal from Azerbaijani territories as a precursor to the deployment of peacekeepers, the placement of a Russian separating force would freeze the situation on the ground—thus cementing the *de facto* separation of Nagorno-Karabakh from Azerbaijan.[8]

While such a situation was unacceptable in itself, Aliyev also feared that the stationing of peacekeepers, followed presumably by the establishment of Russian military bases in the country, would infringe upon Azerbaijan's sovereignty and make Baku dependent upon Moscow to an unacceptable degree. Such sentiments were shared by Azerbaijan's opposition political parties and by a populace still haunted by visions of "Black January."[9]

Unlike the Azerbaijanis, the Armenians were averse neither to the deployment of Russian peacekeepers nor to the establishment of Russian military bases in the region. Despite frequent statements from Moscow expressing concern with Armenian military moves in the Karabakh war and signs of tacit Russian military support for Azerbaijan, warm relations had been cultivated between Armenia and Russia since the breakup of the USSR.[10] As a great power and a fellow Christian country, the Armenians looked to Russia as a "big brother"—a protector from the hostile Turks and Azeris. Thus, Moscow was welcomed by Yerevan as the only power "capable of really playing the role of guarantor in the peace process."[11]

Although small gains in the winter offensive of 1993–1994 gave Aliyev some breathing room at home, Baku continued to face pressure from Moscow on the matter of troop basing rights. In the wake of an 18 January 1994 speech by Russian Foreign Minister Andrei Kozyrev on the necessity of maintaining a Russian military presence in the "Near Abroad" in order to prevent forces hostile to Russia from filling a perceived security vacuum,[12] Defense Minister Pavel Grachev ventured to the Transcaucasus in pursuit of agreement on the establishment of Russian bases in the three states. Specifically, Grachev sought to deploy about 23,000 troops at five military facilities across the region with the mission of "provid[ing] regional security in the former Soviet territory."[13] Whereas Georgia and Armenia agreed in principle to Grachev's proposal, Azerbaijan continued to hold out.

Under what must have been regarded as growing pressure from Russia, Aliyev sought to improve relations with one of his last remaining potential allies in the region: Turkey. Over the course of a four-day official visit to the Turkish capital beginning on 8 February, Aliyev succeeded in achieving a momentous rapprochement with Ankara, thereby putting an end to the falling out between the two countries that had followed Elchibey's ouster eight months earlier.[14] Crowning Aliyev's visit was the signing of a ten-year Treaty of Friendship and Cooperation with Turkey providing for, among other things, mutual assistance in case of aggression by a third party.[15]

Perceiving perhaps that the Azerbaijani-Turkish rapprochement might impact negatively upon Russia's attempts to monopolize the Karabakh peace process,

Moscow made a major push beginning in mid-February for a cessation of combat operations on its terms, a push that culminated ultimately in the cease-fire of May 1994.[16] In the face of continued Azerbaijani defiance, Russia's mediation stance changed subtly in April 1994.

Perhaps out of recognition of Aliyev's apprehension with the Moscow-dominated peace process, Russia sought to put an "international" face on its mediation efforts. In early April, Russian special envoy Vladimir Kazimirov ventured to the Transcaucasus with a delegation from the CIS Interparliamentary Assembly, where they discussed with the Armenian and Azerbaijani leaders "the role that the CIS can play in achieving peace in this disturbed region."[17] While the move must have been viewed by Aliyev as a thinly veiled bid by Moscow to conceal its continued monopoly on the peace process, the Azerbaijani leader claimed nonetheless that he "pin[ned] great hopes" on the engagement of the CIS.[18]

Lawmakers from Armenia, Azerbaijan, Russia, Kyrgyzstan and the self-styled NKR commenced negotiations in the Kyrgyzstani capital on 4 May under the aegis of the CIS Interparliamentary Assembly. A protocol was proposed that called for a cease-fire to begin on 8 May, to be followed by supplementary talks on the disengagement of the warring parties, withdrawal of military forces from occupied territories, discontinuation of energy and transportation blockades, return of refugees and prisoners of war, and resolution of Nagorno-Karabakh's final legal status.[19]

The Azerbaijani side took issue with a number of the protocol's provisions regarding the proposed supplementary peace talks. Primarily, Baku's delegate complained that the document did not envision the withdrawal of Armenian units from *all* Azerbaijani territory, and a provision suggesting the dispatch of a largely Russian CIS peacekeeping force was also opposed.[20] However, after at first refusing to sign the protocol, the Azerbaijani official initialed the agreement after attaining two minor adjustments to its text.[21]

Aliyev went to substantial risk in endorsing the Bishkek Protocol. The Azerbaijani opposition protested the measure resolutely because it implied the dispatch of largely Russian peacekeeping forces to the country at a future date, thus raising the specter of a loss of sovereignty over Nagorno-Karabakh and over its own affairs in general. Therefore, by accepting the plan, Aliyev risked unifying the opposition at the potential expense of his own political survival.

On the other hand, if the Azerbaijani president had not initialed the protocol, he chanced a backlash from Russia similar to that which had in all likelihood toppled his predecessor. After defying Moscow's demands vis-à-vis the peace process for several months, Aliyev may have come to believe that he was nearing the end of Russia's patience.[22] As it turned out, however, the nature of the Bishkek Protocol offered Aliyev the opportunity to stave off potential challenges from both domestic and external sources—which may explain why he elected to endorse it.

Because the Bishkek Protocol bound Azerbaijan to a cease-fire with only the *promise* of further negotiations, it gave Aliyev a bit of breathing room with which to strengthen his own hand. By committing to a Russian-mediated halt to hostilities, Aliyev may have hoped to put up the facade that he was beginning to heel under to Moscow's demands—thus staving off temporarily any potential threat to his power from that angle.[23] At the same time, the Azeri leader may have sought to use the non-binding aspects of the Bishkek Protocol—that is, the commitment to continued negotiations—to assuage concerns of the domestic opposition over the prospect of Russian peacekeepers. In order to be successful, Aliyev perceived the need to bide for time in hope that the CSCE would become more involved in the mediation process.[24]

Whatever his deeper motives, Azerbaijan's president committed his country first and foremost to a cessation of hostilities in the conflict zone on 12 May. Despite periodic but, in most cases, insignificant violations, the cease-fire has held down to the present. As a consequence, the true struggle for peace in the Transcaucasus began. Having succeeded in eclipsing the CSCE's Minsk Group in the mediation process, Russia pressed forward with its efforts to reach a comprehensive political settlement to the Armenia-Azerbaijan conflict on terms suitable to Moscow. However, a number of obstacles to Russian objectives arose over the next half-year as oil and the CSCE reentered the geopolitical picture.

Pursuit of a Political Settlement, June–August 1994

The first stirring of a renewed CSCE role in the Karabakh mediation process emerged in the aftermath of the Bishkek meeting. In mid May 1994, Minsk Group chairman Jan Eliasson shuttled back and forth between Yerevan and Baku in an effort to convince the sides not to accept hastily the most recent draft Russian peace plan—a plan that minimized the CSCE's role.[25] Eliasson also offered—without consulting Russia—to dispatch a small multinational force of CSCE cease-fire observers to the region within three days of its acceptance by the parties, with the promise of subsequent additional deployments.[26] Thus, it appeared by late spring that the Minsk Group was at last beginning to challenge Russia's effort to shut it out of the Karabakh mediation process.

The CSCE's apparently newfound interest in the peace process emboldened Aliyev noticeably. After noting that he had not consented to Moscow's latest initiative because it provided for the dispatch of a Russian-dominated peacekeeping force,[27] the Azerbaijani president blasted Kazimirov during a one-on-one meeting: "Russia cannot deploy its troops in Azerbaijan by itself. They will have to tread over my dead body first. Russia's troops can be deployed within the framework of an international force, which the CSCE will establish."[28] Grachev received a similar reply when he attempted to persuade Aliyev to reconsider the Russian plan during a visit to Baku on 11 June.[29]

While the Azerbaijani president continued to hold out on a Russian troop presence in his country, Armenia's leader was doing just the opposite. On 9 June, agreement was reached in principle on the establishment of two Russian military bases in the republic for a 25-year period.[30] Thenceforth, joint Russian-Armenian military exercises became a frequent occurence in Armenia.

By the middle of 1994, a comprehensive draft plan for a political settlement of the Armenia-Azerbaijan conflict was taking shape in Moscow. Eliasson ventured to the Russian capital in late June, presumably in hope of having at least some of the CSCE's proposals included in the document. Whereas Kazimirov commented that there were many similarities in the two sides' positions, he made it clear that he wanted the CSCE's role as minimal as possible, claiming that "there is no alternative to the Russian draft."[31]

Details of Russia's plan for a comprehensive political settlement began to emerge by the end of July. In essence, the document envisaged a six-part process by which a resolution of the Nagorno-Karabakh dispute would be achieved. Because the document's provisions offered revealing insights into Moscow's objectives in the region, a brief summary of its elements is necessary:

1. Withdrawal of all military forces to a separating distance of 5 to 20 kilometers within 3 days of the accord's signing, followed by the pullout of Armenian troops from the Agdam and Fizuli districts of Azerbaijan and the deployment of primarily Russian disengagement forces in the separation strip.[32]

2. Withdrawal of Armenian units from Jebrail within 10 days, followed by the exchange of prisoners of war, the lifting of all transportation, communication, and energy blockades, and the return of Azeri refugees and police units to the Agdam and Fizuli districts.[33]

3. Withdrawal of Armenian forces from the Zangelan district within 15 days.

4. Withdrawal of Armenian units from the Kubatly district within 20 days, followed by the commencement of repair and restoration of transportation links in affected areas and the return of Azerbaijani police units to Jebrail and Zangelan.

5. Withdrawal of Armenian forces from the Kelbajar district within 28 days, followed by the return there of Azerbaijani police; restoration of the all transportation, communication, and energy links within 1 month.[34]

6. Discussion of the ultimate legal and administrative status of Nagorno-Karabakh for an undefined period beginning at the time of the accord's signing.

Despite the open-ended nature of the final status talks, the plan committed the warring parties to a "package" solution of the Nagorno-Karabakh question by obligating them to observe a permanent cessation of hostilities during good-faith negotiations on all remaining issues.

Among the key matters to be settled during the all-important final status negotiations were the fate of the Armenian-controlled towns of Lachin and Shusha. Lachin was contentious because it offers a strategic land link between Armenia and Nagorno-Karabakh but is situated outside the boundaries of both; Shusha was important because it has been the historical center of Azeri culture and nationalism within Nagorno-Karabakh since being sacked by the Turks in 1920. While the draft agreement made no specific prescriptions on the outcome of these crucial and contentious issues, its provisions painted a clear picture of Russia's vision for a Karabakh peace settlement.

Although unstated, the plan assumed a commanding role for Russia in the negotiation process both leading up to and following its signing, thereby strengthening Moscow in its quest to become the chief guarantor of peace and stability in the FSU. Moreover, with the indefinite presence in the area of a Russian-dominated disengagement force upon which the preservation of peace would presumably depend, Moscow would gain a degree of leverage over the warring parties—particularly Azerbaijan—to be used in the lead-up to a final Nagorno-Karabakh resolution and beyond. However, because the draft settlement was indeed only a draft, its provisions became the subject of heated debate over the next several months as the warring sides argued their relative positions and the CSCE tried to clarify and expand its role.

The laborious process of ironing out disagreements over the provisions of the Russian draft plan began in Moscow on 5 August. The first matter of contention in the Moscow round of talks was the composition of the proposed peacekeeping force to be deployed in the conflict zone. As before, Azerbaijan rejected as unacceptable the deployment of a Russian-dominated force as envisioned by the plan. The second major obstacle to progress was the timing of the proposed Armenian withdrawal from Shusha and Lachin. While the draft agreement called for the two contentious areas to remain under Armenian control until their status could be determined, Baku insisted that the Armenians agree to pull out completely from Shusha and Lachin—as well as all other occupied territories—as a precondition for Azerbaijan's signing of a peace agreement.[35] The Karabakh Armenian side rejected out of hand Baku's attempt to link the two issues.

Because Shusha lay within the boundaries of Nagorno-Karabakh, Stepanakert argued that Azerbaijan's insistence on a Karabakh Armenian withdrawal from the city was "out of place."[36] As regards Lachin, the Karabakh side claimed that the strategic town's fate could be decided "only under the condition of final settlement of the conflict and with [the] existence of guarantees of non-renewal of military actions."[37] Thus, little common ground was found during the first round of discussions on a political settlement of the Nagorno-Karabakh dispute.

The Moscow talks ended on 13 August without agreement on the draft plan. Importantly, however, all three parties endorsed the idea of "international" peacekeepers being dispatched to the conflict zone, but the size and composition of the force and the timetable for its deployment were left for future discussion.[38] Thus, the stage was set for further bickering over the peacekeeping issue— primarily, bickering over what constituted an "international" force.

Although little concrete progress was made toward a political settlement during the Moscow talks, Russia remained committed to ensuring its monopoly over the Karabakh mediation process. At the behest of Minsk Group chairman Eliasson, who wished "to unite the mediation efforts by the CSCE and Russia and work out a single political solution,"[39] CSCE representatives took an active role in the next round of peace talks held in Moscow on 1 September.[40] Annoyed clearly with the CSCE's renewed activism, Kazimirov complained that: "There are constant attempts to formalize the [Minsk] Group's primacy, to emphasize the CSCE's leading role . . . Some countries are trying to use the CSCE as a cover for their geopolitical interests, rather than as a conflict resolution mechanism. Some people would like to minimize Russia's role and exclude the CIS from the process."[41] In a demonstration of the hypocrisy of this statement, Russia hosted a two-day summit meeting between the presidents of Armenia and Azerbaijan while the second round of Moscow talks was still ongoing, and the CSCE was not invited to participate.

Russia's attempt to emerge as the dominant peacemaker in the Armenia-Azerbaijan conflict made little real headway in the late summer of 1994. While the draft comprehensive political agreement was a creation of Moscow, the conflicting parties continued to adopt stances that precluded compromise, and the CSCE took on a more active role in the negotiation process that was unwelcome by Russian officials. A further obstacle to Russia's designs in the region was erected in late September with the conclusion of the long-delayed oil contract between Azerbaijan and a consortium of mostly Western oil companies.

Impact of the "Oil Factor," September–November 1994

As noted previously, Heydar Aliyev put on hold plans to sign a major contract with a consortium of global oil companies upon his ascension to power in Azerbaijan in June 1993. The move was perceived by many observers to be a display of the new Azerbaijani leader's plans to eschew ties with Turkey and the West and improve relations with Russia that were strained under his predecessor. However, the oil deal was not canceled outright by Aliyev, and jockeying over its terms continued through 1993 and on into 1994.

From the thirteenth century, when Marco Polo wrote of springs near Baku that produced oil, the region in and around the present-day capital of Azerbaijan has been known to be rich in oil. A fledgling oil industry began to grow up in the area in the early 1800s, and by 1880 nearly two hundred oil refineries were operating in Baku, earning it the nickname "Black Town."[42] In the first year of the twentieth century, oil output from Azerbaijan was 81 million barrels out of a total of 84.5 million for all of the Russian Empire.[43]

Production declined substantially with the revolutions of 1905 and 1917, and the Bolsheviks nationalized the oil industry after recapturing Baku in 1920.[44] Under the Soviet system, Azerbaijan was a key source of crude production, but Moscow's emphasis on development of the oilfields of Siberia caused Azerbaijan's share of total Soviet crude output to fall steadily from the late 1960s. By the time of the Soviet Union's dissolution, the Kremlin's indifference to the Azerbaijani oil industry—reflected by frequent and costly accidents, a shortage of spare parts and equipment, outdated technology, and a steady drop in oil production—made newly independent Azerbaijan a shadow of its former self as a great oil producing nation.

With the breakup of the USSR, Azerbaijan found itself in control of its own energy resources for the first time in seven decades. Because the export of energy was the main potential source of hard currency for the republic, development of the oil industry became vital to economic restructuring and integration with the world market. Additionally, energy production and export would be fundamental in forging new regional economic and political linkages, thus strengthening Baku's sovereignty and independence. However, a number of obstacles to the potential benefits of oil export were also raised when Azerbaijan became independent.

Due to its geographic position, Azerbaijan's ability to export oil is inhibited severely. While export by sea is the preferred option, the Caspian Sea is virtually an inland lake with no outlet to the ocean, and both the Mediterranean Sea and the Persian Gulf lay hundreds of miles away. Thus, in order to get oil out of the country, pipelines are necessary to carry the oil to suitable ports. Because Soviet-era pipelines have become increasingly unreliable and unsuitable for the transportation of substantial volumes of oil, Azerbaijan was faced with major difficulties in getting its energy resources to the world market.

The second potential barrier to the realization of Azerbaijan's oil wealth was derived from the nature of Transcaucasia's post-Soviet geopolitics. Once Azerbaijan achieved independence, regional states began to look to its energy resources as a source of potential influence and wealth. Influence upon, if not *de facto* control over, the production and export of Baku's oil would be vital in shaping regional economic and political linkages at the expense of surrounding states. "By 1993," according to Stephen J. Blank, "this struggle over energy resources . . . had become a basic feature of international politics and rivalries [in the Transcaucasus], linking local struggles over land and nationality . . . with control over energy."[45]

As Moscow lobbied to conclude its version of a comprehensive political settlement to the Armenia-Azerbaijan conflict in the summer of 1994, talks between the State Oil Company of the Azerbaijan Republic (SOCAR) and a consortium of international oil majors picked up speed—due possibly to Aliyev's growing disenchantment with the Russian-dominated Nagorno-Karabakh peace process. Viewing a major contract with global oil giants as a way to bolster Azerbaijani sovereignty vis-à-vis Russia and demonstrate its growing international prestige, Aliyev presided over the signing of the so-called "Contract of the Century" on 20 September 1994.

The $8 billion contract, which included oil companies from the United States, the United Kingdom, Norway, Turkey, Russia, Saudi Arabia, and Japan, called for the exploitation of the giant offshore Guneshli, Azeri, and Chirag fields on the Caspian shelf near Baku. Total projected profits from the venture, which will produce an estimated 650 million metric tons of crude over a 30-year period, have been pegged at $100 billion or more at current prices—80 percent of which will go to the Azerbaijani treasury.

The signing of the "Contract of the Century" was greeted with elation in Azerbaijan. The infusion of billions of dollars of foreign capital and technology promised to offer major long-term benefits to the republic's economy; in addition to providing oil revenues, development of the Azerbaijani oil industry promised to bring major new employment opportunities and infrastructure improvements for the republic and its citizens.[46] Furthermore, both Aliyev and his domestic opposition claimed that the deal would strengthen the republic's sovereignty as well as its ties with the West.[47] However, the oil agreement was not welcomed as warmly elsewhere in the region.

Soon after the oil contract was signed between Azerbaijan and the consortium on 20 September, Russian Foreign Ministry spokesman Grigoriy Karasin decreed that his ministry would not recognize the deal. Citing solemn agreements signed between Iran and the Soviet Union in 1921 and 1940, Karasin claimed that the Caspian Sea and its resources are the joint property of the states bordering upon the body of water. As such, he argued that Azerbaijan had no legal right to conclude a contract to exploit oilfields on the Caspian shelf without consulting the other littoral states.[48] Until such consultations are held and new agreements are drawn up on the use of the Caspian's resources, Karasin argued that Russia would not recognize the deal.[49]

The Russian Foreign Ministry's response came as a surprise to many analysts in light of the fact that the giant Russian oil company Lukoil held a 10 percent share in the Azerbaijani contract. Signaling possible embarrassment over the contradiction, the Foreign Ministry attacked the Fuel and Energy Ministry for "failing to coordinate its position with that of the Foreign Ministry and damaging Russian interests by approving the terms of Russian participation in the project."[50] However, the apparent dissension within the Russian government reflected more than mere embarrassment; it indicated a clash between the desire to gain profit by participating in the oil deal and the desire to block the spread of Western influence in the "Near Abroad."

By asserting its non-recognition of Azerbaijan's oil deal, Russia likely sought to block the ultimate realization of the contract's terms. Claiming that the fate of the Caspian shelf's resources is not to be decided unilaterally by any of the littoral states, Moscow aimed to open the matter for debate that could be carried out largely on its own terms, thus forestalling potentially the entrance of Western companies into Russia's self-perceived sphere of influence in the "Near Abroad."[51] A natural ally for Moscow in this endeavor was Iran, which also sought to keep Western influence out of the region.

Evidence of Russian-Iranian collusion to undermine the Azerbaijani-Western oil deal emerged mere weeks after its signing, when Tehran adopted the Russian position on the status of the Caspian Sea. Both governments proposed that the Caspian littoral states meet to update the 1921 and 1940 agreements with a draft Treaty on Regional Cooperation in the Caspian Sea, which stated that no single littoral state could exploit the Sea's resources without obtaining the prior consent of the others.[52]

In what was likely meant to be an implicit threat to encourage Azerbaijan's cooperation, Moscow issued a demarche at the United Nations claiming:

[Russia] reserves the right to take necessary measures at a time it considers best to restore the broken order and eliminate the consequences of unilateral actions [on the Caspian shelf] . . . All the responsibility . . . *including possible material damage*, will rest on those taking unilateral actions and showing their contempt for the nature of the Caspian Sea and obligations on international treaties [emphasis added].[53]

However, Azerbaijan chose not to join the treaty, and in doing so received the ready support of the Western governments whose companies are participants in the oil deal. In a further display of defiance to Russia's demands, Azerbaijan's parliament ratified the oil contract almost unanimously on 15 November, thus removing any doubt of the republic's commitment to oil development and integration with the global economy.[54]

While Russia and Iran took up opposition to the Azerbaijani oil deal through the fall of 1994, the contract's signing had further repercussions across the region. On 30 September, two close associates of President Aliyev were gunned down within two hours of one another by unidentified gunmen.[55] Within days, turmoil gripped Baku as a group of nearly one hundred special-purpose police loyal to Deputy Interior Minister Rovshan Dzhavadov seized control of the Public Prosecutor's Office after several of its members were arrested for alleged involvement in the murders.[56] Among the demands forwarded by the group was the convocation of an emergency session of parliament to discuss the situation in Azerbaijan—a move interpreted by some observers to mean a reassessment of the oil deal.[57]

Aliyev responded to the crisis by declaring a state of emergency in the capital, but the rebellion soon spread to Ganja. On the night of 4–5 October, rebel units seized the city's airport and administrative buildings in what Aliyev described as the beginning of "a coup attempt in Azerbaijan."[58] Only after government forces stormed the facilities occupied by the rebels did the rebellion die down.[59]

Aliyev was quick to level blame for the alleged coup attempt. Several interior ministry officials were toppled for their role in the Baku events, and Prime Minister Surat Huseinov was implicated in the Ganja episode. Huseinov, who had launched the June 1993 rebellion that prompted Aliyev's rise to power, had been a vocal critic both of the president and the oil deal in the weeks leading up to the October incident.[60] Although he denied the charges, Huseinov was sacked from his post in disgrace for allegedly masterminding the Ganja episode in an effort to take power.[61]

Aliyev's wrath did not focus entirely, nor primarily, on domestic actors, however. Drawing a direct link between the attempted putsch and the signing of the oil contract, Aliyev implied that Russia was responsible ultimately for the coup due to his support of the oil deal and his continuing refusal to accept a

Russian troop presence in the country. In the Azerbaijani president's own words, "It is possible to think that the events which followed the signing of the contract are merely coincidental. But they can also be seen as a logical progression . . . All these facts come together and aim to threaten Azerbaijan's independence by overthrowing the existing government which is its guarantor."[62] An unnamed Western diplomat went further, claiming just after the coup attempt that "there's either a concerted campaign being waged [against Aliyev] by Moscow or [the] last week has been an incredible string of coincidences."[63]

Whatever the role and motives of Russia, the October 1994 coup attempt failed to oust Aliyev or undermine his power. At the third round of talks on the provisions of Russia's draft comprehensive political settlement held in Moscow on 15 November, which followed a failed Russian bid to wrest control of the mediation process from the CSCE,[64] Azerbaijan reiterated that only a peace agreement within the framework of the CSCE was acceptable. Furthermore, Baku continued to insist on the unconditional liberation of Shusha and Lachin without offering security guarantees to the Armenians of Nagorno-Karabakh.[65] A tough and seemingly uncompromising stand in itself, Azerbaijan also issued two completely new demands at the Moscow talks.

First, Baku sought the participation of representatives of Karabakh's former Azeri community in the talks, and second, it sought the inclusion of a provision specifying a fixed time period for observance of any peace agreement. Although the Moscow discussions ended without achieving any progress, Azerbaijan's toughened stance appeared to reflect newfound self-confidence in the wake of the September oil deal.

By the closing months of 1994, it appeared that joint Azerbaijani-CSCE resolve had been successful in thwarting Moscow's attempts to be the sole mediator and enforcer of a settlement to the Nagorno-Karabakh dispute. While the Armenian side was inclined to accept a dominant Russian role, neither Azerbaijan nor the Minsk Group were willing to yield to Moscow's exclusionary demands. Although Russia may or may not have backed a coup to unseat the Azerbaijani leader in October, Aliyev remained securely in power and emboldened by his success with the Western oil deal, thereby precluding apparently the potential success of further Russian pressure. Therefore, at the landmark CSCE summit in Budapest in December 1994, Moscow appeared to give in finally to demands that it relinquish its self-perceived role as the dominant peacemaker and peacekeeper in the Transcaucaus.

The December 1994 CSCE Summit and Beyond

Heads of state and government from the fifty-three member states of the CSCE met in Budapest from 5 to 6 December 1994 to discuss strengthening the body's role in the resolution of conflicts in Europe and the FSU. Among the issues dealt with were the conflict in Bosnia and the future of European security arrangements, but the dispute over Nagorno-Karabakh took center stage.

After many months of resisting the deployment of a multinational peacekeeping force to the Nagorno-Karabakh conflict zone, Russia dropped its insistence on having the dominant responsibility for policing a political settlement during the first day of the Budapest summit. With the revelation by Yeltsin that Russia would be willing to participate in an international peacekeeping force under CSCE auspices,[66] the path was cleared for agreement on the dispatch of a 3,000-strong CSCE force to the region following the signing of a peace agreement between the warring parties. The composition of the force and questions of its command and control were left aside for future discussion, but a tacit agreement appeared to emerge that no single country would contribute more than 30 percent of the troops for the proposed operation.[67]

The Budapest summit concluded on 6 December with the approval of a document changing the CSCE's name to that of the Organization for Security and Cooperation in Europe (OSCE). As regards the Armenia-Azerbaijan clash, the document contained two crucial provisions. First, support was expressed for the four UN Security Council resolutions on Nagorno-Karabakh that call for the liberation of occupied Azerbaijani territory, and speedy negotiations toward a political settlement under OSCE auspices were urged. Second, the document called for the deployment of a multinational OSCE peacekeeping force following agreement between the warring parties on a peace settlement.[68] (See Appendix I.)

The Budapest summit marked a potential watershed in the Karabakh conflict. Whereas the body had taken a back seat to Russia in the mediation process for more than a year, the OSCE promised to emerge in 1995 as the group responsible ultimately for negotiating a peaceful settlement of the Nagorno-Karabakh dispute. Moreover, Moscow seemed to drop its insistence that it be the dominant mediator and enforcer of peace among the parties. In essence, it appeared that Western and Azerbaijani intransigence in the face of Russia's demands had finally paid off.

Although hailed widely as a landmark meeting, the December summit left open the possibility for a resurgence of Russian influence in both the Karabakh mediation and peace enforcement processes. In apparent exchange for its agreement on a future multinational peacekeeping force—whose composition was left vague at Moscow's insistence—Russia was granted permanent co-chairmanship of the Minsk Group.[69] Thus, the door was left open for Moscow to exert tangible leverage within the new negotiating format.

The first anniversary of the May 1994 cease-fire was marked by the failure of a new round of negotiations in Moscow. The primary stumbling block was Baku's refusal to recognize Nagorno-Karabakh as an equal party to the talks; Azerbaijan insisted instead that representatives of both the Armenian and Azeri communities of Nagorno-Karabakh be included as armed—but not political—parties to the conflict.[70] The talks' failure was punctuated by a 21 May explosion on Georgian territory that damaged the pipeline carrying Russian natural gas to Armenia. The Armenian Foreign Ministry termed the blast an act of war carried out by "agents of the Azerbaijani Government" and declared the suspension of its participation in the Minsk Group talks.[71] Baku retorted that the Armenian withdrawal from the peace process was carried out in collusion with Russia in an effort to forestall implementation of the Budapest summit resolution.[72]

Armenia returned to the Minsk Group talks after a several-month absence, but the peace process was not given new impetus until the appointment of Yevgeni Primakov as the new Russian Foreign Minister in late 1995. Primakov, a Middle East specialist and close advisor to Gorbachev at the onset of the Karabakh problem, undertook a spate of shuttle diplomacy throughout the first half of 1996. At the minister's behest, several key Armenian demands with regard to the security of Nagorno-Karabakh were inserted as a supplement to the latest draft political agreement in February,[73] and the warring parties were pressed to release all prisoners of war on the occasion of the second anniversary of the cease-fire.[74] The renewed Russian activity produced little further success, however; a round of OSCE-led talks ended in Moscow on 18 June without progress.[75]

The quest for a political settlement to the Nagorno-Karabakh dispute was dealt a serious blow in December 1996 when a clash between the Armenian and Azerbaijani presidents nearly derailed the Lisbon summit of the OSCE. At Aliyev's insistence, a last-minute annex calling for a resolution based on the territorial integrity of Azerbaijan was added to the final summit declaration. Ter-Petrosyan proclaimed that the move wrongly prejudiced future talks on the final status of Nagorno-Karabakh, and the Armenian delegation was the only OSCE member to refrain from signing the summit declaration.[76] (See Appendix J.) The row resulted in a four-month disruption of the OSCE mediation process and, in combination with other events, contributed to a marked rise in tensions between Armenian and Azerbaijan.

RECENT DEVELOPMENTS

In mid 1997, disquiet between Armenia and Azerbaijan reached its highest level since the achievement of the May 1994 cease-fire. At the heart of the tensions was the 14 February allegation of Russia's Minister for Cooperation with CIS Countries, Aman Tuleyev, that 86 T-72 tanks, 50 APCs, and 32 Scud-B missiles were transferred to Armenia from the Russian Defense Ministry—free of charge and without the apparent endorsement of the Russian government—from 1994 to 1996.[77] Baku termed the transfer—the facts of which were conceded by then Russian Defense Minister Igor Rodionov—[78] "a gross violation of the Conventional Forces in Europe Treaty" and a direct threat to the security of Azerbaijan.[79] Armenia's Foreign Ministry refuted the charges and claimed that Azerbaijan had embarked on a major weapons buildup of its own as part of "a preparatory campaign to justify its plans for a military solution to the Nagorno-Karabakh conflict."[80]

The row over the illegal Russian arms transfers was exacerbated by the surprise appointment of self-styled NKR President Robert Kocharyan as Prime

Minister of Armenia on 20 March. The move was interpreted, on the one hand, as an attempt by Ter-Petrosyan to appeal to nationalist sentiments and thus mollify his domestic opposition following rigged September 1996 presidential elections.[81] On the other hand, the appointment was seen as a hardening of Armenia's line on the Karabakh issue since it entailed the appointment of an ostensible citizen of Azerbaijan to the Armenian government. Baku took the latter view, decrying the move as a "provocation" and an attempt "to reinforce [Armenia's] annexation of the territory of Azerbaijan."[82] Kocharyan gave credence to the Azerbaijani claim in May when he noted before the Armenian parliament that "serious discussion" should be given to incorporating Nagorno-Karabakh within Armenia.[83]

The growing turmoil in the region was punctuated by the resurgence of fighting along the Armenian-Azerbaijani border and the Nagorno-Karabakh front in April 1997. The clashes represented the worst fighting since the May 1994 truce, prompting a telephone discussion between the Armenian and Azerbaijani leaders in which both sides reaffirmed their intention to observe the cessation of hostilities.[84] The violence tapered off by early May, but several dozen soldiers were said to have died on both sides.

The warring parties were brought back to the negotiating table in the spring under a revitalized Minsk Group format. A dispute between Armenia and Azerbaijan over the chairmanship of the body had resulted in the creation of a three-way co-chairmanship among Russia, France, and the United States in February.[85] U.S. participation brought new impetus to the talks, and a series of negotiations throughout the summer focused on a new draft political settlement to the Nagorno-Karabakh conflict.

The new Karabakh proposal resembled closely those that had failed in the past. Armenian forces would be withdrawn from Azerbaijani territories outside Nagorno-Karabakh as well as the town of Shusha within the enclave, after which OSCE peacekeeping forces would be deployed in the formerly occupied areas. Nagorno-Karabakh would be allowed to retain its own constitution, anthem, flag, and military police force. The OSCE force would ensure the safe return of refugees and oversee the down-sizing of the Karabakh Armenian military. Although returned to Azerbaijan, the Lachin corridor would be leased by the OSCE to ensure road communications between Armenia and Karabakh until agreement is reached on the region's final status.[86]

While Armenia and Azerbaijan accepted the proposal in principle as a basis for further negotiation, the leadership of Nagorno-Karabakh declined. Within a week of Karabakh's 25 August rejection of the peace plan, elections elevated self-styled NKR Foreign Minister Arkadiy Gukasyan to the vacant post of president. Gukasyan iterated that "any status for Nagorno-Karabakh within Azerbaijan is impossible" and pledged to expand the Karabakh military and broaden economic integration with Armenia.[87]

The Karabakh Armenians' rejection of the latest OSCE peace plan marked a further watershed in the mediation process. Recognizing ostensibly that all attempts since 1992 to sign a single, comprehensive document providing for the resolution of all major issues in the conflict have failed, OSCE negotiators turned to a so-called "step-by-step" or phased approach in September 1997. In essence, the phased approach sought to separate the military and political issues related to conflict resolution. A suggested first step would involve the withdrawal of ethnic Armenian forces from Azerbaijani territories outside of Nagorno-Karabakh, followed in subsequent steps by Armenian withdrawal from Lachin and Shusha, deployment of international peacekeeping forces, and return of refugees. The political aspects of a peace settlement, focusing mainly on the future status of Nagorno-Karabakh, would not be put on the negotiating table until after the military aspects have been resolved.[88]

Although the new method resembled closely Azerbaijan's long-standing approach to the peace talks, Armenian policy changed course with Yerevan's endorsement of the phased approach on 26 September. In his first presidential press conference in five years, Ter-Petrosyan declared his administration's support for a step-by-step settlement characterized by mutual compromise and direct talks between Baku and Stepanakert. Although Azerbaijan welcomed the comments as a "constructive change in Yerevan's position,"[89] the president's move opened an immediate split within the Armenian camp.

Armenia's opposition parties rose quickly in objection to Ter-Petrosyan's ostensibly newfound approach to the peace process. National Democratic Union (NDU) leader Vazgen Manukyan decried the president's action as "capitulation" and "treason," while a spokesman of the banned Dashnak party termed the move as "dangerous."[90] On 21 October a group of 10 deputies in the Armenian parliament defected from the majority Hanrapetutyun bloc, leaving pro-government factions with a majority of only two seats in parliament.[91]

Disagreement over the policy change also reached into the government itself. First Deputy Foreign Minister Vardan Oskanyan noted his objections to the phased approach on 6 October,[92] forcing an immediate retraction by the Foreign Ministry and a pledge that differences within the Armenian government "do not and cannot exist."[93] Defense Minister Vazgen Sarkisyan, however, was a vocal opponent of the phased approach. Claiming that "certain people" should not be allowed to resolve the Karabakh problem on behalf of the whole Armenian nation,[94] Sarkisyan argued that Armenia and the "Nagorno-Karabakh Republic" should be prepared for a protracted conflict not only by rejecting concessions to Baku, but also by annexing Shusha and Lachin in the interests of Karabakh's security.[95]

Prime Minister Kocharyan also contradicted the president, asserting that a package solution based on firm security guarantees for Nagorno-Karabakh was preferable to the step-by-step approach. He also warned that "no decision adopted in Armenia will be implemented without Karabakh's consent, irrespective of who is in power in Yerevan."[96] Opposition to Ter-Petrosyan's approach extended further to Interior and National Security Minister Serzh Sarkisyan—the third member of the troika of Armenian "power" ministers—as well as to the

Armenian military, much of the intelligentsia, and the worldwide Armenian diaspora.[97]

Tensions rose in January 1998, when a meeting of the Armenian Security Council brought together the top officials of Armenia and the "Nagorno-Karabakh Republic" for a frank discussion of the peace process. A heated debate ensued in which Kocharyan threatened reportedly to resign over the president's Karabakh policy.[98] Two weeks later, three officials close to Ter-Petrosyan were fired on by unidentified gunmen in separate incidents, and accusations were lofted by both sides in the growing rift.[99]

The political crisis came to a head in the first week of February, when Yerevan mayor Vano Siradeghian and Foreign Minister Alexander Arzumanian, both Ter-Petosyan allies, resigned. Their departures were followed by the defection of 40 of the 96 deputies of the ruling bloc in parliament to the opposition, and a new National Council of intellectuals and members of public-political organizations was formed to combat the "heavy moral and socio-economic crisis" facing Armenia.[100] A uneasy mood also settled over the republic with the arrest of 25 militiamen suspected of participation in the three shootings and the publication of an unsubstantiated report alleging a plot by Karabakh officials to overthrow the Armenian government.[101]

Defense Minister Vazgen Sarkisyan played ultimately the principal role in inducing the president's resignation. Ironically, it was Sarkisyan who had saved the Ter-Petrosyan regime with the dispatch of troops to Yerevan following the disputed presidential elections of September 1996, but the Armenian leader's support for concessions in the Karabakh peace process cost him Sarkisyan's support. Amid the growing crisis, the defense minister claimed that he would not step aside, even if asked to do so by the president, and his control over the 50,000-strong Armenian military gave the opposition great leverage.[102] Under overwhelming pressure to step down, Ter-Petrosyan went before the nation to announce his resignation on 3 February, declaring defeat for Armenia's "party of peace."[103] Following the resignation of the speaker of parliament, Prime Minister Kocharyan was next in line to assume the post of acting president until new elections could be held on 16 March.

Ter-Petrosyan's resignation produced a major shift in the political balance of forces in the republic. Shortly after becoming acting president, Kocharyan backed the re-legalization of the Dashnak party, which had been banned by Ter-Petrosyan in 1994 for alleged involvement in subversive activities. The Dashnak party—Armenia's oldest political movement—has long been a powerful supporter of Nagorno-Karabakh's separation from Azerbaijan, and its reentry into Armenian political life was welcomed as a necessary step toward restoring national unity.

In parliament, defections from the ruling faction elevated the Union of Yerkrapah ("Volunteers"), which represents a group of 6,000 Karabakh war veterans led by Defense Minister Sarkisyan, to a position of strength.[104] At the group's annual congress held in November 1997, chairman Albert Bazeyan noted that Yerkrapah is prepared to battle for a "victorious settlement of the Nagorno-Karabakh issue" based on self-determination for the region's Armenian population.[105] Ironically, the Armenian National Movement (ANM), which came to power in 1990 on just such a platform, has not only been discredited but its very future as a political force is in question. Indeed, "the most significant result of the departure of Ter-Petrosyan and the decline of the ANM is that there is no remaining leader or political movement of any significance that advocates significant concessions to Azerbaijan over Nagorno-Karabakh."[106]

Armenia's run-off election of 30 March produced a victory for Robert Kocharyan. His rise to the presidency was important not only because of the prominence of the Karabakh issue but also because Kocharyan became the only man to be elected leader of both Armenia and Nagorno-Karabakh. Kocharyan's opponents in the election campaign failed ultimately to argue that he was unable to contest the presidency due to the constitutional requirement that a presidential candidate must be a citizen of the Republic of Armenia for at least ten years. His election—allowed to take place after a favorable ruling on the citizenship issue by the Armenian Central Election Commission—was tantamount to a declaration that Karabakh Armenians are considered by Armenia to be citizens of the republic. Despite the obvious challenge to its sovereignty, Baku was largely silent on the issue.

The Karabakh peace process was put on hold with the onset of the political crisis in Armenia, and the time frame for its resumption was, at the time of this writing, uncertain. Kocharyan has pledged to continue talks within the Minsk Group format, but his regime will almost certainly jettison the more comprising attitude of its predecessor. This need not mean that renewed warfare is likely, as many in the Western press have predicted, but it is important to recognize that sentiments do exist in Armenia that new military operations might be necessary to break the current stalemate.

In September 1997, self-styled NKR Defense Minister Samvel Babayan indicated the growing dissatisfaction with the *status quo* in some Armenian circles. In an interview with *Noyan Tapan*, Babayan remarked that renewed hostilities in the region "are quite possible":

If the war begins [again], it will solve the [Karabakh] problem. Why? Because this time it is going to be the final one: whether they beat us, or we beat them. Agreements on conflict solution must be reached during hostilities, and not after they are stopped . . . If no corrections are made in the mediators' proposals by the end of [1998], or maximum before spring 1999, one of the sides will have to either yield, or start hostilities. I do not see any other way out.[107]

The view that a solution of the Nagorno-Karabakh question is likely to be reached only by force—i.e., that military action will either produce the outright defeat of one of the parties or create the necessary conditions for genuine compromise—is not limited to the Armenian side.

Late 1997 also witnessed the emergence in Baku of a vocal opposition to the policies of the Aliyev regime vis-à-vis Nagorno-Karabakh. In October, a spokesman of the Musavat party, one of the leading Azerbaijani opposition parties, assailed the phased approach to the Karabakh peace process for being contrary to the republic's interests because it purportedly does not guarantee the liberation of all Azerbaijani land.[108] This sentiment was echoed by the Azerbaijani Popular Front, whose former leader Abulfaz Elchibey returned to Baku from internal exile in the same month to head the party and possibly to run against Aliyev in presidential elections scheduled for October 1998. Not only did Elchibey warn that an APF-led government would "reconsider Azerbaijan's oil contracts if the U.S. and the West do not change their approach to the resolution of the Armenian-Azerbaijani conflict,"[109] but he also advocated a military solution to the Karabakh problem if mediation efforts do not produce the desired result.[110]

Such sentiments reflect not only the growing disenchantment of both sides with the *status quo*, but also the recognition of a new geopolitical order that is forming in Eurasia. As the next chapter will argue, the changing dynamics of the Armenia-Azerbaijan conflict are pushing the sides closer to renewed hostilities. What is different in 1998 than 1994, however, is that external powers, including the United States and Europe, now have important interests at stake in the region.

NOTES

1. Elizabeth Fuller, "Mediators for Transcaucasia's Conflicts," *World Today* 49, no. 5 (May 1993): 89; and Konrad J. Huber, "The CSCE's New Role in the East: Conflict Prevention," *Radio Free Europe/Radio Liberty* (hereafter RFE/RL) *Research Report* 3, no. 31 (12 August 1994): 27.

2. Such a tactic had been rejected consistently by previous Azerbaijani leaders because it was believed that direct talks implied *de facto* recognition of Nagorno-Karabakh's sovereignty. Elizabeth Fuller, "Russia's Diplomatic Offensive in the Transcaucasus," *RFE/RL Research Report* 2, no. 39 (1 October 1993): 34.

3. *Interfax,* 15 August 1993, in Foreign Broadcast Information Service—Central Eurasia (hereafter FBIS-SOV), #93–158 (16 August 1993): 57; and *Interfax*, 11 October 1993, in FBIS-SOV, #93–197 (14 October 1993): 87.

4. *Radio Yerevan International Service*, 26 July 1993, in FBIS-SOV, #93–142 (27 July 1993): 61.

5. Via a series of Russian-mediated agreements, the Nagorno-Karabakh cease-fire was extended ultimately to early November 1993. In general, the measure was observed by the parties, and the enclave remained relatively peaceful until the onset of the Azerbaijani winter offensive in December. *ITAR-TASS*, 5 October 1993, in FBIS-SOV, #93–192 (6 October 1993): 23.

6. *Turan*, 8 October 1993, in FBIS-SOV, #93–195 (12 October 1993): 2.

7. Daniel Sneider, "Russia Vies to Halt Lengthy Karabakh War," *Christian Science Monitor* (19 November 1993): 6.

8. Daniel Sneider, "Russia as Big Brother to Neighboring States," *Christian Science Monitor* (2 March 1994): 3.

9. *Radio Baku International Service*, 10 December 1993, in FBIS-SOV, #93–237 (13

December 1993): 95.

10. H. Huseyinoglu Kuliyev, "Rusya'nin Azerbaycan Stratejisi," *Avrasya Dosyasi* 3, no. 4 (Winter 1996): 193.

11. Spokesman for Armenian President Ter-Petrosyan quoted in Elizabeth Fuller, "The Karabakh Mediation Process: Grachev Versus the CSCE?" *RFE/RL Research Report* 3, no. 23 (10 June 1994): 15.

12. See *ITAR-TASS*, 18 January 1994, in FBIS-SOV, #94–011 (18 January 1994): 1–2.

13. Fred Hiatt, "Russia Seeks Bases in Former Soviet Republics," *Washington Post* (3 February 1994): A21.

14. Elizabeth Fuller, "Aliyev in Turkey," *RFE/RL News Briefs* 3, no. 7 (7–11 February 1994): 9.

15. *Cumhuriyet*, 11 February 1994, in Foreign Broadcast Information Service— Western Europe (hereafter FBIS-WEU), #94–031 (15 February 1994): 56.

16. Yasin Aslan, *Ununcu Roma'nin Jeopolitik Arzulari* (Ankara: Avrasya Stratejik Arastirmalar Merkezi, 1995): 103.

17. *ITAR-TASS World Service*, 2 April 1994, in FBIS-SOV, #94–064 (4 April 1994): 55.

18. Quoted by *ITAR-TASS*, 1 April 1994, in ibid., p. 59.

19. *Interfax*, 5 May 1994, in FBIS-SOV, #94–088 (6 May 1994): 1; and *Snark*, 6 May 1994, in FBIS-SOV, #94–089 (9 May 1994): 2.

20. *Turan*, 6 May 1994, in ibid., p. 3.

21. Elizabeth Fuller, "Azerbaijan Belatedly Signs Bishkek Karabakh Protocol," *RFE/RL News Briefs* 3, no. 20 (9–13 May 1994): 7.

22. Fuller, "The Karabakh Mediation Process," p. 16.

23. Umit Ozdag, "SSCB'den Rusya Federasyonu'a," *Avrasya Dosyasi* 3, no. 4 (Winter 1996): 184.

24. It may have also been in Aliyev's mind that his recent rapprochement with Turkey might soon pay off. At the 4 May ceremony in which Azerbaijan became a member of the Partnership for Peace, Aliyev expressed hope that closer cooperation with Turkey and NATO could "enable us as quickly as possible to achieve a just peaceful settlement of the Armenia-Azerbaijan conflict, the liberation of the occupied Azerbaijani territory, and the elimination of all the consequences of the war. The high authority of NATO could be a telling factor in an end to this bloody war." *Azerbaydzhan*, 14 May 1994, in Foreign Broadcast Information Service—Central Eurasia (FBIS-USR), #94–056 (26 May 1994): 83.

25. *Turan*, 24 May 1994, in FBIS-SOV, #94–101 (25 May 1994): 65.

26. *Die Presse*, 20 May 1994, in FBIS-WEU, #94–099 (23 May 1994): 1.

27. *Turan*, 24 May 1994, in FBIS-SOV, #94–101 (25 May 1994): 65.

28. Quoted in *Hurriyet*, 5 June 1994, in FBIS-WEU, #94–110 (8 June 1994): 53.

29. Elizabeth Fuller, ". . . and Azerbaijan," *RFE/RL News Briefs* 3, no. 25 (13–17 June 1994): 7.

30. An agreement had already been reached three months earlier legalizing the presence of Russian border guards along Armenia's frontier with Turkey. *Ostankino Television First Channel*, 23 March 1994, in FBIS-SOV, #94–064 (4 April 1994): 57. For an account of the June agreement, see *Interfax*, 10 June 1994, in FBIS-SOV, #94–113 (13 June 1994): 75.

31. *Segodnya*, 19 July 1994, in FBIS-SOV, #94–138 (19 July 1994): 2.

32. *Interfax*, 22 July 1994, in FBIS-SOV, #94–142 (25 July 1994): 68.

33. *Kommersant Daily*, 26 July 1994, in FBIS-SOV, #94–144 (27 July 1994): 54.

34. *Interfax*, 22 July 1994, in FBIS-SOV, #94–142 (25 July 1994): 68.

35. *Interfax*, 11 August 1994, in FBIS-SOV, #94–156 (12 August 1994): 37.

36. Karabakh Armenian spokesman quoted by *Interfax*, 11 August, in ibid., p. 36.

37. *Snark*, 10 August 1994, in FBIS-SOV, #94–155 (11 August 1994): 38.

38. Elizabeth Fuller, "Karabakh Mediation Update," *RFE/RL Daily Report*, no. 154 (16 August 1994); and *Interfax*, 12 August 1994, in FBIS-SOV, #94–157 (15 August 1994): 1.

39. Quoted by *Interfax*, 26 August 1994, in FBIS-SOV, #94–167 (29 August 1994): 50.

40. Elizabeth Fuller, "Karabakh Talks Resume," *RFE/RL Daily Report*, no. 167 (2 September 1994).

41. Quoted in Vladimir Socor, "Russia Challenges CSCE Over Karabakh," *RFE/RL Daily Report*, no. 190 (6 October 1994).

42. Daniel Yergin, *The Prize: The Epic Quest for Oil, Money, and Power* (New York: Simon & Schuster, 1991): 57–59.

43. Congressional Research Service, "Petroleum in the Muslim Republics of the Commonwealth of Independent States: More Oil for OPEC?" *Congressional Research Service Report for Congress* 92–684SPR (1 September 1992): 14.

44. Yergin, *The Prize*, p. 238.

45. Stephen J. Blank, *Energy and Security in Transcaucasia* (Carlisle Barracks, PA: Strategic Studies Institute, 7 September 1994): 4.

46. It is predicted that eventually 90 percent of the professional staff and 95 percent of the unprofessional staff working on the September 1994 contract will be Azerbaijanis. There has also been a surge in construction and renovation in Azerbaijan as foreign investors have begun to build infrastructure including pipelines, roads, railroads, office buildings, and hotels. Services necessary for business like a reliable phone service and the Internet are also becoming available. Einar Bergh, "AIOC Current Developments," *Azerbaijan International* 4, no. 2 (Summer 1996): 44.

47. *Turan*, 20 September 1994, in FBIS-SOV, #94–183 (21 September 1994): 81; and Bess Brown, "Aliyev Defends Oil Deal," *RFE/RL Daily Report*, no. 183 (26 September 1994).

48. *Turan*, 21 September 1994, in FBIS-SOV, #94–184 (22 September 1994): 67–68.

49. Bess Brown, "Russia Refuses to Recognize Caspian Oil Deal," *RFE/RL Daily Report*, no. 180 (21 September 1994).

50. Vladimir Socor, "Russian Foreign Ministry Attacks Energy Ministry, Azerbaijan Over International Oil Deal," *RFE/RL Daily Report*, no. 191 (7 October 1994).

51. Sanobar Shermatova, "Oil Fuels Russia's Caspian Cold War," *Moscow News*, no. 42 (21–27 October 1994): 4.

52. Aidyn Mekhtiyev, "Chernomyrdin Has No Complaints Against 'Contract of the Century,'" *Current Digest of the Post-Soviet Press* 46, no. 41 (9 November 1994): 26.

53. Quoted by Joseph de Courcy, "Developments to Watch," *Intelligence Digest* (14 October 1994): 12.

54. Elizabeth Fuller, "Azerbaijan's Parliament Ratifies Oil Deal," *RFE/RL Daily Report*, no. 218 (17 November 1994).

55. Bess Brown, "Top Officials Assassinated in Azerbaijan," *RFE/RL Daily Report*, no. 187 (30 September 1994).

56. Pyotr Yudin, "Azeri Troops in Standoff with Rebels," *Moscow Times* (5 October 1994): 4.

57. *Turan*, 3 October 1994, and *Izvestiya*, 4 October 1994, in FBIS-SOV, #94–192 (4

October 1994): 50–52.

58. Quoted by *Agence France Presse*, 5 October 1994, in FBIS-SOV, #94–193 (5 October 1994): 36.

59. Sanobar Shermatova, "President of Azerbaijan Retains Power," *Moscow News*, no. 41 (14–20 October 1994): 4.

60. *Le Figaro*, 11 October 1994, in FBIS-SOV, #94–197 (12 October 1994): 60–61.

61. Elizabeth Fuller, "More Repercussions in Azerbaijan," *RFE/RL Daily Report*, no. 197 (17 October 1994).

62. See Aliyev interview with *Le Figaro*, 11 October 1994, in FBIS-SOV, #94–197 (12 October 1994): 60–61.

63. Quoted in Chris Bird, "Rebels Reject Talks As Blast Rocks Baku," *Moscow Tribune* (5 October 1994): 2.

64. At a meeting of the CSCE in Vienna on 24 October 1994, the Russian delegation made the case that the Minsk Group had not been imparted with legal status at the time of its formation in 1992 and that it should consequently abdicate to Moscow in the Karabakh mediation process. Russia demanded that the body draw up a legal mandate for the peace negotiations in which Moscow would be given sole responsibility for settling the conflict under the banner of the CSCE. Once again, the CSCE balked at Moscow's proposals, and it reaffirmed its earlier claim that Russia would have to allow the body's participation both in the mediation and the peace enforcement process. *Turan*, 25 October 1994, in FBIS-SOV, #94–207 (26 October 1994): 51; and Georgy Plekhanov, "Karabakh Settlement: Moscow Still Wants to be Chief Player," *Current Digest of the Post-Soviet Press* 46, no. 46 (1994): 11.

65. *Interfax*, 15 November 1994, in FBIS-SOV, #94–220 (15 November 1994): 12.

66. *Agence France Presse*, 6 December 1994, in FBIS-WEU, #94–234 (6 December 1994): 1.

67. *Turan*, 6 December 1994, in FBIS-SOV, #94–235 (7 December 1994): 55; and Carlotta Gall, "Russia Made Compromise on Karabakh, Say Analysts," *Moscow Times*, no. 609 (10 December 1994): 6.

68. Organization for Security and Cooperation in Europe, "Towards a Genuine Partnership in a New Era: Final Decision of the 1994 Budapest Summit," OSCE DOC.RC/1/95 (21 December 1994).

69. Gall, "Russia Made Compromise on Karabakh, Say Analysts," p. 6.

70. *Turan*, 17 May 1995, in FBIS-SOV, #95–096 (18 May 1995): 78–79.

71. Text of Armenian Foreign Ministry statement as read by *Radio Yerevan International Service*, 23 May 1995, in FBIS-SOV, #95–100 (24 May 1995): 68.

72. *Turan*, 25 May 1995, in FBIS-SOV, #95–102 (26 May 1995): 74.

73. *Interfax*, 15 January 1996, in FBIS-SOV, #96–010 (16 January 1996): 15.

74. The exchange was questioned by the International Committee of the Red Cross, which claimed that all sides continued to hold prisoners of war. Armenia and Azerbaijan levied the same charge at each other. Elizabeth Teague, Vladimir Socor, and Stephen Foye, "Azerbaijani-Armenian Prisoner Exchange Questioned," *Jamestown Foundation Monitor* 2, no. 100 (21 May 1996).

75. "No Progress as Karabakh Talks End in Moscow," *British Broadcasting Corporation* (hereafter BBC) *Summary of World Broadcasts* (19 June 1996).

76. Timothy Heritage, "Nagorno-Karabakh Row Almost Wrecks Lisbon Summit," *Reuters* (3 December 1996).

77. Vladimir Semiryaga, "Aman Tuleyev Says There Are Forces in Russia Interested in Undermining the CIS Integration Process," *Russian Information Agency Novosti* (14

February 1997).

78. "Russian Defense Minister Admits Facts of Arms Supplies to Armenia," *Interfax* (13 March 1997).

79. "Armenians, Azeris Trade Weapons Build-up Charges," *Reuters* (4 March 1997); and Hafiz M. Pashayev, "Russian Arms Shipments to Armenia Are a Major Threat to Azerbaijan," *Washington Times* (15 April 1997),

80. "Statement by the Ministry of Foreign Affairs of the Republic of Armenia," *Armenpress* (1 March 1997).

81. Elizabeth Teague, Vladimir Socor, and Stephen Foye, "Armenia's New Prime Minister is Karabakh's President," *Jamestown Foundation Monitor* 3, no. 57 (21 March 1997).

82. "U.S., Azerbaijan React to Kocharian Appointment," *Asbarez On-Line* (21 March 1997).

83. Quoted by Elizabeth Fuller, "Armenian Premier Raises Possibility of Annexing Nagorno-Karabakh," *RFE/RL Newsline* 1, no. 32 (16 May 1997).

84. Elizabeth Teague, Vladimir Socor, and Stephen Foye, "Armenian, Azerbaijani Presidents Clear the Air After Armed Clashes," *Jamestown Foundation Monitor* 3, no. 79 (22 April 1997).

85. Rovshan Aliev, "OSCE Proposes Troika to Co-Chair Minsk Group," *Open Media Research Institute Daily Digest* 3, no. 23 (3 February 1997).

86. Elizabeth Fuller, "More Details on New Karabakh Proposals," *RFE/RL Newsline* 1, no. 44 (4 June 1997).

87. Quoted by Elizabeth Fuller, "Nagorno-Karabakh's New President and the Peace Process," *RFE/RL Newsline* 1, no. 109 (3 September 1997).

88. Roland Eggleston, "Negotiators Try New Approach to Karabakh," *Radio Free Europe/Radio Liberty* (30 September 1997).

89. Unnamed Azerbaijani government official quoted by Elizabeth Fuller, ". . . But Baku Makes Positive Assessment," *RFE/RL Newsline* 1, no. 129 (1 October 1997).

90. Quoted by Elizabeth Fuller, "Armenian Opposition Slams President's Karabakh Policy," in ibid., and "ARF Leader Responds to Ter-Petrosyan Comments," *Noyan Tapan* (1 October 1997).

91. Elizabeth Fuller, "Ten Deputies Quit Ruling Armenian Parliamentary Bloc," *RFE/RL Newsline* 1, no. 144 (22 October 1997).

92. Elizabeth Teague, Vladimir Socor, and Stephen Foye, "Karabakh Signals New Flexibility On its Future Political Status," *Jamestown Foundation Monitor* 3, no. 186 (7 October 1997).

93. Foreign Ministry spokesman quoted by Elizabeth Fuller, "'No Differences' Over Karabakh Between Armenian President, Foreign Ministry," *RFE/RL Newsline* 1, no. 134 (8 October 1997).

94. Quoted in "Defense Minister: 'Levon Ter-Petrossian Only Says What He Ought to Say,'" *Respublisca Armenia*, 14 October 1997.

95. Elizabeth Fuller, "But Armenian Defense Minister Non-Conciliatory", *RFE/RL Newsline* 1, no. 142 (20 October 1997).

96. Quoted by Elizabeth Teague, Vladimir Socor, and Stephen Foye, "Top Armenian Officials Contradict Ter-Petrosian on Karabakh," *Jamestown Foundation Monitor* 3, no. 201 (28 October 1997).

97. David Petrosyan, "Political Vectors of the Armenian Society Pressuring President," *Noyan Tapan Highlights*, no. 42 (1997).

98. Elizabeth Fuller, "Serious Differences Surface at Security Council Meeting," *RFE/*

RL (14 January 1998).

99. Marcel Petrosian, "Nagorno-Karabakh Blasts Armenia's Ruling Party over Terrorist Attacks," *RFE/RL Armenia Report* (24 January 1998).

100. National Council member Raphael Ghazarian quoted in "New National Council Formed," *Noyan Tapan* (2 February 1998).

101. Elizabeth Fuller, "Nagorno-Karabakh Denies Plotting Armenian President's Ouster," *RFE/RL Newsline* 2, no. 20 (30 January 1998).

102. David Petrosyan, "Armenia's Big Power Shift?" *Noyan Tapan Highlights*, no. 3 (1998).

103. Text of presidential address in *Noyan Tapan* (3 February 1998).

104. "'Yerkrapah' Becomes Largest Deputy Group," *Noyan Tapan* (3 February 1998).

105. Quoted by Elizabeth Fuller, "Armenia's Karabakh War Veterans Hold Congress," *RFE/RL Newsline* 1, no. 169 (1 December 1997).

106. Michael P. Croissant, "Armenian President Quits as Line Hardens Over Nagorno-Karabakh," *Jane's Intelligence Review* 10, no. 4 (April 1998): 20.

107. "Probability of War is Rather High, Karabakh Defense Minister Says," *Noyan Tapan* (11 September 1997).

108. "Opposition Activist Warns Against OSCE Karabakh Proposals," *BBC Summary of World Broadcasts* (31 October 1997).

109. Quoted by Elizabeth Teague, Vladimir Socor, and Stephen Foye, "Elchibey Warns West He Would Reconsider Oil Contracts," *Jamestown Foundation Monitor* 3, no. 207 (5 November 1997).

110. Elizabeth Fuller, "Elchibey Criticizes OSCE Karabakh Peace Plan," *RFE/RL Newsline* 1, no. 151 (3 November 1997).

6

Future Prospects and Conclusions

When will the blood cease to flow in the mountains? When the sugar-canes grow
in the snows.

— Caucasian proverb

The year 1998 marked the tenth anniversary of the reawakening of the Armenia-
Azerbaijan conflict from 70 years of slumber under Soviet rule. In Stepanakert,
the anniversary was marked by celebrations of victory in achieving Nagorno-
Karabakh's *de facto* independence from Azerbaijan; in Baku, reaction to the
anniversary was decidedly more low-key, with emphasis on remembrance of the
victims of "Black January," Khojaly, and other deadly incidents over the past 10
years. Markedly absent was any sign that reconciliation is near. Below the nationalistic passions that manifest themselves continually, however, is a growing recognition that a new geopolitical order is emerging in Eurasia. This order— spawned
in part by Baku's efforts to develop its oil resources—is not only cementing the
divide between Armenia and Azerbaijan but is also increasing both the chances
and risks of renewed conflict between the two republics.

THE CHANGING GEOPOLITICAL ENVIRONMENT

Since September 1994, Azerbaijan has attracted more than $35 billion in
investment by international oil companies for the development of its vast oil
reserves, and billions more in oil revenues are expected to flow into the Azerbaijani treasury over the next 30 years. Baku's efforts to tap its oil reserves have
been a source of concern for Yerevan. Possessing few natural resources, Armenia
has generated little interest among international businessmen while Western
oilmen have flocked to Baku and other regional capitals. Armenia thus sees the
rise of a potentially strong, wealthy nation as the logical result of Azerbaijan's oil

development. Moreover, Armenian leaders have viewed with dismay at the impact of oil on Baku's attitude toward the Nagorno-Karabakh dispute. Emboldened by the belief that Western governments, especially those whose oil companies are engaged in the Caspian basin, will help Azerbaijan achieve diplomatically what it failed to achieve on the battlefield,[1] Azerbaijani leaders have adopted a maximalist approach to the peace talks.

In the OSCE-led peace negotiations, Azerbaijan has sought essentially to restore the *status quo ante* in Nagorno-Karabakh. Baku has offered autonomous status for Nagorno-Karabakh within Azerbaijan and security guarantees for the region's population, but it has demanded the unconditional withdrawal of ethnic Armenian forces that now control 20 percent of its territory as a precondition to its signing of a political settlement. Independence for Nagorno-Karabakh has been explicitly ruled out, and Azerbaijan has refused to recognize the Karabakh Armenians as an equal negotiating entity.

In addition, Azerbaijan has used to its benefit the world community's prefer-ence for the principle of territorial integrity over that of self-determination. Talks have focused not on whether Nagorno-Karabakh's right to decide its own future independent of Baku will be recognized but on what status it will be accorded as a constituent region of Azerbaijan. Azerbaijani leaders thus appear willing to sit back and allow the republic's increased importance to Western governments translate gradually into increased pressure on the Armenian side.

This is not to say, however, that oil has been a factor working solely against compromise between the two rivals. Because the routing of a pipeline south to Iranian ports on the Persian Gulf is a non-option due to the U.S. government's ban on U.S. firms or their subsidiaries doing business with Iran, Azerbaijan's only viable export options are to route pipelines north through Russia or west through Turkey via either Georgia or Armenia.

During the spring and summer of 1995, the pros and cons of constructing a pipeline from Azerbaijan to the Turkish Mediterranean port of Ceyhan via Armenia were a topic of discussion in capitals from Washington to Baku. It was conceptualized that such a pipeline could contribute to a resolution of the Nagorno-Karabakh dispute by prompting the warring parties to settle their differences in order to realize the joint benefits of oil export. In exchange for hard currency revenues from the transit of Azerbaijani oil across Armenian soil, Baku would secure the withdrawal of ethnic Armenian forces from Azerbaijani territories outside of Nagorno-Karabakh. Azerbaijan's newfound dependence on Armenian goodwill would then allow Yerevan to hold Baku to its promises of security and autonomy for Nagorno-Karabakh.

Despite its conceptual attractiveness, the so-called "peace pipeline" was a non-starter for the simple reason that the warring parties have been unwilling to make the necessary compromises and conclude a political settlement in a timely manner. Because a permanent pipeline for the export of Caspian oil must be in place and operational in order to meet projected full-scale Azerbaijani production in 2005, a decision on the route of the pipeline is expected sometime in 1998 or 1999.

Without a peace agreement in Nagorno-Karabakh, the Armenian option for oil export is simply not feasible and has thus been shelved by international investors.

Developments since late 1995 have virtually assured that Armenia will be bypassed in the export of Caspian oil. On 9 October 1995 Azerbaijan and a group of mostly Western oil companies announced plans to adopt a two-route strategy for exporting early amounts of Azerbaijani oil to market. The first interim pipeline, which will carry the bulk of so-called "early" oil, traces a northern route from offshore Azerbaijan to the Russian Black Sea port of Novorossisk and has been operational since late 1997. The second system, due to come on-line in 1999, will carry oil west to the Georgian port of Supsa. Although it is as yet uncertain whether Turkey will be chosen as the final destination of a main export pipeline, Aliyev has remarked publicly that the pipeline "will certainly cross Georgia" and thus avoid Armenia.[2] Yerevan therefore appears to have lost out on the lucrative transport of major energy reserves to the West in the twenty-first century.

With the "peace pipeline" a dead issue, Armenia has been sidelined as a player in the development and export of Caspian oil. Thus, as Azerbaijan—a country with more than twice the population of its western neighbor—stands to receive vast economic and political benefits from its oil development, Armenia will gain little; Yerevan therefore cannot fail to see the strategic situation in the region changing in Baku's favor. Moreover, Armenia knows that Azerbaijan is winning the public relations war being waged in the media and in diplomatic circles.

With 20 percent of its territory under the control of forces hostile to the central government, Baku has been able to portray itself as a victim of Armenian aggression. This claim has found a receptive audience among Western mediators unwilling to alter inter-state borders for fear of opening a Pandora's Box of territorial irredentism in the post–Cold War world. Thus, there is likely a growing realization in Yerevan that the West's instinctive support for the territorial integrity of Azerbaijan—reflected in the 1996 OSCE Lisbon conference decision—has ended the possibility of international recognition of either an independent "Nagorno-Karabakh Republic" or a union between Armenia and Karabakh.[3]

The looming security environment is thus one of an increasingly strong Azerbaijan confronting an isolated and weak Armenia. Baku makes no secret of its plans to use oil revenues and increased military-technical cooperation with Turkey and other states to rebuild its military might. A parallel between the Croatian reconquest of the Serbian enclave of Krajina in 1995 and the developing situation in Nagorno-Karabakh cannot fail to be drawn by Armenian and Azerbaijani leaders alike. Barring one side's outright submission to the other's demands, which at this point seems unlikely, the continuation of the *status quo* not only favors Azerbaijan in the long term, but increases the likelihood of renewed violence in the region.[4]

Armenia's response to the developing security situation has been apparent in its foreign policy. In June and September 1996, respectively, Yerevan signed military cooperation agreements with Greece and Bulgaria; Armenia is also reported to have held discreet talks with Syria on military cooperation.[5] Although Yerevan claimed these activities were not directed against a third party, the moves no doubt aimed to counter the growing Turkey-Azerbaijan axis.[6]

By far the most important of Armenia's external relationships, however, has been its ties with Moscow. Despite Armenia's negative experiences with Soviet rule, Russia has reprised its role as a close friend of the Armenian people. A close military relationship between the two countries has emerged, including the operation of two Russian military bases in Armenia, the frequent conduct of joint exercises, and growing cooperation in military industries (not to mention the "gift" of $1 billion in Russian arms to Armenia from 1994 to 1996). The emphasis on the military aspect of Russian-Armenian relations was enshrined in the Treaty of Friendship, Cooperation, and Mutual Assistance signed in August 1997, which provides for, *inter alia*, mutual military support if either side is attacked or threatened by a third party.[7] Although both governments claim the alliance is not directed against a specific country or countries, Armenia clearly views its ties with Moscow as a guarantee of its security vis-à-vis Turkey and Azerbaijan.[8]

Notwithstanding its frequent meddling in the Karabakh conflict, which has tended to benefit Armenia at Azerbaijan's expense, Russia is becoming displeased increasingly with the emerging geopolitical environment in the Transcaucasus. In defiance of Moscow's attempts to monopolize the flow of oil from the Caspian and retain a foothold in the strategic region, Azerbaijan has succeeded brilliantly in its efforts to keep Russian influence at a minimum.[9] Although Baku has accepted a token role by Russian companies in its oil development efforts and agreed to ship much of its "early" oil through the Russian pipeline, Azerbaijan has moved vigorously to strengthen its independence from Moscow by broadening its external ties, denying basing rights for Russian military forces, and seeking long-term oil export options that bypass Russian territory.

The person largely responsible for this success is President Aliyev, who has remained in power despite three attempted coups (the second and third being in March 1995 and August 1996, respectively) and a handful of assassination bids. Realizing that during a single 15-month period following independence, no less than four Azerbaijani leaders were toppled as a result of popular uprisings or military revolts, Aliyev has ruled with a strong hand, tolerating little opposition. It is believed widely that the 75-year-old leader's eventual departure from office will hasten a power struggle, and possibly a civil war, in Azerbaijan due to the fact that his entire regime is reliant on a network of clan contacts and favoritism from his years as *de facto* ruler of Nakhichevan.[10] Possessing neither viable political institutions nor a functioning civil society, Azerbaijan is ill prepared to deal with the question of political succession in a peaceful and democratic way. Aliyev's replacement with a pro-Russian—or at least a less anti-Russian—leader would no doubt be looked upon favorably by Moscow.

Azerbaijani officials have suggested that the illicit Russian arms transfers to Armenia represented an effort by Moscow to trigger a new round of fighting and depose Aliyev. There is certainly logic to this argument. Aliyev's replacement with a ruler more responsive to Russian interests would alter the strategic situation in the region almost overnight. Moscow would likely be called upon to impose a *pax Rus* in Nagorno-Karabakh, especially if Azerbaijan were to lose additional territories to Russian-backed Armenian forces. Moreover, the eruption of renewed violence would no doubt stir unease among international investors at work in Azerbaijan and possibly delay the development of the republic's energy resources, thus opening the door for a Russian power grab in the region.

The renewal of the Nagorno-Karabakh war would also have implications throughout the region. Turkey has used the past four years of relative calm in the Transcaucasus to increase its economic, political, and security links to Georgia and Azerbaijan while promoting itself as a transit point for the export of oil and gas from the Caspian Sea basin to the West. Despite signs of growing cooperation with Russia, particularly in the supply of Russian natural gas to Turkey and in increasing inter-state trade, Ankara would no doubt look unfavorably on the return of Russian influence to Azerbaijan.

The downfall of Aliyev would strike a serious blow to Turkey's ambitions as a power-broker in the Transcaucasus and Central Asia, particularly if it disrupted the development of oil and gas in the Caspian region. Although unlikely, it is possible that large Azerbaijani losses on the battlefield could also stir public opinion in favor of Turkish military intervention as was almost the case in the spring of 1993. Five years later, Turkey has far more at stake in the region, and it is unlikely that Ankara would remain passive in the face of renewed hostilities in Nagorno-Karabakh, particularly if Russia was involved openly on the side of Armenia. In such a case, Turkey would, at the very least, file a serious diplomatic protest and possibly campaign for international sanctions against Russia.

Iran, too, would not welcome the renewal of warfare in Karabakh. Although Iranian leaders would no doubt look favorably on the fall of Aliyev, who has kept Iran at arms length while seeking close ties with the United States, Tehran has broader concerns vis-à-vis Azerbaijan. Iran continues to fear that the growth of nationalistic feelings among its Azeri populace—possibly prompted by renewed warfare in Azerbaijan—could result in an Azeri separatist movement and the dismemberment of Iran. Tehran thus remains wary of the potential security threats of a reawakened Karabakh clash.

Although Russia may or may not attempt to foment new violence in the Transcaucasus in order to forward its strategic agenda, it would react negatively to any participation in future hostilities by an outside power. There is virtual unanimity in Moscow on the necessity of maintaining in the region a sphere of influence in which Russia is entitled to act without external interference. Moreover, Russia is bound under the terms of both the 1992 Tashkent Collective Security Treaty and the 1997 Treaty of Friendship, Cooperation, and Mutual Assistance with Armenia to come to its defense if attacked by a third party. Thus, Moscow would no doubt oppose Turkey militarily in an expanded regional clash.

Whereas the Nagorno-Karabakh dispute was transformed from an internal Soviet problem in 1988–1991 to a regional problem in 1992–1993, the potential is great for it to take on a larger and more dangerous scope in the future. In addition to Turkey, Russia, and Iran, other external powers have entered the regional scene in the past three years. With an eye on the huge oil and gas reserves of the Caspian Sea basin, which could become the West's second most important energy source in the next century, Japan, Germany, France, Italy, the United Kingdom, and the United States have heightened their economic engagement in the Transcaucasus and Central Asia through investment and joint ventures.[11] As plans go forward to expand NATO eastward, regional countries have also assumed a more important place in the political-security calculations of Europe and the United States. Thus, a renewed war in Nagorno-Karabakh is likely to matter far more to the West than it did prior to 1994.

The United States increased its presence in the Transcaucasus substantially beginning in late 1996. In response to a Russian proposal for limited division of the Caspian Sea into national sectors, U.S. Special Ambassador to the Newly Independent States, James Collins, noted in a message to Aliyev that the United States "support[s] our investment companies and uphold[s] the idea of the sectoral division of the Caspian Sea."[12] Because Washington had declared previously that the Sea's status was a matter to be resolved by mutual agreement of the littoral states, this unambiguous stand against joint sovereignty over the Caspian—in direct opposition to Russia's position on the issue—marked a sea change in U.S. policy.

U.S. engagement in the region was deepened in February 1997, when the United States joined France and Russia as co-chairmen of the Minsk Group.[13] Whereas the U.S. role in the Karabakh negotiations was a secondary one prior to its ascension to co-chairmanship of the body, Washington assumed an active role as mediator throughout 1997 and 1998. Accompanying the elevated U.S. diplomatic profile were increasing calls for the repeal of Section 907 of the Freedom Support Act of 1992, which bars U.S. governmental assistance to the government of Azerbaijan until the latter takes "demonstrable steps to cease all blockades and other offensive uses of force against Armenia and Nagorno-Karabakh."[14] (See Appendix K.) Critics claimed that Section 907 marked a *de facto* American bias toward Armenia and thus impeded the United States' ability to act as an impartial mediator of the Nagorno-Karabakh conflict.[15]

Indicative further of the United States' increased interest in the Transcaucasus was Heydar Aliyev's visit to Washington in August 1997—the first of any Azerbaijani leader. To complement the four oil contracts signed with American oil companies totaling $8 billion in investment, Aliyev came away from the visit with the rhetorical support of top U.S. officials for the reversal of Section 907 as well as with promises of increased defense cooperation with the United States.[16] The visit marked a new chapter in U.S. policy toward the Transcaucasus, thus demonstrating greater recognition in Washington of the region's importance— and Azerbaijan's in particular—for U.S. interests.

Although the United States has done little to challenge directly Russia's position in the region, the growth of U.S. engagement in the Caspian basin has stirred concern in Moscow. In August 1997 Yeltsin slammed the United States for "declaring that [the Transcaucasus] is in [its] zone of interest. Our interest is weakening but the Americans, on the contrary, are beginning to penetrate this zone."[17] The statement reflected displeasure with the perceived U.S. encroachment into Moscow's self-declared sphere of influence as well as apprehension that Russia's own position in the region is becoming insecure. Although U.S. officials responded that Washington's only interest is in promoting genuine independence for the states of the region,[18] Russia continues to grow dissatisfied with the emerging geopolitical situation in the Transcaucasus.

Were Moscow to foment new hostilities in Nagorno-Karabakh, intervention by U.S. or other Western military forces is neither likely or foreseeable. Nonetheless, a renewal of the clash is sure to stir concern over its possible negative implications for regional energy development. Moreover, an enlargement of the clash to include Turkey and Russia could certainly eclipse the Persian Gulf crisis of 1990–1991. Whereas the Gulf crisis pitted initially a regional power against a weak and tiny neighbor, the internationalization of the Karabakh war would pit a NATO member against a nuclear-armed former superpower. Barring their outright intervention, Russia and Turkey would likely seek to influence the war by offering arms and assistance to the respective combatants. Whatever the case, a bloody round of fighting would ensue. Although the Western response to such a development is difficult to project, U.S. and European interests in the Transcaucasus are too important at this point for the West to remain indifferent to a reignited and escalated conflict in the region.

While Armenia and Azerbaijan have found it difficult to make meaningful compromises on the path to a peace settlement, it should not be regarded as an impossibility that an agreement will be signed in the near future. The bloodshed that has stained the region for the past 10 years has blinded most Armenians and Azeris to the fact that, before being subjected to Russian rule and czarist policies aimed at promoting jealousy and division among ethnic groups, their peoples lived together in peace for hundreds of years prior to the twentieth century. Although collective memories of recent brutalities will not be undone easily, reconciliation should be regarded as an attainable goal.

If there is any single factor—barring complete military defeat of one of the sides—that will hasten a political settlement, it is the realization that rapprochement will allow the republics to emerge into a new era of peace and prosperity together. Despite Russian efforts to maintain hegemony in the region, the Transcaucasus has in the past four years become increasingly integrated with the West. The trickle of oil from the Caspian Sea that began in late 1997 is expected to become a gusher early in the next century, and the influx of major oil revenue, international investment, and new trade ties will present the countries of the region with an unprecedented opportunity for achieving prosperity after centuries of subjugation to foreign rule. Although the window of opportunity for a "peace pipeline" has closed, it is not too late for Armenia to enjoy some of the benefits of regional oil development. Proposals for a common Caucasian market and a Eurasian transport corridor depict the Transcaucasus as a region of vigorous East-West economic activity in the twenty-first century. Such a vision is based, however, on the resolution of regional conflicts.

Although Baku lost the battle for Nagorno-Karabakh in 1992–1994, it has yet to lose the war. Rightly or wrongly so, future negotiations will proceed from the premise that Azerbaijan's borders are inviolable, and thus that the "Nagorno-Karabakh Republic" will be re-subordinated eventually to Baku's sovereignty. However, Azerbaijan will continue to be acutely aware of the impact of its dealings with the Karabakh Armenians on its relations with the country's other nationalities. Any peace deal that is seen as curtailing Azerbaijani sovereignty over Karabakh will cause anxiety in Baku over the perceived prospects for the republic's federalization or outright disintegration. Thus, there is likely to be continued opposition to concessions to the Karabakh Armenians, and the growing support for Azerbaijan in international diplomatic circles will only harden attitudes against compromise.

Although the fissure that emerged within the Armenian camp in late 1997 was healed ostensibly with President Ter-Petrosyan's February 1998 departure from office, there is still no consensus on both the means and ends of the Armenians' negotiating strategy. In October 1997 Karabakh leader Arkadiy Gukasyan offered Baku a compromise: In exchange for reliable and effective guarantees of its security, Nagorno-Karabakh would be willing to jettison its independence drive and enter into a confederative relationship with Azerbaijan.[19] Although the proposal received little attention at the time due to the dormancy of the OSCE talks and the emerging crisis of the Ter-Petrosyan regime, it indicated that there is a growing, if unspoken, recognition within Armenian society that the dream of self-determination for the Karabakh Armenians is likely to go unfulfilled.

At the same time, notwithstanding, "there is no organized force in Armenian society that favors the return of Nagorno-Karabakh to Azerbaijani rule . . . And, if there is one point on which the various political and intellectual elites both inside Armenia and in the diaspora agree, it is that Nagorno-Karabakh must never again be part of Azerbaijan."[20] Thus, there is likely to be continued uncertainty as to how to proceed, and, as time goes on, the Karabakh question will tear increasingly at the soul of the Armenian nation.

The Nagorno-Karabakh issue is of far greater gravity than any other problem of post-Soviet transition in Armenia and Azerbaijan. In Armenia, the fall of the Communist regime as well as its successor were related directly to the Karabakh question; whereas in Azerbaijan, four administrations have been toppled since 1992 at least in part as a result of the Karabakh dispute. Thus, regardless of who holds the organs of power in Yerevan and Baku at any given time, the Nagorno-Karabakh question will not lend itself to quick or easy resolution.

CONCLUSIONS

Since its violent resurgence in 1988, the dispute between Armenia and Azerbaijan has brought untold destruction and hardship to the region. More than twenty-five thousand lives have been lost, and scores of towns and villages have been utterly destroyed. The conflict's drain on the Azerbaijani economy has been worsened by the estimated 500,000 to 800,000 Azeris displaced from their homes during the fighting and forced to live a squalid existence in Baku and other cities and towns. Armenia, too, faces a large refugee burden as well as a devastating blockade that has aggravated the effects of the Soviet economic collapse and produced a severe energy shortage. Indeed, the Karabakh conflict has amplified substantially the negative effects of the Soviet breakup in both republics. More importantly, it has struck at the heart of both peoples' sense of identity and state-hood.

Although the dispute over Nagorno-Karabakh is steeped in the language of self-determination and the inviolability of borders, the conflict is a struggle for the soul of the Armenian and Azerbaijani peoples. The Armenians evoke images of Karabakh as a bastion in which Armenian culture and autonomy were shielded over countless centuries of foreign rule. Their view of the mountainous region as an indelible part of Armenia is symbolized in the flag of the "Nagorno- Karabakh Republic," in which a jagged white line divides the tri-color standard of Armenia to denote the division of Armenia and Karabakh by Stalin in 1923. The separation of Karabakh from Armenia has been and will continue to be a gaping wound in the Armenian national consciousness.

The Azeris view Nagorno-Karabakh as a heartland of the Turkic presence in the mountains and the birthplace of Azerbaijani nationalism. Because, unlike the Armenians, the Azerbaijanis lack a strong sense of historical continuity as a distinct people, territory has become a central criterion of national identification. To challenge Baku's sovereignty over the territory of Azerbaijan is, in the view of the Azeris, to challenge the very foundation of Azerbaijani identity.[21]

National historiographies have been created to legitimate both sides' claims, and they have been influenced greatly by collective memories of history as interpreted through the eyes of the Armenians and Azerbaijanis. These collective memories, which draw on personal, family, and community experiences and recollections, shape the national consciousness of both peoples and provide a lense through which they view current events. New situations are absorbed into familiar paradigms, and new developments are often interpreted as the continuation of historical injustices. All too often, on each side attention focuses on the destruction and injustice they have suffered as a people, while the suffering they inflicted is ignored.

For the Armenians and Azerbaijanis, as Nora Dudwick points out,

historic memories of victimization and oppression have dominated their views of each other and prevented both peoples from grasping the subjective significance Karabakh holds for each other. Where Armenians see a continuation of Turkic aggression and genocidal oppression, Azerbaijanis perceive ruthless nationalism and expansionism. For Armenians, Azerbaijanis are "Turks"; for Azerbaijanis, Armenians are arrogant "westerners" who look down on Muslims as backward and fanatic. Escalation of political conflict into bloodshed has only reinforced these stereotypes.[22]

Indeed, mutual hostility has become a major facet of the Armenians' and Azerbaijanis' identities in the twentieth century.

International efforts of the past six years to mediate an end to the Nagorno-Karabakh clash have been predicated on the notion that a political document providing for such tangible things as the withdrawal of military forces, the return of refugees, and the deployment of multinational peacekeepers will produce peace between the Armenians and Azerbaijanis. This notion is deeply flawed; true peace must not be confused with peaceful coexistence, which is what a political settlement aims essentially to achieve. Genuine peace will only come when there is mutual respect for each other's aims and aspirations and mutual willingness to live and work together in pursuit of constructive ends. If such a peace is to come to the region, it must spring from the collective realization that the Nagorno-Karabakh conflict need not have a zero-sum outcome in which a gain for one side is perceived as a loss by the other. This is something that no political agreement can hasten.

Sadly, there is little indication of a change of attitudes in either republic. Indeed, if there is anything on which the government and opposition in both countries agree, it is on where to draw the line vis-à-vis Nagorno-Karabakh: The Armenians are united in the belief that Karabakh must never again be subject to Baku rule, while the Azeris will settle for nothing less than the re-subordination of Karabakh to Azerbaijani sovereignty.[23] It goes without saying that a wide gulf must be bridged for there to be even a chance for true peace. In the meantime, a new generation of Armenians and Azerbaijanis is growing up under conditions in which hostility toward each other is accepted—if not promoted—and conciliation is rejected.

Even if left to themselves, the Armenians and Azerbaijanis would not have an easy time resolving their differences and overcoming the ill will that has colored their relations for a century. Unfortunately, the strategic location and resources of the Transcaucasus will virtually guarantee the continued interest of outside powers seeking influence in the area at the expense of their rivals. Although there is no doubt a genuine desire among external powers to see an end to the human suffering loosed by the Armenia-Azerbaijan conflict, the continuation of hostility between the two fledgling countries provides a means of manipulating the situation in the region for those seeking to reassert their influence. The Armenians and Azerbaijanis have become pawns in a larger geopolitical contest that will have wide implications through the next century. Consequently, until such a time that cooperation rather than competition and confrontation between those involved becomes the norm in this region situated at the crossroads of Europe and Asia, the Armenia-Azerbaijan conflict is likely to remain a dark and unfinished chapter in human history.

NOTES

1. Aliyev stated in January 1997 that "the great powers which make use of our oil . . .

can use their influence to persuade Armenia to negotiate." Quoted in Lowell Bezanis, "Aliyev on 'Oil Weapon,'" *Open Media Research Institute Daily Digest* 3, no. 10 (15 January 1997).

2. Jennifer DeLay, "Aliyev Says Main Export Pipeline to Cross Georgia," *Pipeline News*, no. 48 (15–21 February 1997).

3. Levon Ter-Petrosyan, "War or Peace? Time for Thoughtfulness," *Armenpress* (3 November 1997).

4. Michael P. Croissant, "Tensions Renewed in Nagorno-Karabakh," *Jane's Intelligence Review* 9, no. 7 (July 1998): 310.

5. Elizabeth Teague, Vladimir Socor, and Stephen Foye, "Armenian-Syrian Military Talks Reported," *Jamestown Foundation Monitor* 2, no. 165 (6 September 1996).

6. Elizabeth Teague, Vladimir Socor, and Stephen Foye, "Armenia, Greece Sign Military Pact," *Jamestown Foundation Monitor* 2, no. 121 (20 June 1996); and "Armenia, Bulgaria Sign Military Agreement," *Noyan Tapan* (3 September 1996).

7. Elizabeth Teague, Vladimir Socor, and Stephen Foye, "Armenia Signs Military Alliance with Russia," *Jamestown Foundation Monitor* 3, no. 161 (2 September 1997).

8. Then-Deputy Foreign Minister Vardan Oskanyan wrote that the agreement "clearly strengthens our security in the regions and shields us from any possible attack by our non-CIS neighbors, Turkey and Iran. Armenia is not now threatened by Iran, but Turkey is another matter . . . Turkey remains a potential military threat. For this reason alone, Armenia must continue to cultivate military cooperation with Russia." Oskanyan became acting Foreign Minister following the resignation of President Ter-Petrosyan. Vardan Oskanyan, "A New Security Agenda for Armenia," *Transitions* 4, no. 4 (September 1997).

9. Jim MacDougall, "Russian Policy in the Transcaucasian 'Near Abroad': The Case of Azerbaijan," *Demokratizatsiya* 5, no. 1 (Winter 1997): 92, 99.

10. Joseph A. Kechichian and Theodore W. Karasik, "The Crisis in Azerbaijan: How Clans Influence the Politics of an Emerging Republic," *Middle East Policy* 4, no. 1–2 (September 1995): 70–71.

11. By late 1997, more than 50 companies from 22 different countries had invested in the development of the Caspian basin's oil and gas resources. Joan Beecher, "Caspian Pipelines and the U.S.," *Voice of America Background Report*, no. 5–38158 (21 November 1997).

12. Quoted in "U.S. Official Arrives in Azerbaijan," *United Press International* (13 November 1996).

13. Rovshan Aliev, "OSCE Proposes Troika to Co-Chair Minsk Group," *Radio Free Europe/Radio Liberty* (4 February 1997).

14. *Freedom for Russia and Emerging Eurasian Democracies and Open Markets Support Act of 1992*, U.S. Public Law 102–511, 102nd Cong., 3d sess., 24 October 1992.

15. S. Frederick Starr, "Power Failure: American Policy in the Caspian," *The National Interest*, no. 47 (Spring 1997): 31.

16. Jennifer DeLay, "Caspian Sea Change Seen in U.S.-Azerbaijan Relations," *Pipeline News*, no. 70 (2–8 August 1997).

17. Quoted in "Yeltsin Says U.S. Influence Increasing in Caucasus," *Reuters* (20 August 1997).

18. "U.S. Responds to Russia on Caucasus Sphere of Influence," *Reuters* (21 August 1997).

19. Elizabeth Teague, Vladimir Socor, and Stephen Foye, "Karabakh Signals New Flexibility on its Future Political Status," *Jamestown Foundation Monitor* 3, no. 186 (7 October 1997).

20. Emil Danielyan, "Nagorno-Karabakh: Imminent Breakthrough or Yet Another Stalemate?" *Prism* 3, no. 18 (7 November 1997).

21. Nora Dudwick, "Armenian-Azerbaijani Relations and Karabagh: History, Memory, and Politics," *Armenian Review* 46, no. 1–4 (1993): 86.

22. Ibid., p. 89.

23. On 6 May 1997, 12 Azerbaijani political parties issued a statement expressing their willingness to unite with the government in the event of renewed war with Armenia. Aliyev was emboldened by the show of support, noting the next day that "we favor a peaceful settlement to the problem, but if it does not happen, we will definitely take back our lands under occupation using every method no matter what this will cause." Quoted in "Azeris Pledge to Take Back Armenian-held Enclave 'Through All Means,'" *Agence France Presse* (7 May 1997); and "Azeri Government and Opposition to Unite Against Armenia," *Turan* (5 May 1997).

APPENDIXES

Appendix A

**Text of resolution by the Soviet of the Autonomous Region of Mountainous Karabakh requesting incorporation into the Armenian SSR
(Adopted on 20 February 1988)**

Regarding mediation for the transfer of the Autonomous Region of Mountainous Karabakh (ARMK) from the Azerbaijani SSR to the Armenian SSR:

After listening to and reviewing the statements of the people's deputies of the Autonomous Region of Mountainous Karabakh Soviet "regarding the mediation of the SSR Supreme Soviet between the Azerbaijani SSR and Armenian SSR for the transfer of the Autonomous Region of Mountainous Karabakh from the Azerbaijani SSR to the Armenian SSR," the special session of regional soviet of the 20th regional soviet of Mountainous Karabakh *resolves*,

Welcoming the wishes of the workers of the Autonomous Region of Mountainous Karabakh to request the supreme soviets of Azerbaijani and Armenian SSRs that they appreciate the deep aspirations of the Armenian population of Mountainous Karabakh and to transfer the Autonomous Region of Mountainous Karabakh from the Azerbaijani SSR to the Armenian SSR, at the same time to intercede with the Supreme Soviet of USSR to reach a positive resolution regarding the transfer of the region from the Azerbaijani SSR to the Armenian SSR.

Source: Gerard J. Libaridian, ed. *The Karabakh File: Documents and Facts on the Question of Mountainous Karabakh, 1918–1988* (Cambridge: The Zoryan Institute, 1988): 90.

Appendix B

Resolution of the Presidium of the USSR Supreme Soviet regarding the decisions of the Supreme Soviets of Azerbaijan and Armenia on Nagorno-Karabakh (Adopted on 18 July 1988), abridged

The Presidium of the USSR Supreme Soviet, having examined the 15 June 1988 request from the Supreme Soviet of the Republic of Armenia for the Nagorno-Karabakh autonomous region to be united with Armenia in conjunction with an application by the Soviet of People's Deputies of Nagorno-Karabakh and the 17 June 1988 decision of the Supreme Soviet of the Republic of Azerbaijan that making the Nagorno-Karabakh autonomous region part of Armenia is unacceptable, deems a change of borders and an ethnic-territorial division of Azerbaijan and Armenia on a constitutional basis impossible.

Making this ruling, the Presidium of the USSR Supreme Soviet is guided by a provision in the Constitution of the USSR (Article 78), under which the territory of a union republic may not be altered without the latter's consent.

A different decision would contradict the fundamental interests of the peoples of both republics and cause serious harm to inter-ethnic relations in the area.

The Presidium of the USSR Supreme Soviet notes that over the years of Soviet Government the working people of Nagorno-Karabakh have achieved significant success in developing the economy and science and in other spheres of social life on the basis of implementing Lenin's nationalities policy and under the guidance of party and local government organizations.

At the same time no action has been taken in the autonomous region for a long time to solve many issues affecting the national interests of the Armenian population, especially in the fields of culture and education and in personnel policy. The autonomous region's constitutional rights have been breached.

The authorities of Azerbaijan, Armenia and the Nagorno-Karabakh autonomous region have taken a superficial attitude to assessing the situation, failed to realize the political danger of unfounded calls for reviewing the existing ethnic-territorial arrangement in the area and adopted a passive, wait-and-see posture.

The situation in the republics has grown tense and heavy damage has been done to the economies and inter-ethnic relations of the peoples of Armenia and Azerbaijan.

With a view to rectifying the situation in Nagorno-Karabakh and overcoming the serious shortcomings, the Central Committee of the Communist Party of the Soviet Union, the Presidium of the USSR Supreme Soviet and the USSR Council of Ministers have passed resolutions outlining far-reaching measures to further the economic and cultural development of the Nagorno-Karabakh autonomous region, improve the well-being of its working people, strengthen socialist legality and public order, and intensify the education of the population of Azerbaijan and Armenia in a spirit of fraternal friendship and cooperation.

Source: *TASS*, 13 July 1988. Abridgement by the author.

Appendix C

Joint resolution of Supreme Soviet of the Armenian SSR and the National Council of the Nagorno-Karabakh Autonomous Oblast on the reunification of Armenia and Nagorno-Karabakh (Adopted on 1 December 1989)

Proceeding from the universal principles of national self-determination and acceding to legal aspiration for reunification of the two segments of the Armenian people torn apart by force, the Armenian Supreme Soviet recognizes the fact of NKAO's self-determination, and the congress of the plenipotentiary representatives of the NKAO and the National Council it has elected as the sole legal authority in force in the oblast. The Armenian Supreme Soviet and NKAO National Council declare the reunification of the Armenian republic and the NKAO. The Armenian republic citizenship rights extend over the population of the NKAO. The Supreme Soviet and the National Council hereby set up a joint commission to formulate practical steps to realize reunification. They assume the obligation to represent the national interests of the Armenian population in northern Artsakh (NKAO), Shaumyan rayon, and Getashen districts.

Source: *Yerevan International Service*, 3 December 1989.

Decision of the Supreme Soviet of the Azerbaijan SSR in connection with the decision of the Supreme Soviet of the Armenian SSR on uniting the Armenian SSR and the Nagorno-Karabakh Autonomous Oblast (Adopted on 6 December 1989)

The decision adopted by the Armenian SSR Supreme Soviet on 1 December 1989 to unite the Armenian SSR and NKAO is regarded as an impermissible interference in the Sovereign Azerbaijan SSR's affairs and a measure aimed at encroaching on the Azerbaijan SSR's territorial integrity, which does not contribute toward the effort made to stabilize the situation in the region and restore normal conditions.

Source: *Baku Domestic Service*, 6 December 1989.

Appendix D

Relevant principles of the Helsinki Final Act of the Conference on Security and Cooperation in Europe (Adopted on 1 August 1975)

Declaration on Principles Guiding Relations between Participating States

III. INVIOLABILITY OF FRONTIERS
The participating States regard as inviolable all one another's frontiers as well as the frontiers of all States in Europe and therefore they will refrain now and in the future from assaulting these frontiers. Accordingly, they will also refrain from any demand for, or act of, seizure and usurpation of part or all of the territory of any participating State.

IV. TERRITORIAL INTEGRITY OF STATES
The participating States will respect the territorial integrity of each of the participating States. Accordingly, they will refrain from any action inconsistent with the purposes and principles of the Charter of the United Nations against the territorial integrity, political independence or the unity of any participating State, and in particular from any such action constituting a threat or use of force. The participating States will likewise refrain from making each other's territory the object of military occupation or other direct or indirect measures of force in contravention of international law, or the object of acquisition by means of such measures or the threat of them. No such occupation or acquisition will be recognized as legal.

VIII. EQUAL RIGHTS AND SELF-DETERMINATION OF PEOPLES
The participating States will respect the equal rights of peoples and their right to self-determination, acting at all times in conformity with the purposes and principles of the Charter of the United Nations and with the relevant norms of international law, including those relating to territorial integrity of States. By virtue of the principle of equal rights and self-determination of peoples, all peoples

always have the right, in full freedom, to determine, when and as they wish, their internal and external political status, without external interference, and to pursue as they wish their political, economic, social and cultural development. The participating States reaffirm the universal significance of respect for and effective exercise of equal rights and self-determination of peoples for the development of friendly relations among themselves as among all States; they also recall the importance of the elimination of any form of violation of this principle.

Source: Conference on Security and Cooperation in Europe Final Act (Helsinki, 1 August 1975)

Appendix E

United Nations Security Council Resolution 822 [1993]
(Adopted on 30 April 1993)

The Security Council,

Recalling the statements of the President of the Security Council of 29 January 1993 (S/25199) and of 6 April 1993 (S/25539) concerning the Nagorno-Karabakh conflict,

Taking note of the report of the Secretary-General dated 14 April 1993 (S/25600),

Expressing its serious concern at the deterioration of the relations between the Republic of Armenia and the Republic of Azerbaijan,

Noting with alarm the escalation in armed hostilities and, in particular, the latest invasion of the Kelbajar district of the Republic of Azerbaijan by local Armenian forces,

Concerned that this situation endangers peace and security in the region,

Expressing grave concern at the displacement of a large number of civilians and the humanitarian emergency in the region, in particular in the Kelbajar district,

Reaffirming the respect for sovereignty and territorial integrity of all States in the region,

Reaffirming also the inviolability of international borders and the inadmissibility of the use of force for the acquisition of territory,

Expressing its support for the peace process being pursued within the framework of the Conference on Security and Cooperation in Europe and deeply concerned at the disruptive effect that the escalation in armed hostilities can have on that process,

1. *Demands* the immediate cessation of all hostilities and hostile acts with a view to establishing a durable cease-fire, as well as immediate withdrawal of all occupying forces from the Kelbajar district and other recently occupied areas of Azerbaijan;

2. *Urges* the parties concerned immediately to resume negotiations for the resolution of the conflict within the framework of the peace process of the Minsk Group of the Conference

on Security and Cooperation in Europe and refrain from any action that will obstruct a peaceful solution of the problem;

3. *Calls* for unimpeded access for international humanitarian relief efforts in the region, in particular in all areas affected by the conflict in order to alleviate the suffering of the civilian population and reaffirms that all parties are bound to comply with the principles and rules of international humanitarian law;

4. *Requests* the Secretary-General, in consultation with the Chairman-in-Office of the Conference on Security and Cooperation in Europe as well as the Chairman of the Minsk Group of the Conference to assess the situation in the region, in particular in the Kelbajar district of Azerbaijan, and to submit a further report to the Council;

5. *Decides* to remain actively seized of the matter.

Source: United Nations Security Council, S/RES/822 [1993] (30 April 1993)

Appendix F

United Nations Security Council Resolution 853 [1993]
(Adopted on 29 July 1993)

The Security Council,

Reaffirming its resolution 822 (1993) of 30 April 1993,

Having considered the report issued on 27 July 1993 by the Chairman of the Minsk Group of the Conference on Security and Cooperation in Europe (CSCE) (S/26184),

Expressing its serious concern at the deterioration of relations between the Republic of Armenia and the Azerbaijani Republic and at the tensions between them,

Welcoming acceptance by the parties concerned of the timetable of urgent steps to implement its resolution 822 (1993),

Noting with alarm the escalation in armed hostilities and, in particular, the seizure of the district of Agdam in the Azerbaijani Republic,

Concerned that this situation continues to endanger peace and security in the region,

Expressing once again its grave concern at the displacement of large numbers of civilians in the Azerbaijani Republic and at the serious humanitarian emergency in the region,

Reaffirming the sovereignty and territorial integrity of the Azerbaijani Republic and of all other States in the region,

Reaffirming also the inviolability of international borders and the inadmissibility of the use of force for the acquisition of territory,

1. *Condemns* the seizure of the district of Agdam and of all other recently occupied areas of the Azerbaijani Republic;

2. *Further condemns* all hostile actions in the region, in particular attacks on civilians and bombardments of inhabited areas;

3. *Demands* the immediate cessation of all hostilities and the immediate, complete and unconditional withdrawal of the occupying forces involved from the district of Agdam and all other recently occupied areas of the Azerbaijani Republic;

4. *Calls on* the parties concerned to reach and maintain durable cease-fire agreements;

5. *Reiterates* in the context of paragraphs 3 and 4 above its earlier calls for the restoration of economic, transport and energy links in the region;

6. *Endorses* the continuing efforts by the Minsk Group of the CSCE to achieve a peaceful solution to the conflict, including efforts to implement resolution 822 (1993), and *expresses its grave concern* at the disruptive effect that the escalation of armed hostilities has had on these efforts;

7. *Welcomes* the preparations for a CSCE monitor mission with a timetable for its deployment, as well as consideration within the CSCE of the proposal for a CSCE presence in the region;

8. *Urges* the parties concerned to refrain from any action that will obstruct a peaceful solution to the conflict, and to pursue negotiations within the Minsk Group of the CSCE, as well as through direct contacts between them, towards a final settlement;

9. *Urges* the Government of the Republic of Armenia to continue to exert its influence to achieve compliance by the Armenians of the Nagorno-Karabakh region of the Azerbaijani Republic with its resolution 822 (1993) and the present resolution, and the acceptance by this party of the proposals of the Minsk Groups of the CSCE;

10. *Urges* States to refrain from the supply of any weapons and munitions which might lead to an intensification of the conflict or the continued occupation of territory;

11. *Calls once again* for unimpeded access for international humanitarian relief efforts in the region, in particular in all areas affected by the conflict, in order to alleviate the increased suffering of the civilian population and *reaffirms* that all parties are bound to comply with the principles and rules of international humanitarian law;

12. *Requests* the Secretary-General and relevant international agencies to provide urgent humanitarian assistance to the affected civilian population and to assist displaced persons to return to their homes;

13. *Requests* the Secretary-General, in consultation with the Chairman-in-Office of the CSCE as well as the Chairman of the Minsk Group, to continue to report to the Council on the situation;

14. *Decides* to remain actively seized of the matter.

Source: United Nations Security Council, S/RES/853 [1993] (29 July 1993)

Appendix G

The Security Council,

Reaffirming its resolutions 822 (1993) of 30 April 1993 and 853 (1993) of 29 July 1993, and *recalling* the statement read by the President of the Council, on behalf of the Council, on 18 August 1993 (S/26326),

Having considered the letter dated 1 October 1993 from the Chairman of the Conference on Security and Cooperation in Europe (CSCE) Minsk Conference on Nagorno-Karabakh addressed to the President of the Security Council (S/26522),

Expressing its serious concern that a continuation of the conflict in and around the Nagorno-Karabakh region of the Azerbaijani Republic, and of the tensions between the Republic of Armenia and the Azerbaijani Republic, would endanger peace and security in the region,

Taking note of the high-level meetings which took place in Moscow on 8 October 1993 and *expressing* the hope that they will contribute to the improvement of the situation and the peaceful settlement of the conflict,

Reaffirming the sovereignty and territorial integrity of the Azerbaijani Republic and of all other States in the region,

Reaffirming also the inviolability of international borders and the inadmissibility of the use of force for the acquisition of territory,

Expressing once again its grave concern at the human suffering the conflict has caused and at the serious humanitarian emergency in the region and expressing in particular its grave concern at the displacement of large numbers of civilians in the Azerbaijani Republic,

1. *Calls upon* the parties concerned to make effective and permanent the cease-fire established as a result of the direct contacts undertaken with the assistance of the Government of the Russian Federation in support of the CSCE Minsk Group;

2. *Reiterates again* its full support for the peace process being pursued within the framework of the CSCE, and for the tireless efforts of the CSCE Minsk Group;

3. *Welcomes and commends* to the parties the "Adjusted timetable of urgent steps to implement Security Council resolutions 822 (1993) and 853 (1993)" set out on 28 September 1993 at the meeting of the CSCE Minsk Group and submitted to the parties concerned by the Chairman of the Group with the full support of nine other members of the Group, and *calls on* the parties to accept it;

4. *Expresses* the conviction that all other pending questions arising from the conflict and not directly addressed in the "Adjusted timetable" should be settled expeditiously through peaceful negotiations in the context of the CSCE Minsk process;

5. *Calls for* the immediate implementation of the reciprocal and urgent steps provided for in the CSCE Minsk Group's "Adjusted timetable," including the withdrawal of forces from recently occupied territories and the removal of all obstacles to communications and transportation;

6. *Calls also* for an early convening of the CSCE Minsk Conference for the purpose of arriving at a negotiated settlement to the conflict as provided for in the timetable, in conformity with the 24 March 1992 mandate of the CSCE Council of Ministers;

7. *Requests* the Secretary-General to respond favorably to an invitation to send a representative to attend the CSCE Minsk Conference and to provide all possible assistance for the substantive negotiations that will follow the opening of the Conference;

8. *Supports* the monitoring mission developed by the CSCE;

9. *Calls on* all parties to refrain from all violations of international humanitarian law and *renews its call* in resolution 822 (1993) and 853 (1993) for unimpeded access for international humanitarian relief efforts in all areas affected by the conflict;

10. *Urges* all States in the region to refrain from any hostile acts and from any interference or intervention which would lead to the widening of the conflict and undermine peace and security in the region;

11. *Requests* the Secretary-General and relevant international agencies to provide urgent humanitarian assistance to the affected civilian population and to assist refugees and displace persons to return to their homes in security and dignity;

12. *Requests also* the Secretary-General, the Chairman-in-Office of the CSCE and the Chairman of the CSCE Minsk Conference to continue to report to the Council on the progress of the Minsk process and on all aspects of the situation on the ground, and on present and future cooperation between the CSCE and the United Nations in this regard;

13. *Decides* to remain actively seized of the matter.

Source: United Nations Security Council, S/RES/874 [1993] (14 October 1993)

Appendix H

United Nations Security Council Resolution 884 [1993]
(Adopted on 12 November 1993)

The Security Council,

Reaffirming its resolutions 822 (1993) of 20 April 1993, 853 (1993) of 29 July 1993 and 874 (1993) of 14 October 1993,

Reaffirming its full support for the peace process being pursued within the framework of the Conference on Security and Cooperation in Europe (CSCE), and for the tireless efforts of the CSCE Minsk Group,

Taking note of the letter dated 9 November 1993 from the Chairman-in-Office of the Minsk Conference on Nagorno-Karabakh addressed to the President of the Security Council and its enclosures (S/26718, annex),

Expressing its serious concern that a continuation of the conflict in and around the Nagorno-Karabakh region of the Azerbaijani Republic, and of the tensions between the Republic of Armenia and the Azerbaijani Republic, would endanger peace and security in the region,

Noting with alarm the escalation in armed hostilities as consequence of the violations of the cease-fire and excesses in the use of force in response to those violations, in particular the occupation of the Zangelan district and the city of Goradiz in the Azerbaijani Republic,

Reaffirming the sovereignty and territorial integrity of the Azerbaijani Republic and of all other States in the region,

Reaffirming also the inviolability of international borders and the inadmissibility of the use of force for the acquisition of territory,

Expressing grave concern at the latest displacement of a large number of civilians and the humanitarian emergency in the Zangelan district and the city of Goradiz and on Azerbaijan's southern frontier,

1. *Condemns* the recent violations of the cease-fire established between the parties, which resulted in a resumption of hostilities, and particularly *condemns* the occupation of the

Zangelan district and the city of Goradiz, attacks on civilians and bombardaments of the territory of the Azerbaijani Republic;

2. *Calls upon* the Government of Armenia to use its influence to achieve compliance by the Armenians of the Nagorno-Karabakh region of the Azerbaijani Republic with resolutions 822 (1993), 853 (1993) and 874 (1993), and to ensure that the forces involved are not provided with the means to extend their military campaign further;

3. *Welcomes* the Declaration of 4 November 1993 of the nine members of the CSCE Minsk Group (S/26718) and *commends* the proposals contained therein for unilateral cease-fire declarations;

4. *Demands* from the parties concerned the immediate cessation of armed hostilities and hostile acts, the unilateral withdrawal of occupying forces from the Zangelan district and the city of Goradiz, and the withdrawal of occupying forces from other recently occupied areas of the Azerbaijani Republic in accordance with the "Adjusted timetable of urgent steps to implement Security Council resolutions 822 (1993) and 853 (1993)" (S/26522, appendix) as amended by the CSCE Minsk Group meeting in Vienna of 2 to 8 November 1993;

5. *Strongly urges* the parties concerned to resume promptly and to make effective and permanent the cease-fire established as a result of the direct contacts undertaken with the assistance of the Government of the Russian Federation in support of the CSCE Minsk Group, and to continue to seek a negotiated settlement of the conflict within the context of the CSCE Minsk process and the "Adjusted timetable" as amended by the CSCE Minsk Group meeting in Vienna of 2 to 8 November 1993;

6. *Urges again* all States in the region to refrain from any hostile acts and from any interference or intervention, which would lead to the widening of the conflict and undermine peace and security in the region;

7. *Requests* the Secretary-General and relevant international agencies to provide urgent humanitarian assistance to the affected civilian population, including that in the Zangelan district and the city of Goradiz and on Azerbaijan's southern frontier, and to assist refugees and displaced persons to return to their homes in security and dignity;

8. *Reiterates* its request that the Secretary-General, the Chairman-in-Office of the CSCE and the Chairman of the CSCE Minsk Conference continue to report to the Council on the progress of the Minsk process and on all aspects of the situation on the ground, in particular on the implementation of its relevant resolutions, and on present and future cooperation between the CSCE and the United Nations in this regard;

9. *Decides* to remain actively seized of the matter.

Source: United Nations Security Council, S/RES/884 [1993] (12 November 1993)

Appendix I

CSCE Budapest summit decision on the intensification of CSCE action in relation to the Nagorno-Karabakh conflict (Adopted on 6 December 1994)

1. Deploring the continuation of the conflict and the human tragedy involved, the participating States welcomed the confirmation by the parties to the conflict of the cease-fire agreed on 12 May 1994 through the mediation of the Russian Federation in co-operation with the CSCE Minsk Group. They confirmed their commitment to the relevant resolutions of the United Nations Security Council and welcomed the political support given by the Security Council to the CSCE's efforts towards a peaceful settlement of the conflict. To this end they called on the parties to the conflict to enter into intensified substantive talks, including direct contacts. In this context, they pledged to redouble the efforts and assistance by the CSCE. They strongly endorsed the mediation efforts of the CSCE Minsk Group and expressed appreciation for the crucial contribution of the Russian Federation and the efforts by other individual members of the Minsk Group. They agreed to harmonize these into a single co-ordinated effort within the framework of the CSCE.

2. To this end, they have directed the Chairman-in-Office, in consultation with the participating States and acting as soon as possible, to name co-chairmen of the Minsk Conference to ensure a common and agreed basis for negotiations and to realize full co-ordination in all mediation and negotiation activities. The co-chairmen, guided in all of their negotiating efforts by CSCE principles and an agreed mandate, will jointly chair meetings of the Minsk Group and jointly report to the Chairman-in-Office. They will regularly brief the Permanent Council on the progress of their work.

3. As a first step in this effort, they directed the co-chairmen of the Minsk Conference to take immediate steps to promote, with the support and co-operation of the Russian Federation and other individual members of the Minsk Group, the continuation of the existing cease-fire and, drawing upon the progress already

achieved in previous mediation activities, to conduct speedy negotiations for the conclusion of a political agreement on the cessation of the armed conflict, the implementation of which will eliminate major consequences of the conflict for all parties and permit the convening of the Minsk Conference. They further requested the co-chairmen of the Minsk Conference to continue working with the parties towards further implementation of confidence-building measures, particularly in the humanitarian field. They underlined the need for participating States to take action, both individually and within relevant international organizations, to provide humanitarian assistance to the people of the region with special emphasis on alleviating the plight of refugees.

4. They agreed that, in line with the view of the parties to the conflict, the conclusion of the agreement mentioned above would also make it possible to deploy multinational peacekeeping forces as an essential element for the implementation of the agreement itself. They declared their political will to provide, with an appropriate resolution from the United Nations Security Council, a multinational CSCE peacekeeping force following agreement among the parties for cessation of the armed conflict. They requested the Chairman-in-Office to develop as soon as possible a plan for the establishment, composition and operations of such a force, organized on the basis of Chapter III of the Helsinki Document 1992 and in a manner fully consistent with the Charter of the United Nations. To this end the Chairman-in-Office will be assisted by the co-chairmen of the Minsk Conference and by the Minsk Group, and be supported by the Secretary General; after appropriate consultations he will also establish a high-level planning group in Vienna to make recommendations on, *inter alia,* the size and characteristics of the force, command and control, logistics, allocation of units and resources, rules of engagement and arrangements with contributing States. He will seek the support of the United Nations on the basis of the stated United Nations readiness to provide technical advice and expertise. He will also seek continuing political support from the United Nations Security Council for the possible deployment of a CSCE peacekeeping force.

5. On the basis of such preparatory work and the relevant provisions of Chapter III of the Helsinki Document of 1992, and following agreement and a formal request by the parties to the Chairman-in-Office through the co-chairmen of the Minsk Conference, the Permanent Council will take a decision on the establishment of the CSCE peacekeeping operation.

Source: Conference on Security and Cooperation in Europe, Budapest Document 1994 (DOC.RC/1/95, 21 December 1994)

Appendix J

Relevant provisions of the OSCE Lisbon summit declaration
Annex 1: Statement of the OSCE Chairman-in-Office
(Submitted on 3 December 1996)

You all know that no progress has been achieved in the last two years to resolve the Nagorno-Karabakh conflict and the issue of the territorial integrity of the Republic of Azerbaijan. I regret that the efforts of the Co-Chairmen of the Minsk Conference to reconcile the views of the parties on the principles for a settlement have been unsuccessful.

Three principles which should form part of the settlement of the Nagorno-Karabakh conflict were recommended by the Co-Chairmen of the Minsk Group. These principles are supported by all member States of the Minsk Group. They are:

- territorial integrity of the Republic of Armenia and the Azerbaijan Republic;
- legal status of Nagorno-Karabakh defined in an agreement based on self-determination which confers on Nagorno-Karabakh the highest degree of self-rule within Azerbaijan;
- guaranteed security for Nagorno-Karabakh and its whole population, including mutual obligations to ensure compliance by all the Parties with the provisions of the settlement.

I regret that one participating State could not accept this. These principles have the support of all other participating States.

This statement will be included in the Lisbon Summit documents.

Annex 2: Statement of the delegation of Armenia
(Submitted on 3 December 1996)

With regard to the statement by the Chairman-in-Office of the OSCE, the Delegation of Armenia wishes to express its concern over the following issues:

1. The statement does not reflect either the spirit or the letter of the Minsk Group's mandate

as established by the Budapest Summit 1994, which proposed negotiations with a view to reaching a political agreement. The problem of status has been a subject of discussion in direct negotiations which have yet to be concluded.

2. The statement predetermines the status of Nagorno-Karabakh, contradicting the decision of the OSCE Ministerial Council of 1992, which referred this issue to the competence of the OSCE Minsk Conference, to be convened after the conclusion of a political agreement.

3. The Armenian side is convinced that a solution of the problem can be found on the basis of international law and the principles laid down in the Helsinki Final Act, above all on the basis of the principle of self-determination.

4. In the interests of reaching a compromise solution, the Armenian side is prepared to continue with the most intensive negotiations, both within the Minsk Group and on the basis of direct contacts coordinated by the Co-Chairmen of that Group.

I request that this statement be annexed to the Lisbon Summit Declaration.

Source: Organization for Security and Cooperation in Europe, Lisbon Document 1996 (DOC.S/1/96, Annex 1–2, Appendix I)

Appendix K

Section 907 of the Freedom Support Act of 1992
(Adopted on 24 October 1992)

United States assistance under this or any other Act (other than assistance under title V of this Act) may not be provided to the Government of Azerbaijan until the President determines, and so reports to the Congress, that the Government of Azerbaijan is taking demonstrable steps to cease all blockades and other offensive uses of force against Armenia and Nagorno-Karabakh.

Source: *Freedom for Russia and Emerging Eurasian Democracies and Open Markets Support Act of 1992 (Freedom Support Act)*. U.S. Public Law 102–511, 102d Cong., 3d sess., 24 October 1992

Selected Bibliography

Adalian, Rouben P., ed. *Armenia and Karabagh Factbook*. Washington, DC: Armenian Assembly of America, 1996.

Akiner, Shirin. "Melting Pot, Salad Bowl—Cauldron? Manipulation and Mobilization of Ethnic and Religious Identities in Central Asia." *Ethnic and Racial Studies* 20, no. 2 (April 1997): 362–398.

Aliev, Igrar. *Daghlyg Garabagh: tarikh, faktlar, hadisalar*. Baku: Elm, 1989.

Aliev, Kemal. *Kavkazskaia Albaniia: I v. do n. e. - I v. n. e.* Baku: Elm, 1974.

Aliev, Saleh M. "The Crisis in Azerbaijan: Origins and Outcomes." *Journal of the Institute for Muslim Minority Affairs* 12, no. 1 (January 1991): 69–76.

Altstadt, Audrey L. "The Azerbaijani Turks' Response to Russian Conquest." *Studies in Comparative Communism* 19, no. 3–4 (Autumn–Winter 1986): 267–286.

——. "Nagorno-Karabakh: 'Apple of Discord' in the Azerbaijan SSR." *Central Asian Survey* 7, no. 4 (1988): 63–78.

——. *The Azerbaijani Turks: Power and Identity Under Russian Rule*. Stanford: Hoover Institution Press, 1992.

Anassian, H.S. "Une Mise Au Point Relative À L'Albanie Caucasienne." *Revue Des Études Arméniennes*. 6 (1969): 299–330.

Aras, Bulent. "Iran'in Orta Asya ve Kafkasya ile Iliskileri." *Avrasya Dosyasi* 3, no. 3 (Fall 1996): 167–180.

——. "The Importance of Turkey to Relations Between Europe and the Turkic Republics of the Former Soviet Union." *UCLA Journal of International Law and Foreign Affairs* 2, no. 1 (Spring–Summer 1997): 91–112.

Arslanian, Artin H. "Britain and the Question of Mountainous Karabagh." *Middle Eastern Studies* 16, no. 1 (January 1980): 92–104.

Aslan, Yasin. *Ucuncu Roma'nin Jeopolitik Arzulari*. Ankara: Avrasya Stratejik Arastirmalar Merkezi, 1995.

Atabaki, Touraj. *Azerbaijan: Ethnicity and Autonomy in Twentieth-Century Iran*. London: British Academic Press, 1993.

Atkin, Muriel. *Russia and Iran: 1780–1828*. Minneapolis: University of Minnesota Press, 1980.

Bremmer, Ian and Ray Taras, eds. *Nation and Politics in the Soviet Successor States.* Cambridge: Cambridge University Press, 1993.

Broxup, Marie Bennigsen, ed. *The North Caucasus Barrier: The Russian Advance Towards the Muslim World.* New York: St. Martin's Press, 1992.

Buniatov, Z. M. *Azarbaijan VII–IX asrlarda.* Baku: Elm, 1988.

Chorbajian, Levon, Patrick Donabedian, and Claude Mutafian, eds. *The Caucasian Knot: The History and Geopolitics of Nagorno-Karabagh.* London: Zed Books, 1994.

Chubin, Shahram. "The Geopolitics of the Southern Republics of the CIS." *Iranian Journal of International Affairs* 4, no. 2 (Summer 1992): 313–321.

Cockburn, Patrick. "Dateline USSR: Ethnic Tremors." *Foreign Policy,* no. 74 (Spring 1989): 168–184.

Cox, Caroline and John Eibner. *Ethnic Cleansing in Progress: War in Nagorno-Karabakh.* London: Institute for Religious Minorities in the Islamic World, 1993.

Croissant, Michael P. "Turkey and NATO After the Cold War." *Strategic Review* 23, no. 4 (Fall 1995): 66–71.

——. "Tensions Renewed in Nagorno-Karabakh." *Jane's Intelligence Review* 9, no. 7 (July 1997): 308–311.

——. "Armenian President Quits as Line Hardens Over Nagorno-Karabakh," *Jane's Intelligence Review* 10, no. 4 (April 1998): 18–20.

Dudwick, Nora. "The Case of the Caucasian Albanians: Ethnohistory and Ethnic Politics." *Cahiers du Monde russe et sovietique* 31, no. 2–3 (April–September 1990): 377–384.

——. "Armenian-Azerbaijani Relations and Karabagh: History, Memory, and Politics," *Armenian Review* 46, no. 1–4 (1993): 79–92.

Freedman, Robert O. "Russia and Iran: A Tactical Alliance." *SAIS Review* 17, no. 2 (1997): 93–109.

Fuller, Graham E. and Ian O. Lesser, eds. *Turkey's New Geopolitics: From the Balkans to Western China.* Boulder: Westview Press, 1993.

Goble, Paul A. "Coping with the Nagorno-Karabakh Crisis." *Fletcher Forum of World Affairs,* no. 16 (Summer 1992): 19–26.

Goldstein, Lyle. "Flashpoint: Conflict in the Caucasus May Escalate." *Harvard International Review* 16, no. 1 (Fall 1993): 42–43, 70–71.

Hadjibeyli, Timoutchine. "La Question du Haut Karabagh: Un point de vue azerbaidjanais." *Le Monde Musulman a l'épreuve de la frontière,* no. 48–49 (1988): 281–290.

Halbach, Uwe, and Heinrich Tiller. "Russia and Its Southern Flank." *Aussenpolitik* 45, no. 2 (1994): 156–165.

Helsinki Watch. *Bloodshed in the Caucasus: Escalation of the Armed Conflict in Nagorno-Karabakh.* New York: Helsinki Watch, September 1992.

Hostler, Charles Warren. *The Turks of Central Asia.* Westport: Praeger Publishers, 1993.

Hovannisian, Richard G. *Armenia on the Road to Independence, 1918.* Berkeley: University of California Press, 1967.

——. *The Republic of Armenia, Volume I: The First Year, 1918–1919.* Berkeley: University of California Press, 1971.

——. *The Republic of Armenia, Volume II: From Versailles to London, 1919–1920.* Berkeley: University of California Press, 1982.

——. "Nationalist Ferment in Armenia." *Freedom at Issue,* no. 105 (November–December 1988): 29–35.

——. "Mountainous Karabagh in 1920: An Unresolved Contest," *Armenian Review* 46, no. 1–4 (1993): 1–35.

Hovannisian, Richard G., ed. *The Armenian Genocide in Perspective.* New Brunswick:

Transaction Books, 1986.

Hunter, Shireen T. "The Emergence of Soviet Muslims: Impact on the Middle East." *Middle East Insight* 8, no. 5 (May–June 1992): 32–40.

____. *The Transcaucasus in Transition: Nation-Building and Conflict.* Washington, DC: Center for Strategic and International Studies, 1994.

Karam, Patrick and Thibaut Mourgues. *Les guerres du Caucase: Des tsars à la Tchétch-énie.* Paris: Perrin, 1995.

Kazemzadeh, Firuz. *The Struggle for Transcaucasia, 1917–1921.* New York: Philosophical Library, 1951.

Kechichian, Joseph A. and Theodore W. Karasik. "The Crisis in Azerbaijan: How Clans Influence the Politics of an Emerging Republic." *Middle East Policy* 4, no. 1–2 (September 1995): 57–71.

Kovner, Milton. "Russia in Search of a Foreign Policy." *Comparative Strategy* 12, no. 3 (July–September 1993): 307–320.

Kuliyev, H. Huseyinoglu. "Rusya'nin Azerbaycan Stratejisi," *Avrasya Dosyasi* 3, no. 4 (Winter 1996): 191–206.

Kushen, Robert. *Conflict in the Soviet Union: Black January in Azerbaijan.* New York: Helsinki Watch, May 1991.

Lapidus, Gail W. "Gorbachev's Nationalities Problem." *Foreign Affairs* 68, no. 4 (Fall 1989): 92–108.

Lemercier-Quelquejay, Chantal. "Islam and Identity in Azerbaijan." *Central Asian Survey* 3, no. 2 (1984): 29–55.

Libaridian, Gerard J., ed. *The Karabakh File: Documents and Facts on the Question of Mountainous Karabakh, 1918–1988.* 1st ed. Cambridge: The Zoryan Institute, March 1988.

MacDougall, Jim. "Russian Policy in the Transcaucasian 'Near Abroad': The Case of Azerbaijan," *Demokratizatsiya* 5, no. 1 (Winter 1997): 89–101.

Malkasian, Mark. *Gha-ra-bagh! The Emergence of the National Democratic Movement in Armenia.* Detroit: Wayne State University Press, 1996.

Mamedova, Farida. *Politicheskaia istoriia i istoricheskaia geografiia Kavkazskoi Albanii.* Baku: Elm, 1986.

Mandalian, James G. "The Transcaucasian Armenian Irredenta." *Armenian Review* 14, no. 2–59 (Summer 1961): 3–29.

Masih, Joseph R. and Michael P. Croissant. "Pipeline Politics in the Transcaucasus." *National Security Studies Quarterly* 3, no. 1 (Winter 1997): 61–74.

Meister, Ulrich. "Islam in Azerbaijan." *Swiss Review of World Affairs*, no. 37 (April 1987): 10–11.

Mesbahi, Mohiaddin. "Russia and the New Muslim States: Change or Continuity." *Central Asian Survey* 12, no. 2 (1993): 117–121.

____. "Russian Foreign Policy and Security in Central Asia and the Caucasus." *Central Asian Survey* 12, no. 2 (1993): 181–215.

Mikaelian, Vardges and Lendrush Khurshudian. "Several Issues Concerning the History of Mountainous Karabagh." *Armenian Review* 43, no. 2–3 (Summer–Autumn 1990): 51–65.

Minassian, Anahide Ter. "The Revolution of 1905 in Transcaucasia." *Armenian Review* 42, no. 2 (Summer 1989): 1–23.

Mouradian, Claire. "The Mountainous Karabagh Question: Inter-Ethnic Conflict or Decolonization Crisis?" *Armenian Review* 43, no. 2–3 (Summer–Autumn 1990): 1–34.

Murphy, David E. "Operation 'Ring': The Black Berets in Azerbaijan." *Journal of Soviet*

Military Studies 5, no. 1 (March 1992): 80–96.

Nassibian, Akaby. *Britain and the Armenian Question, 1915–1923*. New York: St. Martin's Press, 1984.

Nolyain, Igor. "Moscow's Initiation of the Azeri-Armenian Conflict." *Central Asian Survey* 13, no. 4 (1994): 541–563.

Pipes, Richard. *The Formation of the Soviet Union: Communism and Nationalism, 1917–1923*. Cambridge, MA: Harvard University Press, 1964.

Ramazani, R. K. "Iran's Foreign Policy: Both North and South." *Middle East Journal* 46, no. 3 (Summer 1992): 393–412.

Robins, Philip. "Between Sentiment and Self-Interest: Turkey's Policy Toward Azerbaijan and the Central Asian States." *Middle East Journal* 47, no. 4 (Autumn 1993): 594–610.

Samuelian, Thomas J., ed. *Classical Armenian Culture: Influences and Creativity*. Pennsylvania: Scholars Press, 1982.

Saroyan, Mark. "The 'Karabakh Syndrome' and Azerbaijani Politics." *Problems of Communism*, no. 39 (September–October 1990): 14–29.

Shahmuratian, Samvel, ed. *The Sumgait Tragedy: Pogroms Against Armenians in Soviet Azerbaijan, Volume I: Eyewitness Accounts*. Cambridge: The Zoryan Institute, 1990.

Starr, S. Frederick. "Power Failure: American Policy in the Caspian." *The National Interest*, no. 47 (Spring 1997): 20–31.

Suny, Ronald G. "The Revenge of the Past: Socialism and Ethnic Conflict in Transcaucasia." *New Left Review*, no. 184 (November–December 1990): 5–34.

——. *Looking Toward Ararat: Armenia in Modern History*. Bloomington: Indiana University Press, 1993.

——. *The Revenge of the Past: Nationalism, Revolution, and the Collapse of the Soviet Union*. Stanford: Stanford University Press, 1993.

Suny, Ronald G., ed. *Transcaucasia: Nationalism and Social Change*. Ann Arbor: Michigan Slavic Publications, 1983.

Swietochowski, Tadeusz. *Russian Azerbaijan, 1905–1920: The Shaping of National Identity in a Muslim Community*. Cambridge: Cambridge University Press, 1985.

——. "Azerbaijan: Between Ethnic Conflict and Irredentism." *Armenian Review* 43, no. 2–3 (Summer–Autumn 1990): 35–49.

Vorochil, G. "De l'histoire de l'Albanie caucasienne et de l'écriture albanaise." *Bedi Kartlisa: revue de karvélologie* 32 (1974): 275–284.

Walker, Christopher J. *Armenia: The Survival of a Nation*. New York: St. Martin's Press, 1980.

——. *Armenia and Karabagh: The Struggle for Unity*. London: Minority Rights Publications, 1991.

Yacoub, Mir. *Le Problème du Caucase*. Paris: Librairie Orientale et Américaine, 1933.

Index

About the Author

MICHAEL P. CROISSANT is an Earhart Fellow in the Department of Central Eurasian Studies at Indiana University. He has published numerous articles on the southern former Soviet republics in *Strategic Review, Eurasian Studies, National Security Studies Quarterly, Comparative Strategy*, and other journals.

ISBN 0-275-96241-5

90000>

EAN

9 780275 962418

HARDCOVER BAR CODE